PRAISE FOR GREGG OLSEN

If You Tell

"This riveting account will leave readers questioning every odd relative they've known."

—*Publishers Weekly* (starred review)

"Olsen presents the story chronologically and in a simple, straightforward style, which works well: it is chilling enough as is."

—*Booklist*

"An unsettling stunner about sibling love, courage, and resilience."

—*People* magazine (Book of the Week)

"*If You Tell* accomplishes what it sets out to do. The result is a compelling portrait of terror and a powerfully honest, yet still sensitive, look at survival."

—*Bookreporter*

"This disturbing book recounts the unimaginable abuse and torture three sisters Nikki, Sami, and Tori Knotek endured from their own mother, Shelly . . . The strong bond they form to survive and defy their mother's sadistic tendencies is inspiring."

—*BuzzFeed*

"A true crime tour de force."

—Steve Jackson, *New York Times* bestselling author of
No Stone Unturned

"Even the most devoted true crime reader will be shocked by the maddening and mind-boggling acts of horror that Gregg Olsen chronicles in this book. Olsen has done it again, giving readers a glimpse into a murderous duo that's so chilling, it will have your head spinning. I could not put this book down!"

—Aphrodite Jones, *New York Times* bestselling author

"A suspenseful, horrific, and yet fascinating character study of an incredibly dysfunctional and dangerous family by Gregg Olsen, one of today's true crime masters."

—Caitlin Rother, *New York Times* bestselling author

"There's only one writer who can tell such an intensely horrifying, psychotic tale of unspeakable abuse, grotesque torture, and horrendous serial murder with grace, sensitivity, and class . . . A riveting, taut, real-life psychological suspense thrill ride . . . All at once compelling and original, Gregg Olsen's *If You Tell* is an instant true crime classic."

—M. William Phelps, *New York Times* bestselling author

"We all start life with immense promise, but in our first minute, we cannot know who'll ultimately have the greatest impact on our lives, for better or worse. Here, Gregg Olsen—the heir apparent to legendary crime writers Jack Olsen and Ann Rule—explores the dark side of that question in his usual chilling, heartbreaking prose. Superb and creepy storytelling from a true crime master."

—Ron Franscell, author of *Alice & Gerald: A Homicidal Love Story*

"A master of true crime returns with a vengeance. After a decade detour into novels, Gregg Olsen is back with a dark tale of nonfiction from the Pacific Northwest that will keep you awake long after the lights have gone out. The monster at the heart of *If You Tell* is not your typical boogeyman, not some wandering drifter or man in a van. No. In fact, they called her . . . mother. And yet this story is about hope and renewal in the face of evil and how three sisters can find the goodness in the world after surviving the worst it has to offer. Classic true crime in the tradition of *In Cold Blood* and *The Stranger Beside Me*."

—James Renner, author of *True Crime Addict*

"This nightmare walked on two legs and some of her victims called her mom. In *If You Tell*, Gregg Olsen documents the horrific mental and physical torture Shelly Knotek inflicted on everyone in her household. A powerful story of cruelty that will haunt you for a long time."

—Diane Fanning, author of *Treason in the Secret City*

"Bristling with tension, gripping from the first pages, Gregg Olsen's masterful portrait of children caught in the web of a coldly calculating killer fascinates. A read so compelling it kept me up late into the night, *If You Tell* exposes incredible evil that lived quietly in small-town America. That the book is fact, not fiction, terrifies."

—Kathryn Casey, bestselling author of *In Plain Sight*

I Know Where You Live

"In *I Know Where You Live*, master of suspense Gregg Olsen peels back layer after layer to reveal an ugly underbelly of family secrets and revenge. This unbearably tense, serpentine tale probes the darkest corners of the heart and mind. The suspense never wavers in this electrifying page-turner, guaranteed to keep your heart pounding until the very last page."

—Heather Gudenkauf, *New York Times* bestselling author

The Hive

"Readers who relish the aftershocks of cult exploitation will turn every page with keen anticipation."

—*Kirkus Reviews*

"*The Hive* is Gregg Olsen at his finest. Exciting, anxiety provoking, and twisty . . . You will stay up all night reading . . . not wanting to put it down until the final and shocking conclusion. This book will take you right down a rabbit hole you never suspected."

—*Mystery and Suspense Magazine*

"Mesmerizing! Gregg Olsen tautly reveals layer after layer of lies, secrets, and betrayals in an increasingly horrifying exposé of one cult leader and her terrible sway over others. Forget the evil men do. These women will have you fearing for your life."

—Lisa Gardner, #1 *New York Times* bestselling author

"*The Hive* is a riveting thriller, a tsunami of a story that starts out strong and absolutely knocks you over at the end. The characters are fascinating, their world so real and absorbing—I was transfixed from the very start. Gregg Olsen is such a compelling writer."

—Luanne Rice, *New York Times* bestselling author

"In this gripping thriller, everything is not as it seems, and beauty is only skin deep. *The Hive* is a brilliantly engrossing read—exactly what we have come to expect from Gregg Olsen."

—Karin Slaughter, *New York Times* and internationally bestselling author

"A charismatic wellness guru, a dead young journalist, and a slew of secrets are the ingredients that make up this fiendishly fun thriller. *The Hive* will have readers buzzing."
—Greer Hendricks, #1 *New York Times* bestselling coauthor of *The Wife Between Us*

"Gregg Olsen's *The Hive* is a fast-paced, intriguing, intense, and suspenseful read that is as creepy as it is fantastic. Brilliant, thought-provoking, heartbreaking, and original, *The Hive* will keep you up at night and leave you reeling long after you've finished it. Every page carries weight in this novel. There are plenty of twists and turns to satisfy even the most seasoned crime fiction reader, and the characters feel authentic and alive in ways that only Olsen can achieve."
—Lisa Regan, #1 *Wall Street Journal* bestselling author of the Detective Josie Quinn series

"Die-hard Gregg Olsen fans will love *The Hive*; new readers will become fans. Olsen deftly guides the reader through the pages, cranking up the suspense as long-held secrets rise to the surface. The result is compulsively page turning as Olsen keeps the reader's mind buzzing in suspense. He hooks the reader as a dark crime from the past collides with a crime from the present."
—Kendra Elliot, *Wall Street Journal* bestselling author

"Gregg Olsen's *The Hive* begins with a fascinating premise and a spellbinding opening scene that held me in its grip as I flew through the pages. Olsen expertly weaves together a multilayered tale told by a complex array of unforgettable characters in his latest jaw-dropping thriller. In this dark and dangerously addictive read buzzing with secrets, betrayal, and murder, queen bees and wannabes take on a whole new meaning. Not to be missed."

—Heather Gudenkauf, *New York Times* bestselling author of *This Is How I Lied*

Lying Next to Me

"*Lying Next to Me* is a clever, chilling puzzle of a tale. A riveting, sharp-edged page-turner, it's Gregg Olsen's best book yet."

—A. J. Banner, *USA Today* bestselling author

"A dark, claustrophobic thriller filled with twists and turns. A brilliant book."

—Caroline Mitchell, #1 international bestselling author

"In *Lying Next to Me*, [Olsen] has given us a first-rate work of psychological complexity as well as a mystery that is full of twists and is quite a grabber."

—Popular Culture Association

The Last Thing She Ever Did

"Gregg Olsen pens brilliant, creepy, page-turning, heart-pounding novels of suspense that always keep me up at night. In *The Last Thing She Ever Did*, he topped himself."

—Allison Brennan, *New York Times* bestselling author

"Beguiling, wicked, and taut with suspense and paranoia, *The Last Thing She Ever Did* delivers scenes as devastating as any I've ever read with a startling, pitch-perfect finale. A reminder that evil may reside in one's actions, but tragedy often spawns from one's inaction."

—Eric Rickstad, *New York Times* bestselling author of *The Silent Girls*

"Olsen's latest examines how a terrible, split-second decision has lingering effects, and the past echoes the present. Full of unexpected twists, *The Last Thing She Ever Did* will keep you guessing to the last line."

—J.T. Ellison, *New York Times* bestselling author of *Lie to Me*

"Master storyteller Gregg Olsen continues to take readers hostage with another spellbinding tale of relentless, pulse-pounding suspense."

—Rick Mofina, international bestselling author of *Last Seen*

"Tense. Well-crafted. Gripping."

—Mary Burton, *New York Times* bestselling author

"With *The Last Thing She Ever Did*, Gregg Olsen delivers an edgy, tension-filled, roller-coaster ride of a novel that will thrill and devastate in equal measure."

—Linda Castillo, *New York Times* bestselling author

THE
AMISH
WIFE

ALSO BY GREGG OLSEN

Fiction

Nonfiction

THE
AMISH
WIFE

UNRAVELING THE LIES, SECRETS,
AND CONSPIRACY THAT LET
A KILLER GO FREE

GREGG OLSEN

Published by Thomas & Mercer, Seattle

www.apub.com

Amazon, the Amazon logo, and Thomas & Mercer are trademarks of Amazon.com,
Inc., or its affiliates.

ISBN-13: 9781662514180 (hardcover)
ISBN-13: 9781542016506 (paperback)
ISBN-13: 9781542016490 (digital)

Cover design by Jarrod Taylor
Cover images: © MMerc / Shutterstock;
© SimplyCreativePhotography / Getty Images; © photka / Shutterstock;
© LittlePerfectStock / Shutterstock; Amish quilt, c. 1920, with a double wedding-
ring pattern © Granger / Bridgeman Images

Printed in the United States of America

First edition

For Daniel Gingerich,
a loving brother and uncle who sought the truth

PART ONE

SUMMER 2022

CHAPTER ONE

It took some doing to respond to Daniel Gingerich's message.

It was first relayed via email from a Plainview, Minnesota, librarian named Alice Henderson.

Dan wanted to talk with me and since he didn't have a phone, I'd have to wait for his call.

I knew it must be something important. We hadn't talked, written, or seen each other for more than three decades, though I had thought of Dan often.

The last time I'd seen him was on a dark and frigid winter day in 1989 at his farm in Harmony, Minnesota, south of Rochester and its famed Mayo Clinic. He was the picture-postcard image of an Amishman—if picture postcards were allowed among his people, that is. His wavy brown hair and full beard brushed against the light-blue fabric of his shirt. His eyes were bright and alert, and his smile was genuine. Even to a stranger like me. A kerosene lamp illuminated the kitchen as we sat at a big wood-planked table. He ate sunflower seeds and spat the shells on the floor. His wife, Salome, had a shy but wary smile. Our eyes seldom met. I can't recall if she said a single word. They are Swartzentruber Amish, which is considered Low Amish, or the most conservative. No electricity, of course, hence the lamps. Muscled teams of horses plow fields of corn, hay, and soybeans. Women secure dark-blue or black dresses with straight pins. Men fasten their plain attire—pants, cotton shirts, dark coats—with hooks and eyes. Buttons are too militaristic and zippers, well, too worldly. Women wear bonnets and prayer caps to conceal the glory of their hair, a sight only for their husbands. Men don dark, wide-brimmed hats in the winter, straw hats in the summer.

I had come to talk with Dan about his nephew and namesake, Danny Stutzman, whose body had been found in a Chester, Nebraska, cornfield on Christmas Eve 1985. Only nine at the time of his death, Danny was clad in a blue Carter's blanket sleeper. The members of the community called him Little Boy Blue. His identity remained a mystery until a magazine article prompted the Amish in Ohio to ask first among themselves, and later a sheriff in Thayer County, Nebraska, if Little Boy Blue was Ida and Eli Stutzman's missing boy, Danny.

Dan and I spoke for hours about his nephew, but also about his sister Ida and the barn fire that took her life. He didn't talk in circles, and yet he didn't lay specific blame—only hints—on anyone but his brother-in-law. Dan was torn about how much to tell me. Church leadership is clear about the Amish staying away from the world of the "English," which is the Amish term for outsiders.

My little Craig tape recorder and airport rental car were decidedly the trappings of the English.

I remember standing outside after the interview, ice crystals forming on our facial hair. Puffs of white vapor followed each word. Truly, I don't think I've ever felt that cold in my entire life, and I've been to North Pole, Alaska, in December. I was about to leave when Dan said something that'd stick with me for years. We had been speaking about some of the things I'd learned about Eli. It was dark stuff.

Dan stretched out his arms, palms up, and looked me in the eye.

"I'd rather hold shit in my hands," he said, "than do what you do."

I understood. I think so anyway. Crime is depressing. In a lot of ways, it is dirty work. Dredging up stuff. Bringing back terrible memories that people want to keep buried. And this was what I did to earn a living, or it would be. I was writing what would become my debut book, *Abandoned Prayers*.

Research for the book took me from Ohio to Michigan, Minnesota, Wyoming, Texas, Colorado, and Indiana in what felt like a never-ending quest for the truth. If I can be forgiven for being sentimental, part of the pull into the story was the pale-blue footed pajamas that Danny was clad in when he was found. My twins were born in 1985, and those Carter's sleepers were what they wore at the time. Most parents have touchstone memories of their children. I can still hear the sliding noise of my twin daughters' feet as they shuffled over the tiles of our kitchen floor. Danny and that Carter's sleeper broke my heart.

Because of the mystery. Because it involved a child. Because it felt so unresolved, more so than any other book I'd written, my first one continued to haunt me. So many unanswered questions lingered. Eli Stutzman was convicted only of murdering his Texas roommate, Glen Pritchett. Two murders in Colorado—David Tyler and Dennis Sleater—were connected to Eli in time, place, and signature. Little Danny's cause of death remained undetermined. Eli only served a short sentence in the prison near Lincoln, Nebraska, for failing to report his son's death and abandoning a human body.

And then there's Ida, which is where Eli's string of crimes started. The cause of her death during a barn fire in 1977 was deemed natural causes and attributed to a weak heart. Eli wasn't questioned as a suspect, despite suspicious circumstances. Instead, he was free to excise himself from the Amish and take Danny on a trail of destruction and murder out west.

To switch up Dan's memorable line, I'd rather eat a handful of shit than let go of what I know to be the truth.

When Dan and I finally connect over the phone in August 2022, we compare notes on our lives. Our children and grandchildren. That he moved. That I am still writing. There is nothing awkward. Small talk. Friendly. He tells me that he'd been in Seattle a time or two over the years and had tried to find me in the phone book but hadn't found the right Gregg Olsen. I ask about his parents, Amos and Lizzie, whom I'd interviewed at their farm near Gladwin, Michigan. He said they'd both passed. Lizzie, at ninety-two, earlier in the year.

Then the reason for the phone call.

"I have a box of things," he says. "Things about Eli."

"What kinds of things?"

"Letters," he says. "I haven't read them all. You might want to take a look. Might interest you some."

"Interest" was putting things mildly.

In reality, I couldn't book a flight to the airport in Marquette, Michigan, fast enough. I didn't care about layovers, stops, whatever.

I wrote about Eli's life and crimes decades ago, and yet Ida remained somewhat of a mystery. Her death, her life. I'd wondered about her over the years, this devoted Amish wife and mother who had no idea of the true nature of the man beside her. I hoped that the box of letters—though Dan had said they were about and from Eli—would tell me about her.

During my layover in Detroit, I kill time at the P.F. Chang's counter, reacquainting myself with key dates in the lives of Eli and Ida Stutzman. The full chronology, in which I logged every detail that had a date associated with the Stutzman family, was as long as Santa's wish list. The devil is in the details, right? In this case of true crime, quite literally so. When I trace Eli's spiral into crime, I keep coming back to 1977, the year Ida died in a barn fire.

The letters could give me a new way in, to secrets that have been buried now for over forty years.

1975

- December 25—Eli Stutzman and Ida Gingerich marry.

1976

- September 7—Ida gives birth to Danny.

1977

- July 12—Ida dies in a barn fire.

1982

- July 16—Eli and Danny relocate to Colorado.
- November 8—Eli and Danny move to Austin, Texas.

1985

- May 12—Glen Pritchett, Eli's roommate, is found murdered.
- June 15—Eli is interviewed by Tarrant County detectives about Glen's murder. Eli drops off Danny in Wyoming with foster parents.
- December 13—Eli returns to Wyoming to get Danny.
- December 24—Little Boy Blue is found in Chester, Nebraska.

1986

- Spring—Eli moves to Fort Worth/Azle, Texas.

1987

- December 11—Little Boy Blue is identified as Danny, and a warrant is issued for Eli's arrest.
- December 14—Eli is taken into custody in Azle, Texas.

1988

- January 11—Eli pleads guilty in a Nebraska courtroom for abandoning a body and concealing a death.

1989

- July—Convicted of killing Glen Pritchett, Eli is sentenced to forty years.

2002

- March—Eli moves to Fort Worth, Texas, on parole.

2007

- January 31—Eli is found dead.

CHAPTER TWO

As my flight skims over quilted farm fields of russet and green on the way from Detroit to Marquette, I try to make the best of my airplane coffee and Biscoff cookie while continuing my review of Ida and Eli's story.

On Ida's side, it was, without a single doubt, a love story.

On Eli's side, well, that's where true crime comes in.

Amos and Lizzie Gingerich's daughter Ida, then sixteen, met Eli at a youth gathering of Swartzentrubers in the summer of 1966. Eli, with a muscular frame and glacial-blue eyes, and Ida, with her ash-blonde hair and radiant smile, had the makings of a striking couple. In Amish Country, especially among the Swartzentruber Order, there is supposedly nothing as unwelcome as pride. And yet, attraction and looks do matter. Ida was smitten. Eli seemed so too.

Their attraction, however, was at once a magnet and a barrier. Over the next few years, Ida would find herself waiting and hoping for Eli to come around and be the man she wanted, a husband. Eli didn't appear to be so serious about his affections, bragging to other Amish boys that Ida "was a good girl" who let him do "everything" during bed courtship, a ritual that has teenage couples—fully clothed—under the covers together. In bed courtship the girl is in charge; she decides among her suitors who visits her at night. A lamp in her bedroom window alerts young men that she's ready for courting, and ready for marriage.

Ida had no idea that her beloved was more than a mere cad, conflicted about other things, including his sexuality. Eli also had a history of mental instability and what his own parents described as "nerve troubles." Indeed, in the summer of 1972, Eli broke Ida's heart when he left the Amish and, subsequently, was put under the bann, or expelled from the church and barred from all personal interactions with church members, including family. I remember talking to Ida's family about that time. While there were a great many tears and lots of headshaking, for Ida, they said, the bann brought hope. It was a tool the church used to force a wayward person to repent and return to the Order.

Ida prayed and waited.

For the next few years Eli enjoyed his freedom, buying a car and traveling to places like Florida and Georgia. It looked as though he'd never come back to the Swartzentruber church.

But that's just what he did.

In the spring of 1975, Eli announced his plan to rejoin the church, which implicitly meant that he was returning for Ida. By the fall, it was announced, or as the Amish church puts it, "published," that Ida and Eli would be married on October 6. Eli was teaching at Cherry Ridge, a one-room schoolhouse, at the time.

As Eli and Ida made wedding plans, news circulated in the community that their marriage had suddenly been put on hold. Some thought maybe Eli had found a new girlfriend or was seeing an old one. The truth, however, was a medical one. The state of Ohio required a blood test to get married at the time, as many states did. Eli's blood test came back with problematic results.

No one can be sure if Ida knew that the test was for gonorrhea and syphilis. It's likely that she didn't. Despite all the talk about bed courtship or "bundling," Amish women know only what they hear from family members when it comes to sex. Venereal disease is not a topic for discussion.

Two memories come to mind of interviewing Ida's sister Lydia in 1989. I drove a rental Geo Metro and was unable to lower the volume on the radio playing Paula Abdul's "Straight Up" as I arrived at Lydia's farm—the knob was stuck!—her wide-eyed kids not sure what to make of me. The other memory was what she said about the blood tests.

That's right.

There was more than one.

Lydia said her sister was beginning to express doubts about her fiancé because of the tests. Ida was a smart young woman. She could see all the reasons why the man she loved was wrong for her, but she hung on. Hope among the Amish is just as powerful as it is in the outside world.

"In some ways," Ida told her sister, "I think Eli is a weak man. I know that I can be a help to him."

Those failing blood tests, however, troubled her. Had they been a message from God?

"Maybe He is telling me it isn't a good idea to marry Eli."

Lydia served me a slice of shoofly pie, a gooey sugar bomb that wept a pool of molasses onto the plate.

Make that *three* memories.

We talked as her barefoot children, curious about me, the Geo Metro, and Paula Abdul, came and went.

"Ida was worried?" I asked.

"Yes."

"Your father too."

"Yes."

"But Eli wasn't worried?"

Lydia shook her head no and told me Eli said he had a doctor who could take the blood and "fix it" so that he and Ida could get married. Despite Ida's love for him, and maybe because some misgivings were settling in, she pushed back on the scheme. It was dishonest. She didn't want to be a part of a lie. But Eli was persistent.

The next thing anyone knew, a big announcement was delivered by a beaming Eli.

"I drank some herb tea a doctor prescribed, and it fixed my blood!"

$$\text{)}\!\text{(}$$

On Christmas Day 1975, Eli and Ida were married at the Gingeriches' home farm in Fredericksburg, Ohio.

A few weeks after they married, Eli and Ida moved into a room at Levi Levi Hershberger's place.

An Amishman told me at the time I wrote *Abandoned Prayers*— in the way Amish do—that this was not a good course of action for anyone.

"I don't want to speak about people in a bad manner. It isn't for me to say," he began, before saying it anyway. "I was suspicious about Levi."

"About what?" I asked.

"I don't want to say. Someone else can."

Fair enough, I thought at the time.

Note to self: *Levi Levi Hershberger, bad.*

Anyway, Ida became pregnant almost right away, and the newlyweds left Hershberger's place for her uncle Gideon Gingerich's fifty-eight-acre farm. No one could tell me why they made the move. Pressure from the bishop? Family? And while Ida was happy to be back with her family, she seemed troubled too. Eli's repeated absences, especially at night, bothered her.

Those worries weighed on Ida throughout the summer of 1976. She was in the last trimester of pregnancy when friends came to visit only to find Ida anxious and alone. She didn't know what she would do if she had to go to Bill-Barb's for the midwife to deliver her first baby.

"I wouldn't know where to find Eli," Ida said.

Whenever Ida said anything of this sort, it was veiled or cast in a roundabout way. She understood her role as a wife. She was not to question but to obey her husband. The acceptance of the role was deep and likely had the unintended consequence of keeping her silent when she really needed help. It also muzzled others from asking too.

People say that the Amish are forgiving, stoic, accepting of God's will. Those attributes are true to some extent. When I met Ida's parents in Michigan, however, I saw two people who had been hurt to the core by their daughter's and grandson's deaths. Faith, and even more so, the bishops who ran their lives with the uncompromising rules of the Ordnung, couldn't hold their emotions captive.

No one can pray away a broken heart or erase a regret.

For their part, Ida's parents knew with certainty something was wrong. They prayed about it. Her father, Amos, even stuck his neck out and directly asked Eli if things were all right between the young couple. Asked, not confronted. Confronting is not the Amish way. In any case, Eli was convincing, and Ida was vague.

"Eli's not doing very good," Ida tearfully confided to her mother, Lizzie, during a visit in 1977.

Lizzie hugged Ida and provided some motherly advice bolstered by the unflinching assurance that all of their prayers would be answered.

"It will be better after the new baby comes," she said.

I remember thinking about that time in Ida's life. She'd wanted nothing more than to be a good wife and mother. She'd loved Eli since she was a teenager. Her parents had told her to forget about him, that he was too troubled and was not going to make a good husband. I wondered if she thought the way women sometimes do in the English world. *Her love would change him. A baby would fortify a shaky union. He'd see that being*

home with their new family would bring joy far greater than whatever he was doing when he was gone.

On September 7, 1976, Eli arranged for a driver to take Ida to Bill-Barb's, where Dr. Elton Lehman was waiting to deliver the baby. Doc Lehman, a Mennonite who made a career out of serving the Amish, handed Ida and Eli Stutzman their firstborn, a son with blue eyes and blond hair. Ida named him Daniel, after her brother.

Around that time, Eli told his family that he'd struck a deal on a ninety-five-acre farm owned by an Amishman named Daniel Swartzentruber. It was a beautiful property on Sand Hill near Dalton. The handshake deal set him back $72,000.

The Stutzmans moved onto the property with six-month-old Danny in the spring of 1977. Ida was pregnant with her second child by then.

During that time, word had gotten around the Amish that there were problems with Eli—again. Now rumors had it that he was training and trading racehorses with Levi Levi—and others that no one in the community knew. Eli's absences associated with the horses weighed on Ida. Eli insisted it was only a sidelight, that he was at heart a farmer.

A father.

A devoted husband.

Eli asked Ida's father to build some steps to the well, because Ida's heart was giving her problems. It was the first time Amos Gingerich had heard of any health concerns. He didn't press his son-in-law about it. Ida was pregnant, and maybe it was the strain of that causing her heart to work hard. So he built the steps.

Another time that same spring, Dan Gingerich and his mother, Lizzie, went to see Ida. Eli was nowhere to be found. At the conclusion of the visit, Dan told me later, his sister broke down on the front porch.

"To cry like that was not like Ida," he said. "She was always the happy one."

She was upset about Eli.

"I don't know what to do about him. I try everything I can think of, yet nothing seems to work."

As Lizzie comforted her, Ida revealed the seriousness of her situation. "I don't think Eli loves me," she said.

His sister's words stung Dan back then, as I suspect they still do.

"If Eli didn't love Ida, why did he marry her?" he asked me, on the way to my car parked next to the barn, his lantern swinging with each step into the rural darkness of Harmony, Minnesota. The cold air coiled around my bare neck. A choke hold. My eyes watered. Dan's did too. The frigid air? Emotion? *A little of both,* I thought. This was a brother who mourned his sister and nephew, a man who had known the answer before his sister had cried on her mother's shoulder.

We both knew it.

Eli married Ida to use her, not to love her.

CHAPTER THREE

Unable to secure a rental car in Marquette or anywhere in Michigan, it seems, I arrange for a driver to take me from Marquette south to Escanaba, where Dan and his family recently relocated from southern Minnesota.

The cost for the ride would be $700.

Ouch.

When I get off the plane in Marquette, I plead my case to the manager at the rental car desk and tell her that I'm there for an interview with an Amishman in Escanaba, and the $700 backup plan is going to kill me.

"What's the interview about?" she asks.

"A murder," I say.

I tell her all about Ida, Eli, and Danny while she clacks away on her computer terminal. Turns out she's a true crime fan. Five minutes later, I'm in my car.

The Midwest gets a bum rap, I must admit. On the drive along Lake Michigan to the dot on the navigation screen that is Dan's new address west of Escanaba, I take in the tidiness of the scenery. Fifty shades of green. No garbage. No graffiti. Homes without posted proclamations about who is right and who is wrong. On a snowy day, it could easily be Wyeth country.

A sign posted near the turnoff to Dan's farm informs me the time zone has changed.

I am stepping back in time.

The Gingerich farm's buggy wheel–rutted gravel driveway is flanked by a massive vegetable garden on one side and a laundry line fluttering with fabrics of indigo, blue, black, and dark green. Behind some ancient chestnut and fruit trees is a white farmhouse. I notice the power lines had been snipped from what had been an English home. Across the road is a phone shack, a bishop's compromise for phone service for the business aspects of Amish life, but not something allowed inside the home.

I park adjacent to a shop, a big, red barnlike building pulsating with the sound of gas-powered air compressors. When Dan emerges from inside, I think I would have known him in a crowd. His eyes are the same. Smile too. He is gray, and his frame, like mine, padded. Thirty years has aged us both, of course. Though he is actually two years younger than I am, I remember thinking when we first met that he'd had a good ten years on me. He had so much responsibility, kids, a farm to run. I had kids too, but a desk job to go to if this writing thing didn't amount to anything. I didn't have to get up at the crack of whatever to milk cows. I didn't have to carry water to the house.

He motions me inside, telling his son-in-law and a gaggle of grand-kids milling hardwood for flooring that he'll be awhile. Then he speaks in *Deutsch*—the German dialect the Amish use—about what I don't know, and we go into his little office. It's like any construction office. Blue vinyl chair on wheels, scuff marks on the floor where wheels trace their movement. A blotter-style calendar with delivery dates and notes sprinkled here and there. All neat. Organized.

Two weeks prior, Dan fell off a wagon—literally, fell off a wagon. He banged his head and even cracked a couple ribs. Despite the mishap, he manages to keep his smile, ignoring the pain while turning his chair to face me.

He fastens his eyes on mine and comes right out with it. "What are you going to try to do?"

"Shake some people loose," I say. "Get them to tell the truth after all these years. I do believe—I *know*—Ida was murdered."

We hold each other's eyes steady, unblinking.

"We know that, right?"

He nods. "Yeah."

"Why can't we get somebody to just say it?"

That "somebody" we're both thinking of all live in Wayne County, Ohio. A few of them, sources who had beat around the bush when I wrote *Abandoned Prayers*, rather than being definitive. No one came out and said what Dan and I knew to be true back then. Now I know the reasons why. None of it had anything to do with the facts of the case surrounding his sister's death, but were the result of secrecy, embarrassment, and shame. To put Ida to rest, officials needed to look at the evidence with unbiased eyes and amend the manner of her death from accidental to homicide.

At the very least, suspicious.

"We know he killed her," Dan says, "but we can't prove it."

I lean into those words. "I think somebody out there could help us."

Quiet fills his little office.

Dan shifts in his chair. "And I don't blame you if you want to try to get to the truth," he says. "I'd like to see the truth. I always said all I want to know is the truth."

"Right," I say.

"But I don't *need* to know it. Yeah. And the reason I say that is, most of my family would say, 'Oh, Dan, don't. Just let it go.'"

"You're different than others in your family. Well, why is that?"

"I don't know the answer."

"I mean, you loved your sister, but is it bigger than that?"

"I can't tell you," Dan says. "I can't answer that question. I, I just always wanted to know the truth."

"So here we are," I say.

Dan is a devout, thoughtful man. He would never seek to hurt anyone involved in the Stutzman saga—Eli's family, friends, members of the church. The very idea of that eats at him as it has since the day of the fire. It is the kind of gnawing, however, that is impossible to ignore. I feel for him. I respect him. Some of what passes between us is unsaid and might always be so.

We talk about how he knows his sister is in heaven and that finding out the truth is of no consequence there. At the same time, Eli may have been consigned to hell.

At this point, the truth can bring only a semblance of justice. No one is going to pay for what he did and nothing can undo what happened.

I had traveled more than a thousand miles to find answers to questions that had occupied my thoughts for more than three decades. I came because I knew that even though Dan couldn't outright say it, he felt the same way. I came because Ida and her unborn baby deserved far better than they got. I also came because the world had changed drastically since Eli Stutzman left a trail of dead bodies from Ohio to Texas.

My theory now is that some secrets don't need to be secrets anymore.

Dan is like a lot of Amish people; in fact, most that I have met over the years share more than just a simple way of life, of loving God, and looking out for each other. Like Ida's brother, they don't like to speak ill of anyone. It is ingrained in every fiber of their being. "Talking bad" about anyone is a poor reflection on the speaker, even greater than transgressions or flaws exposed. Some living among the Amish might scoff at such an assertion—after all, it is doubtful that any electronic or social media is any match for the speed of the Amish grapevine. Their rumor mill is active but for the most part benign. Amish parents raise their children without filling their heads with the ugliness and cruelty that malign our world.

Dan wants me to know something, and I can see it pains him to say it. He speaks in that coded seesaw way that the Amish use when tackling the bad stuff.

"The sister-in-law of a man in Ohio said that her sister's husband confessed before he died."

The word "confessed" halts my breathing and I let him continue without interruption.

"She came to me, and she says, 'Just so you know, he admitted just before he passed that he did not have anything to do with it, I guess, physically, but he knew how it was supposed to happen. And he could have told us who did it and how it was done. But he passed away. And nobody knows for sure.'"

"Did you believe her?" I ask. "Is she trustworthy?"

"Very trustworthy."

Dan withholds his source's name, but I think I know whom he's talking about. In fact, it could be only one person.

Levi Levi Hershberger was a shadowy figure within Eli's life. I'd wondered about his role in what happened the night Ida died. I tried to interview him long ago, but he was never home.

By design, I think now.

"Ida's death was planned, a setup?"

Dan nods. "It had to be. I go as far as saying it had to be, but I leave a little bit of room that I could be wrong. So that's all I can say. But it's annoying. You know, my dad passed away and, you know, he's gone, not forgotten. Ida isn't either. But we can complete this for her."

He slides away from his desk and turns slightly to look out the window. He's thinking of his sister. He's playing all of the circumstances of her life with Eli, as he knew it, and probably in the mix are details

I'd uncovered the first time around. His eyes are damp, and he gives his head a little shake.

"This thing just comes back," he says.

"It just doesn't seem to want to end, Dan. None of this does. It's like a circle."

"Yes," he agrees, "a big circle."

Dan leaves me while he goes into the farmhouse on the other side of the orchard that separates work and home. I sit there, taking in the sounds of his Amish life. The rumbling compressor in the shop, a hen clucking like a metronome on speed as she gets ready to release an egg, the voices of children. When he returns, Dan sets a Wolverine boots shoebox on his desk and removes the lid. "We found this when we settled my parents' estate. Normally we would have put it in the auction. You know, we usually have kids and grandkids, but for some reason this box didn't show up. So, I ended up with it because I was the one that was supposed to settle everything up."

His father, Amos, had put every letter and news clipping about Eli Stutzman inside the box, as he received them.

"Was there anything surprising in there?"

Dan pokes around in the contents.

"I didn't even spend enough time yet in it," he says. "I was going to this winter."

He selects an envelope and looks at the return address. "Oh, here's a letter from Eli's brother-in-law. I don't know what's in there."

He stops talking and lays his eye on me.

"You know, the big thing is, Gregg. I don't want to cause any hard feelings."

"Yeah, I know."

Dan tells me that his wife is skeptical of my intentions. When he went to get the box, she wanted to make sure that I wasn't trying to make a "bunch of money" off of them.

"And don't be offended," he says.

I'm not and I say so. "This is part of my life too. I'm not in as deep as you are because it's your sister. Your namesake nephew. But as an outsider, I'm into finding out the truth more than anybody."

He knows that we have a bond there.

"I guess I feel different about it than some of my family does," he says, indicating the tough spot he's in. His wife, the bishop, and others in his community don't share his compulsion to find out the truth.

We talk a bit more about Levi Levi, though Dan never says his name.

"Why keep the truth hidden all those years if he didn't have a hand in killing your sister?"

"Because he knew that he would be in trouble from the Amish church if he helped with that."

"Well, of course he'd be in trouble with everybody."

I try to scrape off the layers of what I'd learned over the years, looking to Dan for the bottom line, the absolute truth, of what happened.

"What was the reason for all of this?"

"From horse trading, big money to drugs, women. I don't know, but both he and Eli were associated with all of that."

"Right."

"So, it was just a thing when they were young; they had in their heads that 'we're going to do exactly as we please.' So, they did not think they had to abide to any rules. And they got into this way too deep. And all of a sudden, there was no backing out."

I completely agree.

"The truth about some people who commit murder," I say, "it wasn't their ultimate plan. It just seems like the best, though terrible, option at the moment."

"Yeah, I know," he says. "I know. I agree one hundred percent with you. That's why there's no end to this."

I think there could be, but I ask him what an end would look like to him.

"I don't know," he says. "Since Eli is gone, I don't know if there is such a thing."

"What about the truth being known?"

Dan doesn't hesitate.

"Good," he says. "That would be good."

Since he's leaving on a medical trip to Mexico, he apologizes and tells me he needs to leave me alone. I can stay reading as long as I like. Copying the contents is fine too.

I've been in situations like this before with the Amish. They want to help, but they also cannot allow themselves to be a full-on part of helping. Only to a point. Finding how to make that work sometimes takes negotiation.

"Come, but park behind the barn so your car can't be seen."

"Sound is okay to record, but no pictures."

"Milking is at seven, come before that or be prepared to help."

Before Dan leaves, I tell him I wished I lived closer.

"I think we'd be good friends," I say.

A smile takes over his face as he starts to close the door.

"Gregg, we are good friends."

The sound of his grandchildren's voices and the air compressor fades into the background as I start copying letter after letter with my phone's camera. I can't wait to read each one, but there are more than 350 pages in front of me. Letters from Amos, Eli, Danny, family members, strangers; letters from those who knew the family; letters from those who read about the story in *Reader's Digest* before they knew it was Danny or in *People* magazine when Eli had been arrested and was featured in a five-page spread complete with a full-page photo of his face.

There were also letters I'd sent, reminding me that my penmanship hasn't improved over the years.

If the teensiest bit of effort had been applied in the matter of Ida's death, Eli Stutzman would almost certainly have gone to prison, and the falling dominoes of the people in his way would have stopped right there. Danny would have been raised by Amos and Lizzie. The children of Texas murder victim Glen Pritchett would have a father. And, possibly, Dennis Sleater and David Tyler, two unsolved-murder victims tied to Eli in Durango, Colorado, might still be alive.

Later that day, I'm heading home.

CHAPTER FOUR

On the leg to Detroit before the flight home to Seattle, I order a gin and tonic and do my best to read everything I'd copied onto my phone. One letter is of particular interest. Written on January 15, 1978, this is the holy grail of Eli Stutzman missives. It is a letter to an Indiana man whom Eli had never met.

Eli was the consummate liar, an Amish fabulist. He'd changed his story about Ida's death a half dozen times that I knew about, probably more. She'd gone into the milk house to save puppies. Or was it kittens? Or was it to retrieve some milk vats? Whatever. I have known for decades none of those stories were true.

I had worked hard to piece together a case that pointed to his lies. The problem was everything was hearsay. It didn't matter that I trusted the people who told me the versions of what happened that night. It didn't matter if the circumstances of the fire were too far-fetched to be anything but a fabrication.

People could lie. Hell, people *do* lie. All the time. Even when they don't have to.

Dan's father, Amos, told me about this letter, but I'd never actually seen it.

Eli had read an article in an Amish newspaper about this man whose wife had died and felt compelled to write to him.

More than ten years later, when the story of Little Boy Blue became news, the widower mailed a copy to Amos, who put it in the shoebox.

It needs to be noted that not only are the Amish unparalleled letter writers, they are also remarkable letter savers. Their homes are devoid of knickknacks, and I know of no Amish household in which there is a junk drawer, let alone a crafting room piled high with Rubbermaid tubs of projects and keepsakes. On many occasions throughout my research, though, the Amish produced letters that were several decades old. Such communications are cherished.

The letter was written just six months after the fire. It is in Eli's handwriting, no doubt.

And it changes everything.

Dear Unknown Friends,

In days of sorrow & grieves, greeting in our Savior's name. I saw in the Budget that you had something to go through—your dear life's companion left you & your dear little ones are left back in this weary world. But stop and just think there also must be a bright side to it. It might look dark to you at present. I can very easily believe. God can work wonders. There must be a reason to all this. This life on earth is very uncertain. Your wife probably did what she could, or what she was supposed to do. We'll have to believe it must have been God's will.

There's nothing wrong with that, of course. His words are in line with the belief of the Swartzentrubers and others. I'm sure it brought comfort to the Indiana man searching for a reason why a tragedy of that magnitude had come into his life. The next section is the only account of the fire written in Eli's hand.

I have or am having the experiences of losing my companion. This last July one night approx. midnight my wife, woke me up and said there is fire in the barn. She told me then she had also been asleep and was woken up by a bursting sound of some kind from the barns, then looked and saw from where she was lying in our bed, that there were flames in the barn, which she would see through the barn window.

All right, I think, breaking it down. Ida told Eli that she was asleep when wakened by the fire. Okay. Who tells someone, at midnight, that they were sleeping? Then woke up? No one. That's who. It is the beginning of a story Eli carefully crafted. He wanted the recipient to know that Ida was alive. This is the only account mentioning a bursting sound that woke Ida. All others say it was the light coming through the window.

Almost before I was ready to follow, she was ready to leave the house and see if we could stop the fire.

In other recitations of the events of that night, Ida was the first one out the door, fully dressed, with Eli following her. Fully dressed is a key here. Swartzentruber women wear modest nightgowns at bedtime. Ida took the time to pin the kind of dress she'd wear during the day.

But before we got to the barn, I said it looks as if we're too late to stop the flames, as it was burning very brightly on the hay mow, which I could see through from an upper barn window. So, I said I'd like to try and get some implements out which were stored in the barn. She asked what she could do and mentioned that she could go to the neighbors and call the fire department and I agreed and she started to go then turned back and asked if she shouldn't take out the milking bucket before going to the neighbors. She was about to pass the milk house when she asked.

Those were the last words I heard her say.

I then said she could if it was not too hot on that side of the barn. I had noticed that fire was increasing rapid. I got what I could from the upper barn, but I couldn't get very much 'cause this was a lot of smoke and the flames that poured off the main den—where I had the ladder wagon, binder, and hay loaded. So, I decided to get what I could from the ground floor. The first thing I got there was an orphan foal (colt). My thoughts then went to the bull, which was in a back pen. I gave up to let him out as I soon saw that there were flames in the alleys that led to his pen. The fire had already burned through the barn floor in some spots. So, I got some harness and shop tools which were stored in front end of the barn.

Then my thought went to the milk house which was the other side of the barn I had not been to yet. Before I got to the milk house door, I noticed that some things have been removed from the milk house but also saw there was something unusual in the doorway. Then my thoughts flashed to my wife. I found the milk vat standing in the doorway. I put it out of the way. But had a hard time to see anything the milk house was quite dark and contained some smoke. I found my wife lying on the floor not far from the door. I begged her to answer to my call, but there was no answer.

From that instance I felt a lonely feeling which hasn't left me yet. I took her from the milk house and try to put her far enough away so that heat and smoke would surely not touch her. But I didn't take her far enough, as she showed heat burns, that the Dr. said she received after death. The Dr. said the cause of her death was apparent heart attack. She had removed everything from the milk house except the vat, that I think she probably was on her way out when death occurred. The only thing alive that burned in the fire was the bull and a few little puppies. After taking my wife away from the milk house my thoughts soon took me back to our only child a son 10 mo. old, which was in our bed-room in his crib still fast asleep. There [was] also a cousin, 12-year-old boy, which was staying with us and helping along with the farm work. [He] slept upstairs [and] had woken [and] was just ready to leave the house, as I entered it. So, I send him to the neighbors for help.

This last week has seemed to be rather a tough one for me. Just don't want to complaint. It was 6 mos. on Thurs. since my wife passed away. I think it has been the longest 6 mos. I've ever had yet. But I hope it will help me lead a better spiritual life.

My adrenaline wages war with the effects of the gin I'm drinking as I absorb the next paragraph. I know immediately what it was that Amos had found so compelling.

Officials have determined the cause of the fire was lightning. We had a thundershower in the late afternoon that day, but it didn't rain that night at all. They claim lightning must have hit late that afternoon and just smoldered until that night.

Officials determined.
They claimed.

Not true. It was Eli who did all of that. It was also Eli who gave the coroner a potential cause of death.

Something is also missing from Eli's account. There is no mention of CPR. Eli told Ida's family he'd performed CPR on Ida for almost a half hour.

And so it went. Eli Stutzman's version of what happened the night his wife died varied. Wildly. He told one friend that she'd died in a car wreck, another that she went into the barn to save some puppies. Or kittens. Or the milk vats. One of his friends in Texas told me a version that had Ida up feeding Danny when the fire broke out. Instead of waking Eli, she tried to fight the fire all by herself.

As if.

When Eli woke up, he found her in the milk house and carried her across the road.

All right. I admit it. I don't think Ida's death was due to natural causes.

She was murdered.

I had seen a few letters written by Eli before, of course. Amos sent me copies of a handful years ago, but Dan's shoebox contained a veritable archive—stretching more than a decade. The first was mailed from Bradenton Beach, Florida, to Amos, still in Fredericksburg, February 16, 1979. Ida had been gone a year and a half by then.

> *What I'd like to know is who is this I'm getting married to???? Abe said when they came here that day they'd heard before they left the reason I left Ohio and went to Georgia was to get married. This is a shock to me 'cause this was totally news to me, and I can't see why anybody would have decided to make such a thing up.*
>
> *I know that some people think I'm crazy, 'cause I haven't remarried.*

But I think this is my business or between me and God. I do. So far, I don't think it has been God's will for me to get remarried. So, what do I do? Do what people think I should do or try to live after God's will? It is a very touchy situation.

After that rant he writes about Danny not being in diapers anymore and how a neighbor lady has been taking care of him and that he's getting bigger and his clothes are getting small on him. He encloses a picture of Danny in a bathing suit.

On the margin is a note purportedly written by the then two-year-old:

I have lots of fun on beach bye, bye Danny

I order a second gin and tonic on the Seattle-bound flight. The note from Danny was so very much in line with how Eli operated. Later he'd forge other notes, pretending they were written by Danny.

After the boy was dead.

Eli even had the sociopathic gall to put others on the phone pretending to be his son.

The next shoebox letter was almost a year later, on December 17, 1979. In it, Eli writes to Amos and Lizzie from Chicago, where he's sitting at the airport on a plane, and gives a long dissertation about how many people can sit on the plane, what kind of plane it is, how fast it goes, and how the pilots report about how high they are.

I always thought these things would probably roar like a grinder, riding on them, but I sure can't hear much from the inside. I guess they go so fast enough that the noise can't keep up with them.

Next up is a Christmas card, supposedly from Danny, mailed on December 18, 1979.

Hello all, how are you? We both have a little cold but not bad we play a lot and sometimes tease if no buddy else is looking. We have a small Christmas tree in the living room and there are presents underneath. I almost can't wait to open mine. We have to sleep seven times yet.

Here's the thing. It is very hard—no, impossible—to know Eli's motives when he wrote these letters to his in-laws. Did he want to keep them close or keep them away? Letters were a way for Eli to create a story that would appease Amos and Lizzie. Make them think all was well and there was no reason to get on a Greyhound to see what was really going on. I know Amos was suspicious and concerned. He told me so. He told me that he'd heard rumors about things on the farm.

For his part, I can only imagine the annoyance Eli must have felt with the Amish, led by Ida's family, always checking in to see if they could help him through a difficult time. Always suggesting that getting back to the church would be his salvation.

No one, of course, knew what he was really doing.

He sent this letter to his in-laws on Valentine's Day 1980.

Danny is doing his chores in the bathroom. Today I hauled several loads of manure and the rest of the day I worked inside working on a closet in my room. I redid the ceiling and walls. Also I would like to do some of the other rooms the same way. Eli Byler is helping me, whenever the weather is not permissive to work outside. He ordinarily works with a ruff up crew but also has finishing tools and has had them here for a month now for me to use when I get the chance.

Ida's cupboard is still standing where it did that summer and I intend to leave it there if the Lord's will. The sink I've been puzzling with what to do at. And I suppose I'll just keep it in the first backroom for now.

Two weeks ago, I and Danny went to Texas. I did some work on a horse. Danny sure enjoyed the trip. The weather midday by 10 was in the high 60s and sunny. It didn't take Danny long to find some friends to play with.

Eli thanks Ida's sister Susie for sharing a dream she had about Ida. I can only speculate on what she'd written. Maybe a dream in which Ida was in heaven watching over Eli and Danny? Maybe that Ida was still alive. Susie loved Danny. She'd never married and had no children of her own. She'd been there to hear concerns from Ida about whatever it was that Eli was doing. She was too kind a woman. Too Amish, really, to confront Eli.

Yes, Ida is still in my dreams a lot. I have no intentions of moving any of Ida's furniture out of this house. I intend to come to Michigan sometime, but I don't know when I will get there. It seems I've got too many things started now. Thanks for all the invitations anyway.

I scroll through letters to find the ones my younger self sent to the Gingeriches. In the first, on January 17, 1989, I write about returning from the preliminary hearing for Eli's Texas trial for the murder of Glen Pritchett.

I'll keep looking for the truth. Together we might be able to put some of the pieces together.

Next up, a little note written out by their neighbor, Mrs. Calhoun. I guess it's a kind of Amish telegram.

Eli Stutzman convicted of roommate's murder. Sentencing on July 31st. Could get five years to life. Convicted Friday July 21st.

Finally, a letter dated August 14, 1989, in which I inform Ida's family about my latest interview trips.

I am digging very deeply to uncover whatever I can to learn the truth. I know I will find it. One of the most pleasant portions on my trip was a visit with Elmer Miller and his wife Erma. I had my wife and four-year-old twin girls with me at the time. Elmer gave us a buggy ride. He was very kind to us and I am glad that I found him. He took me to see Ida's grave.

I let them know that when I was in Texas, I was unable to find any of the Amish furniture Eli left behind after being questioned by the police.

It all disappeared a couple of days later and no one seems to know where it is but I promise to keep looking. I went to see Eli at the jail, but he didn't want to see me. I'll try again later.

I close by asking for copies of the letters Eli had faked when he pretended Danny was still alive.

That's me then. And now too. I never claimed to be the best true crime writer, like the Seattle area's Jack Olsen and Ann Rule indisputably were, but I did my best to follow their differing approaches on what a true crime book should be.

Jack, though no relation, called me Cousin Gregg. Actually, and with ironic intent, "the loquacious" Cousin Gregg. He was a literary, no-holds-barred kind of writer who dazzled readers with language and smart details. The dean of true crime, without question.

Jack's books were nuanced and meticulously researched, delivering details that no one knew—even on cases in which people thought they'd heard everything.

Ann was a brilliant, cat-sweater-loving crime writer who showed every cop and prosecutor that being on her good side was a very smart thing to do. She was a savvy marketer too, dialing into the emotions of her subjects and her readers like no one else.

Ann's books held no room for any gray areas. Victims were good and beautiful. Perpetrators were nasty and selfish.

Not surprisingly, rivals Jack and Ann hated each other.

When I finished *Abandoned Prayers*, both of my local heroes blurbed the book to launch my career.

Red-letter day that was.

Back home in Olalla, across Puget Sound from Seattle, I send some of the letters to my printer and wait for the sound of the machine as it converts the digital to the tangible. The pages peel into the output tray and I tug at some to force them out quicker. Prosecutors don't get a second chance in a murder case that's gone to trial and ended with an acquittal. What happened to Ida, and eventually Danny, never even made it that far. In a world that calls for justice now on cases long since cold, I know I'm their last chance. This is far from a brag or boast. I don't pretend to be a brilliant investigator. I'm only a writer, a listener. My job is to tell the truth as I find it. My saving grace here is that I have something on my side that allows me a second bite at the apple. No double jeopardy is attached to what I'm doing three decades after I took that first swing at the Stutzman story.

As a writer, I can revisit a case. Go and turn the stones. Ask the same questions. Maybe hold some folks' feet to the fire.

And find out what happened to Ida the night she died.

CHAPTER FIVE

July 11, 1977, was a typical night at the Stutzman farm in Dalton, Ohio. Before bed, Ida sang old German songs and cuddled Danny, who slept in a crib in his parents' room on the main floor.

Eli's cousin, also named Eli Stutzman, twelve, went to bed upstairs about 9:00 p.m. Around midnight, the hired boy's eyes were drawn to a window where he saw the gold and red of flames and a black plume rising from the roof of the barn. Dressing as he went, he hurried downstairs, calling for Eli and Ida. Baby Danny was asleep in his crib, but the Stutzmans were gone.

Why didn't Eli or Ida wake me with the news of the blaze? he wondered. *Where are they? Why didn't they call for me to help?*

On the front porch, he nearly crashed into Eli.

"Go to Harley Gerber's!" Eli said. "Have him call the fire department! Hurry!"

Adrenaline taking over, the boy ran past the south side of the barn, his bare feet pressing hard against the surface of the dirt driveway. Over his shoulder, he caught a glimpse of Stutzman pulling farm machinery from the barn. A box wagon and tools had already been moved.

As he turned the corner where Moser Road connects with the driveway, he saw Ida on her back, motionless. Her eyes were closed. She was only a step or two from the barn.

"Ida! Ida!" he called out, dropping next to her. "What is wrong? Ida, wake up!"

He touched her, but she didn't budge. Although most of the color was washed from her face, her left cheek and her left hand were pink from the heat. He could see that she was too hot, too close to the fire.

He ran back to tell Eli that Ida was hurt.

Stutzman just shook his head. *He already knew.*

"Go to Harley Gerber's now! Get the rescue squad too!" he instructed.

"He seemed mad that I had not done what he told me," Cousin Eli told me, when I was researching *Abandoned Prayers*. He was in his twenties at the time, but the elder Eli's indifference to Ida's condition still rattled him. Why hadn't he mentioned that Ida had been hurt in the first place? Why was he more concerned about the farm equipment than he seemed to be about his pregnant wife?

"I can never understand that," he told me.

There's more that happened that night that no one ever understood. I've racked my brain over the sequence of events. I diagrammed first on paper and then, more recently, with strings of red yarn and white cards pinned to my wall like a member of the FBI's Behavioral Science Unit. I stand by what I have always believed, that Eli moved Ida's body in order to stage a scenario he thought would make the most sense.

The key to understanding Eli's plot is to piece together what Cousin Eli and neighbor Howard Snavely told me in 1989. Based on my research and interviews, the hired boy was the first to observe Ida's body that night. Howard had been the second.

Awakened by the fire and jolted by a gusher of adrenaline, Howard hurried across Moser Road toward the Stutzmans' front door. He assumed that Eli and Ida were unaware of the blaze because he saw no one outside. Just as he arrived, Stutzman came around from the other side of the barn. Howard would tell me later that he wondered if Eli had heard him call out that the barn was on fire. Or maybe he had seen him on the way to the door.

The timing was lucky and remarkable.

Eli seemed frantic. He motioned for Howard to follow.

"We've got to get my wife out! She's trapped!"

More adrenaline surged through Howard's body as he followed his Amish neighbor to the milk house.

"We've got to get her out!" Eli repeated.

Howard noticed some stainless steel three-gallon buckets and a milk strainer outside the door to the milk house. When Eli swung open the door, Howard saw Ida, dressed in her Amish clothes, including her black headscarf, on her back. Her feet were next to the door, her head farther inside the structure.

Stutzman said something about a heart attack as he lifted Ida up by hooking his hands under her arms. Snavely carried the weight of her feet and legs. Ida's uncradled head hung limply as the two men moved her to the night pasture across the road. Eli was quiet, and his body no longer shook in spasms.

Howard reached for Ida's wrist.

No pulse.

When the hired boy returned from the Gerbers, he saw that Ida had been moved to the pasture on the other side of the road. She looked exactly as she had when he saw her slumped outside the milk house. He thought that the fire department, now on the scene, had put her there. He didn't know that it was Eli and English neighbor Howard Snavely who had done it.

Nor did he know that it was *after* he went for help that Eli screamed for Howard to help get his wife out of the milk house.

And when he'd sprinted away, Ida was lying near the barn, not inside the milk house.

)(

Flames roared from the peaked roof of the barn at the Stutzmans' farm. With speed and efficiency, Kidron fire chief Mel Wyss and his crew started pumping from a fifteen-hundred-gallon tanker, the department's only such unit.

Snavely called for Wyss.

"We have an injury! Mrs. Stutzman is hurt!"

When the chief looked at her, he knew Ida was dead.

Wyss, who as a Sugarcreek Township trustee knew Eli Stutzman well enough to recognize him in town, approached him for information for his report. Eli was nervous and excited, and Chief Wyss couldn't blame him for that. His reaction, however, seemed incomplete. He was oblivious to the condition of his wife.

"I told her to go call the fire department and she left for help," Eli told Wyss. "When I came around the barn and went into the milk house, I found her inside. She was lying inside on her back. She must have had a heart attack because of the smoke."

Wyss made notes for his report.

It took Wayne County sheriff's deputy Phil Carr ten minutes to get to the scene from Kidron, where he had been on patrol duty. He arrived at the fire at 12:40 a.m. He was alone, although he knew from the radio dispatcher that his boss, Wayne County sheriff Jim Frost, was on his way. Carr, who had been with the department for two years, was briefed by Mel Wyss.

Wyss instructed the squad led by Wes Hofstetter to take Ida to Dunlap Memorial Hospital. Eli didn't ask about his wife and gave no indication he knew she was dead.

Although Eli Stutzman's reaction seemed off to Hofstetter, Eli was, after all, Amish. Amish, Hofstetter thought, don't show much emotion.

Sheriff Frost arrived about that time and stayed only a few minutes. He left word that he was on his way to the hospital to interview the victim's husband.

Another who showed up then was attorney Tim Blosser.

"You aren't going to believe this," he told Deputy Carr. "I was here earlier in the evening helping the Stutzmans write their will!"

That's right.

A lawyer had been at the farm working on the Amish couple's will. That night.

No one considered that a red flag at the time.

As I go over Eli's description of the night of the fire in his letter to the grieving Indiana Amishman, I see the meeting with the lawyer about the will as crucial circumstantial evidence. It was either a coincidence or planned.

From what I've learned of Eli's life before and after the fire, the way he used being Amish as a smoke screen over his true character, I say it was all planned.

CHAPTER SIX

On the phone from Waynesville, Missouri, where he now lives, Tim Blosser, the attorney at the scene of the fire, is all over the place when it comes to recollections about his client Eli Stutzman. In his late seventies, Blosser speaks in awkward fits and starts. Sometimes about what I need to know. Often about the dogs he and his wife rescue and who are clearly more important than anything in their lives.

Keeping him on track is no easy endeavor.

I want to know how the will came about. He thinks a beat and says Eli came to him at Ida's request.

"So, we set up a date that I would go out to his house and do a will. And they invited me to eat, which I didn't. Maybe some water, though I'm not sure. They were shaken up about the lightning. They were saying, 'You can't believe what happened.'"

Eli and Ida even took him to the barn to show him.

"And I saw this with my own eyes. Lightning struck on the header, knocked out the window up in the apex of the barn. Looking down on the floor, covered with hay, about three or four inches of hay, maybe not, not a lot. And it was still over the hill. I saw this. And he said most of them he thought they had extinguished."

Blosser says he saw embers.

"And I think I picked them up and said, 'Eli, you know, this thing's still smoldering.' Because it had happened about 4:00. The lightning went through roughly 4:00 to 4:15 because I got there, let's say around 6:30. I'm trying to keep this straight."

He stops and rethinks.

"I don't remember who picked it up. Maybe Eli went, got a pitchfork, and picked up that part. But then we tramp the straw around because they were still smoldering. I feel like we got to get some water on this deal. Now, who got the water? I don't know. But we saturated it."

Then he returns to the lightning and the burned wood.

"Oh, lightning. Lightning. And I want to go a little further. My mind is going back now. It was definitely dark and . . . it amazes me. I thought, boy, you know, the Lord is looking after them. Yeah."

While his dogs yap in the background, the lawyer digs into his memory, adding a caveat to allow some grace for his lapse in not pressing the audacity of Stutzman's story of the lightning to the authorities.

The Lord was looking after them.

"From that point," he says, "we went back into the house, and I took down the information for a very simple will. And I left. In fact, you won't believe this. But I can look back at the evening much like it is now. Did that happen in July?"

"Yes."

"So anyhow, when I left, they both walked me out to the car. And Amish never show affection. But they were close to each other. Real close."

Blosser disappears on a tangent, this time about his brother being a Secret Service agent. But that's—most definitely—another story.

When he refocuses, he notes, rather offhandedly, that the Stutzmans had a '72 Dodge.

I don't say a word. Instead, I ponder the rumor I'd heard that Eli hadn't ditched his driver's license—something he'd promised the bishop he'd do when he returned to the Order to marry Ida. His cousin Chris

Stutzman told me in a recent phone call that he'd wondered how it was that Eli was able to drive to see him in Greenville, Ohio, just after the fire. Maybe it was a driver's license that Ida had seen when she told her family that Eli was having some problems.

Mentally?

Or with the church?

In the early morning hours of July 12, Blosser ended up back at the farm as the fire burned. All these years later, he wrestles with just how it was that he was alerted to the fire. A call from someone? The sounds of sirens?

"I'm not an ambulance chaser," he says. "Anyhow, I wind up going toward the fire."

The scene was chaotic. As the flames met water from the trucks, smelly plumes of acrid smoke and steam rose above the trees. Cars came. Amish buggies pulled by terrified horses stayed back from the flames. Onlookers peered from the edges of Moser Road. The air was heavy and sad. Tim Blosser approached Eli, who was talking to one of the first responders.

"Well, Blosser was here," Eli said, indicating his lawyer. "He just did a will for us, thank God."

That fact was recorded in reports made that night.

Eli's face registered relief when mentioning his good luck about the will. It was a standard will. In the event of a death, all assets would go to either spouse and, finally, to Danny.

Blosser didn't tell him then that the will wasn't valid. It hadn't even been typed up, nor had it been witnessed by two other parties. Eli might have thought having an English lawyer over to write up the will would be enough, that witnessing it, recording it in court, all of the steps needed to ensure its validity, weren't required.

Tim Blosser is steadfast in his belief that Eli would never hurt his wife—at least, not the Eli he knew. He doesn't consider that someone could be devious and appear gentle and naïve at the same time.

The rest of the world has an idealized perception of the Amish—always truthful, always kind, always forthright when needed. Some who live among the Amish see that the image, the wrapper of blue and black clothing and hats, only makes them appear all the same. In fact, to no one's surprise, they are real people.

Tim Blosser paints his own picture of the way things are in Amish Country.

"There's always a skepticism because they look at us—and you can put this in your book—they look at us, the English, like we're not worthy. Basically, I don't want to make it too strong a term, but we're unrighteous in their eyes.

"His wife seemed very happy that Eli had been able to extinguish the fire before it burned down their barn," Blosser recalls of Ida. "I can picture how the table was set in the house. And I think I noticed that she was pretty. She was holding Daniel. I was looking at Daniel."

He puts the brakes on his stream of consciousness before going on.

"I can still see her. And the fact that she was very concerned. I told you when they walked out now . . . they were closer than any man and woman. There was love at that point. There was a lot of that going on. What happened after I left the house? I have no suspicion. I have no suspicion whatsoever."

X

As our conversation continues, Tim Blosser switches gears and says that he'd met Eli at a sawmill and that Eli knew he was an attorney. The young Amish husband and father said he needed a will. Blosser concedes the request was a little unusual. Many Amish, especially the older ones at that time, didn't bother with the convention of legal documents from the English world. There was no need. When someone died, everything would be sold at auction with the proceeds split among family members—like it had been done for hundreds of years. In reality, the connection between Blosser and Stutzman was made much earlier. Tim's uncle, Horace Blosser, was an avid horseman—as was Eli. Many of the horses Horace Blosser raced were purchased from Amish farms in Ohio and Indiana.

"Eli would go to my uncle for advice," Tim Blosser says. "So, I saw him, you know, two or three times when I was working for my uncle."

During another call from Missouri, a few days later, Blosser alters his story. Or at the very least, adds a layer of information not mentioned before. He says Eli didn't really care about the will. It was Ida who had insisted that it be done.

"He could care less. I think she wanted it more than he did. It was Ida's idea. He was silent. She didn't talk either."

This conversation, brief and strange, ends abruptly.

"Forgive me, but I have to go get my blood taken."

Click.

I look at the timeline fashioned of Post-it notes spreading across the three windows that face the water of Hood Canal at my writing cabin. Little pink and yellow squares. Confetti, I think, though with nothing to celebrate.

I shift my attention back to our recorded conversation and press play. First, according to Blosser, Eli was very concerned about the future and wanted to protect his wife, son, and unborn baby in the event anything happened to him. But after the fire? Eli was silent. Didn't care? If so, then why make such a big deal about it at the fire by telling everyone that his lawyer had just been there writing the will that very night?

It passes through my thoughts that it is another instance of Eli's adroit mimicry of an Amishman, a man in a community with a strong faith in God's divine presence. He's underscoring how everything that happens, good or bad, is God's will. God was watching out for him and his little boy by having the lawyer there hours before the fire.

Eli Stutzman was so blessed, so lucky.

Until he wasn't, of course.

In reality, he was the unluckiest of men. So many of those close to him would die an untimely death. I rethink that prevailing notion, one that I've held inside for all these years. Every single death could have been stopped.

If just one person had done the right thing.

CHAPTER SEVEN

No one will ever know what Sheriff Jim Frost was thinking when he left Eli Stutzman at the hospital early in the morning on July 12, 1977. No one who worked with the Wayne County sheriff in those days recalls anything other than business as usual.

He simply breezed into his office at the Justice Center, shut the door, and tapped out his report on case C950-77:

> *Eli related to me that this evening while he was coming home from Dalton, about late supper time, he thought he saw a flash of lightning strike his barn. He checked the barn and could not find any sign of a fire. He then ate, milked the cows, and when he was done milking the cows, he went up to get some straw and found a spot on the top of the granary, which stores wheat, that appeared to have been burned by a lightning strike. Because of this, approximately every half-hour he checked the area on the west side of the barn, but never found any other evidence of fire. His wife, Ida, woke him in the night and stated, "There looks like there is a fire in the west end of the barn." They both ran outside, and he asked her to call the fire department. She went around one side of the barn and yelled something back to him, which he*

could not understand. He tried to get things out of the barn; however, the fire was too hot and intense. As he went around the side of the milk house, he saw many items out by the side of the road that had been in the milk house. Upon checking in the milk house, he found his wife with her feet toward the door, lying in somewhat of a curled position. Blocking the door was a large milk vat filled with items from the milk house. He indicates the milk house was full of smoke, but there was no fire and no intense heat. He dragged his wife out of the milk house to the other side of the road with her left side toward the fire. He attempted CPR and mouth-to-mouth resuscitation but was unable to revive her. After help began arriving, he noticed that the heat from the fire was apparently burning her face and arms. He got help to drag her further into a field away from the fire.

Though we met more than three decades ago, when I close my eyes, I can still see Ida's parents. Amos Gingerich, rail thin, with Gothic cathedral–window arched eyebrows, and Lizzie with her petite hands and bright-blue eyes. We walked around the place near Gladwin, Michigan, as they filled me in on what it takes to run a farm without the benefit of modern technology. Amos did most of the talking. It was small talk, fascinating in its own way, but a necessary prelude to why I was there.

By then the Gingeriches had long given up believing anything their son-in-law said. Little Boy Blue was all over the news, and the mystery of what had happened to Ida was coming into uncomfortable focus. Amos, like just about every Amish man or woman whom I met, never spoke in the absolutes that English people employ as a matter of course.

We know something.

We are 100 percent convinced.

We flatly refuse to move our positions one way or another.

The Amish have their own unyielding convictions but are less interested in broadcasting things that are out of their hands. In the case of their incarcerated son-in-law, Eli Stutzman, they provided a narrative without personal opinions shaping any of it.

Inside their living room, Amos leaned forward on a hickory rocker and recalled what Eli told the family when they saw him at the hospital.

"It was such a funny thing that we had just finalized our will," he'd said. "God had sent me up to Dalton to take care of the will just before He called Ida home. He was watching out for me and Danny. Our Lord, the one who died for us on the cross, works miracles."

Amos didn't say his son-in-law's story was complete bullshit. Not with words anyway. He recounted it with a kind of subtle shaking of his head and an upward gaze.

Next, he related what Eli had said about the fire itself.

"Ida awoke me up at midnight, telling me the barn was on fire. We both went out. I went to the upper part of the barn. I told her to call the fire department at the neighbors'. She asked if she could save some things out of the milk house first. I told her she could, but hurry. When I was done in the upper barn, I found her. She was in the milk house trying to put the vats out and she was overcome by smoke. Her feet were under the vats."

Lizzie left to join Susie in the kitchen.

"Eli said he had dragged Ida out of the milk house to the night pasture across the road."

"With help?" I asked, thinking of neighbor Howard Snavely.

Amos shook his head. "Alone."

Again, as I had before, I weigh the shifting details. Was Eli making mistakes? Or was it just the trauma's impact on the listener as he or she recalled the story he'd told them?

"Then he put her gently on the grass and tried to awaken her to life, but he failed."

I asked for more about the purported CPR, and Amos leaned back in his rocker.

"He tried for twenty or thirty minutes," he told me.

Eli knew CPR from his days as an orderly, and while Amos and Lizzie accepted God's plan and would not have done anything to tamper with it, they hoped that part of Eli's story had been true.

"He said he tried to save her, but I don't know the truth of it."

Amos didn't want to call his son-in-law an out-and-out liar, which is what he was really saying with the "I don't know the truth of it" add-on.

Amos, actually all of the Gingeriches, knew Eli had lied right to their faces at the hospital, as he had dozens of times before and since the night Ida died. Right in the eyes. He probably didn't even blink.

CHAPTER EIGHT

It's late and the creamer on my afternoon coffee has become a cold oil slick. I drink from my souvenir Alcatraz mug anyway. Ida's autopsy report is on my desk. I'm both horrified and fascinated by the outcome of Ida's autopsy as rendered by Wayne County coroner J. T. Questel.

I can't say Dr. Questel was combative when I interviewed him in 1989, more than a dozen years after Ida's death, but he definitely wasn't forthcoming. Up to that point, everyone that I interviewed had professed a desire to help. The coroner, however, was standoffish at best. Defensive even. Closed up tight. I knew he'd been feeling some heat for his investigation into Ida's death, or rather, the lack thereof.

If he was as decent a fellow as many proclaimed, I suspect he was mortified that he'd failed Ida and her family. His lack of due diligence, for whatever reason, allowed a monster to escape justice.

And to murder again and again.

Dr. Questel wasn't exactly a commanding presence when I met him at his office in Wooster, Ohio. In fact, the coroner was a small-boned eccentric with a white bottle-brush mustache and an NRA dinner plate–size belt buckle. He'd served in the air force and attended medical school at Ohio State, where he met his wife, Wooster native Helen. The couple was well known to law enforcement, though Sheriff Jim Frost held an especially important place in their hearts.

"We both consider Jim to be like a son," Questel told me back then.

He was stiff and perfunctory when we talked. He told me how Deputy Carr briefed him on the case. How Eli said his wife had a weak heart from rheumatic fever when she was a teenager. How Eli said Ida was unconscious when he found her in the milk house and carried her outside. And because it was too hot there, he moved her again.

When we talked about the likelihood of a pregnant woman hauling milk cans from a burning barn in the middle of the night, he stood his ground. It did not strike him as odd. Like other *Englischers* in Wayne County, Questel insisted the thrifty Amish would save whatever they could.

No one, not Sheriff Frost or any investigator, told the coroner about Stutzman's history of violence and deception.

No one mentioned that setups and fabrications had been the Amishman's MO since he was a teenager.

My oil-slick coffee finally, and thankfully, vanquished, I pick through the pages of the autopsy report and pause to write a single word on the outside of the file folder in block letters. For emphasis, I underscore it three times.

"C-o-n-s-p-i-r-a-c-y?"

It was in the basement morgue at Dunlap Memorial that Dr. Questel went about his business in a manner that suggests incompetence at best, negligence at worst.

All right, maybe even worse than that.

Possibly criminal.

The longtime county coroner collected blood samples for carbon monoxide testing, and since Sheriff Frost told him that the Stutzmans had a bottle of Valium in the house, a sample was collected to test for that at a Cleveland lab.

Most of Ida's burns were on the left part of her body, the side closest to the burning barn. Ida's left breast was exposed; Dr. Questel noted that her nipple had been burned to a parchment-like hardness. The left side of her face was also burned, not from flames, Dr. Questel surmised, but from the intense indirect heat of the fire. The left side of her abdomen was parched enough to cause slippage of some skin. Some burns were outlined in white, others in red. Ida Stutzman's nylon headscarf had melted in a number of places; the fabric soldered itself to her neck. Her jacket was also scorched.

When Dr. Questel poked around Ida's dress, he noted she had suffered extensive burns underneath her clothing, which was not unusual given the extreme heat. The coroner also documented mud smears on the front of her dress.

The mud was insignificant enough to suggest that she had not fallen or doubled over and then rolled onto her back.

Additionally, he wrote that Ida's right fingers had been scorched to a deep red, as was the base of her palm. The center of her palm, however, was unburned. Her hand was frozen in an open clench. The burns covered her entire fingers, not just the obvious contact surfaces.

The exposure of Ida's left breast suggested she might not have had time to fully pin her dress when she left the house to fight the fire.

However, if Eli had told her to go to the neighbors, as an extremely modest Amish woman, Ida would have pinned it securely.

Another explanation could be that the dress was unpinned during Eli's rescue effort of performing CPR.

If he'd actually done any.

Most troubling of Questel's findings were the cut and scratches on Ida's face and mouth. Long scratches cut across her forehead from the bridge of her nose to just above her left eyebrow. A bloody laceration from the corner of her mouth was also noted. Blood seeped over her gums and between her teeth. A fall might have caused the injuries. In fact, Eli Stutzman had said his wife had fallen in the milk house. But he was specific: *she was on her back.*

How could she harm her mouth and scratch her forehead falling backward?

The mouth is a very vulnerable and tender part of the human body. It was more likely that she had been struck by something or, in the most chilling scenario, beaten. When a boxer bleeds from a blow, it usually is planted on the mouth, or above the eyes.

This is where I wish I could do a big do-over on my interview with Dr. Questel. I didn't challenge him enough. I didn't push back on his autopsy report and how cursory its contents were. *"Did you take off her headscarf? Did you think she might have been beaten? You tell me that the blood was red, and you say that she'd been alive when she got those injuries; then why in God's name didn't you examine her body for bruises? Her neck for strangulation?"*

Those questions can never be asked. Dr. Questel died six years ago. He was ninety-three.

So I sit here in deep regret that I didn't do enough. That I accepted his findings. While I knew Ida's death was no accident, I didn't believe at the time that Questel's autopsy, as lousy as it was, was a key to unraveling the lies to find the truth.

Now I know better.

I also know that Dr. Questel knew it too.

For the life of me, I can't figure out Mennonite osteopath Elton Lehman, the quintessential country doctor who devoted his life to caring for generations of Amish people. So classic, so exceptional, Dr. Lehman was honored as Country Doctor of the Year and featured in *Parade* magazine and on the *Today* show. He knew all his patients' and their children's names and said hello to everyone in passing. He'd taken care of Ida from sixteen to the birth of her son, Danny.

But he knew nothing about Ida's weak heart from a bout with rheumatic fever.

He was no stranger to Eli either.

I remember sitting with him in his Mount Eaton office. He wore his graying hair combed back and stared me down through large-framed glasses perched on a sharp nose. His mustache was so closely cropped, it looked more like a shadow above his lips.

Dr. Lehman told me it was true that he'd been to Amish neighbor Mose Keim's place to help when Eli was confined to bed in a depressed and nervous state. He'd been out to the Stutzman farm too. In addition, he knew Eli had been admitted to a mental health hospital.

He probably knew much more than that.

I have no idea what reason could be powerful enough to stop a man like Dr. Lehman from voicing doubts over Dr. Questel's ruling in 1977 when he knew it was false.

That's me thinking today, of course. Back then, I accepted that he was haunted by all of the things that had transpired since the night Ida died.

Little Boy Blue's story had been the catalyst for Dr. Lehman's hand-wringing and regret. Ida's death had been put away somewhere, quiet, in the back of his mind until then. After all, it was possible that it could have been an accident. Maybe Dr. Lehman gave himself the false grace of thinking he might have been wrong. Maybe Ida had a bad heart.

How could it be that he would just let this all go? What, if anything, did Coroner Questel say to convince his assistant? What deal did they make? Or was it the Amish? Did, as some have suggested, Ida's bishop or Eli's father ask to keep it quiet out of respect for their people and the harm it would cause the church?

Dr. Lehman was a man of deep faith. He was revered in his community as a doctor, the mayor, and a member of the Kidron Mennonite

Church. And he had more than ten years to do the right thing and speak up about his concerns before Danny's body was identified.

But he didn't.

Not a peep.

And having died in 2016 at age eighty-one, he never can.

I send off a records request to the Wayne County Coroner's Office, seeking a copy of the lab report associated with Ida's autopsy, a document Dr. Questel didn't show me in 1989, though I'd asked for everything on the case.

Records, transcripts, and reports provide the backbone of a true crime book. I have always done my best to log every single date from any documented source as I build out a chronology. For me, and for my readers, those pinpoints of accuracy are essential as layers of details are added by talking to the people associated with the story.

Over the next few weeks, my take-no-prisoners assistant, Robbin Lassen, and I will send out dozens of public document requests to jurisdictions from Ohio to Texas to Florida.

Though only in her midthirties, Robbin exudes the kind of empathy that comes only as a by-product of a lifetime of ups and downs. She's had family drama. And who hasn't? She's worked as a paralegal and a repo gal. She's married to a wonderful guy and the mother of two girls. What's more, she loves true crime.

She's a perfect fit in every way.

Some PDRs will take weeks or months to procure. Once received, each will be analyzed for details, connections, and the bits of information that make the hair on the back of one's neck stand at attention.

Those "holy shit, I didn't know that" moments are what I live for.

And my readers too.

CHAPTER NINE

I'd known about Ida's manner of dress when she was found, but the relevance of it wasn't clear until her Amish neighbors Elmer and Erma Miller visited my family at our suburban Seattle home in 1992. After spending time at their farm in Fredericksburg and letting our girls drive a buggy (the horse was named Scott; in fact, almost all the animals that had names were English ones), we had struck up a friendship based on our mutual desire to figure out what really happened to Ida and Danny.

In the summer of 1992, they took the train from Ohio, and I picked them up at King Street Station in Seattle.

For obvious reasons, the Millers were very easy to spot among the crowd.

Elmer loved to travel, and I expect Erma did too, though she was on the quiet side. In the Little Boy Blue case, Elmer took a bus with Amos Gingerich to Wyoming in search of Danny's grave, which, of course, didn't exist. Neither did the Cox family cemetery, which Eli had said had been Danny's final resting place in a letter from Texas on July 29, 1986.

Dear folks, greeting in His name, who shed his blood for us.

*This is Tuesday morning 10:30 AM [and] the tempera-
ture is 104 degrees already. Hope you're all well. [We]
have not all been well recently but I'm sure our good
heavenly father knows best. He giveth to be taken I just
found out this morning that the message I [sent to you]
last week was returned instead of delivered. The sad news
is about Danny. He was in a car accident near Salt Lake
City on Monday of last week July 21st around 10:00
AM and died at the hospital in Salt Lake City UT on
Tuesday night 11:30 PM July 23rd due to head injuries.
[The] graveside services were held on Tuesday July 24th
for Danny in Kemmerer, Wyoming where Danny is buried at The Cox Family cemetery.*

 *I'm sorry you didn't get my messages, but I tried [and]
when I had the messages sent I was assured that the message will be delivered to you personally by someone from
your local post office no later than Wednesday 10:00 AM
July 23rd.*

 *Danny has been at the children's camp in Lyman,
Wyoming, since June 1st same place as last summer which
is run by the Cox family and was taken to the airport
by Cary Cox to Salt Lake City when they were hit by a
semi-truck. He was going to fly here to Dallas Fort Worth
airport where I was going to pick him up. I received word
of the accident at noon Monday just as I was getting ready
to go pick him up, so I went to Salt Lake City Monday.*

Elmer didn't believe any of it and continued to play Amish detective, making phone calls to the authorities from the sawmill where he
worked, until the truth came out and Eli was arrested and brought to
Nebraska on charges.

When the Millers arrived, Erma went downstairs to the guest bedroom and bathroom to change. She washed her black polyester dress in the sink and hung it over the shower door to dry. And honestly, it looked like it was a cutout for a pattern, not a complete dress.

Erma told my wife, Claudia, that it wasn't so difficult to put together, but it did take some genuine know-how.

"You don't want to get stuck," she said.

After a dinner of Kentucky Fried Chicken, Elmer burped, which our second-grader twins thought was extremely amusing. He gave them each a quarter and a small wine goblet, a gift that always puzzled me a little. Did he think English kids started drinking in elementary school?

The next morning, I took the Millers to the Washington coast so Erma could fulfill a long-held wish to dip her toes in the Pacific. When we stopped to get fuel, I bought Elmer a V8, which he nearly spat out.

"Tastes like tobacco juice!"

"It kind of does," I admitted.

I had only purchased vegetable juice because it was a healthy choice. After the previous night's KFC, I wanted to show that we weren't frivolous.

I should have bought him a Coke.

The coup de grâce of the visit was a walk through the Nordstrom store at Bellevue Square, which was fun for them not because they were doing any shopping, but for the reaction they got.

"They don't see many like us here," Elmer said with a sheepish grin from his Brillo pad beard.

"I can assure you, Elmer, they've never seen anyone like you here."

Two weeks later, a package from Ohio arrived. The Millers thanked us for our hospitality as though our trip to the mall and our "family feast" of KFC was some great treat. Wrapped in brown paper was a Lone Star quilt Erma had sewn, a treasure then and today.

X

While it wasn't fully on my radar in 1989, I now see Ida's dress the night she died as potentially crucial evidence that she'd been murdered. Make that damning evidence that there had been a conspiracy at the Stutzman farm.

Ida was fully dressed.

Not in a nightgown.

While our dogs bark at the Amazon driver, I take my laptop to the bedroom. It has been more than ten days since I'd met up with Dan in Michigan and restarted the investigation into what really happened to his sister.

It's all about the dress.

It takes only a second to find an explainer video on YouTube. I watch as a former Amish woman moves through the arduous process. It isn't easy. And it does take time. Since Ida was a member of the Swartzentruber Order, her dress likely required anywhere from twenty to forty pins. In the video, the woman takes almost five minutes to get dressed. She's doing the whole ensemble, however. Not only that, she's also demonstrating a very specific technique, so that adds a little time.

I consider the complexity behind something supposedly plain and simple.

The skirt is pinned to the bodice, the fabric covering the torso to the neck. The top piece is a cape that has long sleeves; thankfully, those are sewn into the Rubik's Cube garment. Before the dress is worn, the cape and sleeves are secured in the back by multiple pins. Sometimes as many as five. Once secured, the dress is brought up and over the head, and the arms are put through the slits in the bodice. The front of the bodice is pinned closed using either safety pins or straight pins.

The bodice is tightened on the waist with pins—elastic is considered too worldly.

Right now, my heart aches for Swartzentruber women. This is a fashion nightmare.

Once the bodice is pinned and tightened, the arms are inserted through the long sleeves, and the cape is pulled up and over each shoulder and drapes down in the front. Next, the woman ties a shoe-string-like piece of fabric around her neck that allows her to tuck in the cape and secure it even more.

Just as the bodice is pinned closed, the sleeves and cape are too. Once closed, the top is secured with pins around the waist. The residual fabric of the cape is tucked into the shoestring tied around the neck. The final touch to the entire ensemble is an apron tied around the waist.

It, too, is fastened and secured with multiple pins.

None of that is easy or fast. In fact, just viewing the cumbersome process goes beyond non-Adderall-assisted attention spans.

Ida did not wear a bonnet that night, only a headscarf. Dr. Questel makes no mention of a cape. She purportedly had on underclothing, but was it her nightdress or underwear and a camisole-like top? Were the pins still in place fastened properly?

We don't know because Dr. Questel never recorded any such details.

Erma Miller's dress, as it hung over our shower door when she and Elmer visited, comes to mind just then. Ida had on a dress just like that when she died.

Eli said the flames from the barn woke his wife, and she was already dressed and heading out the door. Amishmen often sleep in their shirts. They wear no underwear. All he had to do to get dressed was to pull on a pair of pants and go.

Eli could be ready in ten seconds.

How was it that Ida took the time to dress before waking her husband? That's not only unlikely, it borders on the absurd.

She was wearing the clothes she had on earlier in the day.

☒

I'm driving home from my six-hundred-square-foot writing cabin, which I call the Oyster Bar, when my phone pings. It is one of those rare late summer days when sunglasses are actually warranted—if you can find your pair—and the complaining about the sogginess of the Pacific Northwest is long forgotten. I side-eye my phone and pull over.

It's the autopsy labs from Ida's case.

I turn off the engine and take in the information on that constrained display.

Dr. Questel's report indicated that he considered carbon monoxide poisoning as a cause of Ida's death. That's not a bad supposition, and it made sense to take blood samples to confirm his theory.

It just didn't turn out that way.

When the labs came back from Analytica Laboratories on July 21, 1977, they painted a different picture. The carbon monoxide detected in Ida's blood was 1.6 percent.

As in *only* 1.6 percent.

For comparison, an average adult will have levels of less than 2 percent, and a person who is a heavy smoker has an average of 6 to 8 percent. Ida's was only 1.6 percent. How can that be? Dr. Questel's hypothesis was off by a mile. It did not fit that Ida died from inhaling too much smoke, which in turn exacerbated a heart condition that ultimately led to her untimely death.

What does it mean? I sit here trying to give the coroner some grace. When lab results no longer supported his original theory, why didn't he feel compelled, as a measure of duty, to investigate Ida's death more?

After all, hadn't he worked on other carbon monoxide poisoning cases?

This is where the microfilm department at the Wayne County Sheriff's Office and its extremely helpful staff come in. Once more.

A day or so after a request, autopsy reports arrive for Wayne County individuals whose cause and manner of death dealt with fire.

In those reports, carbon monoxide levels ranged from 40 to 76 percent. Dr. Questel knew what deadly levels of CO_2 poisoning looked like. I can't know for sure; no one can, but as I write this, it seems he was forced to pivot from what he had been thinking as the cause of Ida's death.

In fact, "thinking" is a good word. Thinking is the same as "belief."

In other words, an opinion.

No scientific evidence backs up his conclusions, for the very reason that there had been zero attempt to collect any evidence, other than a vial of blood.

What he wrote was a *belief*. A story. A trumped-up theory.

Further, Dr. Questel never requested Ida's medical records from Dr. Lehman. By all accounts, he ignored Dr. Lehman, the assistant coroner, when he told him no such heart condition existed.

Moreover, Dr. Questel never removed Ida's clothing to examine the full spectrum of her body, despite facial injuries that suggested a struggle. He noted that her dress had become unpinned but took no photographs documenting that fact.

Just two lousy Polaroids. They capture views of Ida's face. The images are in color, but over time they have taken on a sepia tone, making them seem gothic and sad.

He wrote his belief: *"Acute cardiac arrest and physical and emotional stress due to burning of the barn."*

What was it that made a well-respected coroner perform such a half-assed examination?

Or rather, *who*?

When I get home, I tell Claudia about the labs.

"Reminds me of Dawn's story," she says.

"Yeah," I say, thinking of Dawn Hacheney.

I wrote about Dawn more than a decade ago. She was a young minister's wife who'd been found dead in her Bremerton, Washington, home. She didn't have any smoke in her lungs either, something the Kitsap County forensic pathologist put off to the assertion that there had been a flash fire that seared her larynx, thus preventing any smoke inhalation. Her husband, Nick, got away with killing her for five years until someone came forward with the truth that he'd been having an affair with a church secretary.

"Everyone knew what Eli was up to," Claudia goes on, "but no one said anything there either."

People keep their mouths clamped shut for all kinds of reasons. Some good. Some selfish. In the Hacheney case, coming forward helped bring a killer to justice.

No one will go to prison for Ida's death. I know that. The justice that can come, however, is just as meaningful. It's what drives me to find the truth. Keeping a secret can have dire and irrevocable consequences.

Look no further than Chester, Nebraska; Austin, Texas; or Durango, Colorado.

Bodies left in ditches and roadsides.

The signature of a serial killer.

CHAPTER TEN

Jim Frost, the sheriff of Wayne County, was a "love him or hate him" kind of figure.

No shit.

The man who rapidly and summarily shut down Ida's case was extremely demanding, telling dispatchers like Marianne Gasser and Beth Carr that he never wanted to hear anything important on the radio. He needed to be called first. On the occasions when Jim's micromanaging and control freaking was met with defiance, he'd let his staff know about it with a bark into the phone or an in-person visit to dispatch. He was either an ass, or a man who cared so much that he needed to be on the inside of every criminal occurrence in the county. Many deputies and investigators loathed working a case with Frost because he'd insist things were done his way, no matter how weird.

"At a fire scene," a former investigator told me, "Frost was poking around the ashes looking for bones and other traces of a fire victim, and he'd pause every now and then and sniff his fingers to see what smell he could pick up. I've never seen anyone do that. Made me kind of sick to watch."

His ego was legendary too. A trim and fit fellow with dark hair and a mustache, Frost was impeccable in his dress—and indisputably the president and CEO of his own self-admiration society. When a woman at a traffic stop said he looked like Robert Redford, he not only beamed, he sent a dispatcher to a nearby store to buy a poster of Redford. It hung in his office, as a kind of mirror or ego-boost promo. Frost drove a white Corvette with the vanity plate *"SHERIFF."*

There was another side too. A secretive side. He told a close friend, "I am very careful about what I do. I like to get away and go places where people don't know me, sometimes."

As it turns out, it was hardly an understatement.

Frost's rapid rise and dramatic fall is a tale only partially revealed in the sometimes-blurry printouts of newspaper articles. There's no dispute that he'd been a much-loved Orrville schoolteacher and bus driver, but Jim had always wanted to be a cop. He first served his community as an officer in his hometown, Orrville, starting in 1967. By the time he'd set his sights on leading the Wayne County Sheriff's Office, he'd risen to the rank of sergeant. He had ambition by the boatload when, at twenty-eight, he won the election—the youngest in county history. He was forward-thinking, a by-the-book law enforcement officer, and a classic control freak.

That last personality trait escalated over time.

"Frost had big plans," a former county deputy tells me over the phone. "Big ambitions. Frankly, he was on the right track. Department needed a shake-up."

And shake it up, he did. Frost managed to increase the department's annual budget from $180,129 to $333,635 his first year, thus allowing the county to hire thirteen additional deputies and dispatchers, increase salaries, and add four cruisers to the patrol unit. He got the money.

I plow through the articles in which Frost is mentioned and his reputation as a "tough on crime" public persona grows. Big drug raids. Stolen goods recovered. Those kinds of things. Awards too. After only a year in office, Frost won something called the second annual J. Edgar Hoover award.

So much was going on and each item was clearly one for his personal win column, especially the headline that catches my eye next, from the *Akron Beacon Journal*, 1974: "Poison Candy Case Is Solved." It was just eighteen months after his election.

Several deputies had mentioned the story as one of the lingering crime mysteries of the county and how Frost had made solving it a campaign talking point.

"I think his campaign promise was to solve the candy murder," a former deputy told me over the phone early in my reinvestigation into Ida's death. "And Jim said that, you know, using new techniques he was going to bring the sheriff's department into the twentieth century. You know, we were still operating in the very, very old school. And then he started to look at the more modern techniques and things like that. And he was a good investigator at the time. And I think he was a good cop. It's just he had really lousy people and management skills."

I read the article about a farmer who had been poisoned and whose killer had finally been identified, but whose name was never revealed. In red ink, I write a note on the printout's margin: *"Poss. Story?"*

In early 1975, the young sheriff made news by winning a $700,000 government grant to rebuild the antiquated county Justice Center. It was a celebrated moment in Frost's career; in fact, looking back, most would say it was his high-water mark.

His downfall was already coming.

First, on the personal side. In the fall of the year of his triumph with the plans for a new Justice Center, Jim and his wife, Christine, separated. Court filings offer little insight into the reasons behind the divorce finalized on October 22. Christine was a lovely woman, in all ways, and some speculated that she had tired of being married to a man married to his job. Others wondered if he acted at home anything like he did at the office—bossy, bratty, petulant, abusive even.

Outwardly, they'd been a golden couple, strikingly attractive, intelligent, and civic-minded. For many to see the marriage crumble was difficult, especially for Jim's parents.

If Jim thought his reelection would be a slam dunk, it came with an unexpected turn of events when Deputy Jim Taylor announced his candidacy. Members of the department at the time said Frost hit the roof. He was bitter, angry, and embarrassed that someone inside his own circle would dare suggest he should be replaced.

Frost gave Taylor two options: drop out of the race or be fired.

Taylor dropped out, but Frost fired him anyway.

Despite the drama and escalating dissension within the department, Frost, thirty-two at the time, won his second term in the election of 1976. His salary then was $12,700.

Not long after his unopposed reelection, Frost found himself back on the front pages for the misuse of department funds. State auditors concluded that he'd bought items with county money that were considered inappropriate. Case in point, in his quest to modernize, he purchased a helicopter, insisting that despite the small size of the department, it was a good investment. The helicopter had been a financial fiasco. It was used only a couple of times a year.

While most of the sums were not substantial, the question of financial malfeasance was another ding to his reputation. Two weeks later, the proverbial other shoe dropped.

And it dropped with a decided thud.

Four deputies, three dispatchers, and a secretary were furloughed—despite a huge increase in budget from $330,000 to $520,000. Questions arose about where the money was going. Moreover, was the sheriff minding the store or was he in over his head?

Or, some argued, other things were going on, including a distraction that would change the trajectory of his life from a rocket to the sky to a crash into the deepest of chasms.

He'd found his true love.

But before any of that, in 1974, James Frost forged a disastrous relationship with Amishman Eli Stutzman.

CHAPTER ELEVEN

In the autumn of 1974, Jim Frost had it in his mind that he was going to bust a band of brothers allegedly selling marijuana. Rumors were circulating that Earl, Levi, and Les Miller had a grow operation on their farm in Marshallville, a dozen miles northeast of Wooster. Frost, possibly taking a cue from his purported doppelgänger Redford's movie *The Sting*, out the year before, thought a sting operation was the smart solution to the county's growing drug problem.

And this is where Eli Stutzman comes in. Recently excommunicated from the Amish and put under the Order's bann, the Wayne County sheriff convinced Eli to go undercover to entrap the Millers. Why Eli? Why put an ex-Amishman in the position of being the conduit to an important arrest? People can speculate all day on that. And they have. I don't know the answer, except I do know that Eli and Frost were members of a small, closeted community. Both men were gay.

Given the size and times of rural gay America in the mid-1970s, it's not a surprise that the men knew each other. Even so, Eli had to be persuaded to go undercover. Something had to be in it for him. Whether it was sex between the Amishman and the sheriff or the promise of a monetary payoff, well, that'll likely never be known.

The middleman coordinating the drug buy was Jim Board, a bright but inexperienced deputy, having only been with the department a few months. What he thought of his assignment to conduct the sting is another one of those things that can't be known. Eli made the marijuana purchase on October 30, telling Earl Miller that he needed some weed to cure headaches he was experiencing at the time.

The very next day Frost showed up at the Miller farm waving an arrest warrant.

It couldn't have been more obvious to anyone that Stutzman had been the snitch.

The following night, Levi Miller, fresh from the county jail, showed up at Stoll Farms in Marshallville to have a little chat with Stutzman, who was working at the dairy alongside his cousin Abe. Miller wasn't there for small talk, and the decidedly pissed-off look on his face made that abundantly clear.

Stutzman was holed up in bed, playing the innocent Amishman, a role he'd perfected. He insisted he had no clue what Miller was talking about. His face was bright red, and he kept a blanket wrapped tightly around his body as though it offered some protection. Miller didn't touch Stutzman, although he believed a little force might loosen his tongue.

It was what happened next—a series of threatening letters, supposed sightings of an out-of-state car, and a violent attack—that would set the table for everything that was yet to follow in Eli's life.

Three weeks after Eli completed his role in Amish undercover, Ed Stoll, the owner of the dairy, discovered Eli slumped on the floor of the barn. He was weak and glassy-eyed. His arms were bloody. Scattered all around were rocks dripped with blood. Arcs of blood had been sprayed on timber and hay bales.

Eli told Ed that he'd been jumped and stabbed by two men who had been lying in wait. He'd tried to fight them off, managing to injure one with a pitchfork, but he was outnumbered. They'd left him for dead and if Ed hadn't come into the barn, they'd likely have succeeded.

Oddly, the first thing Eli said when his rescuer arrived was "What took you so long?"

It was a reference to the fact that his boss was a half-hour late on a routine that normally worked like, well, clockwork.

That statement would gain importance later.

Eli's cousin Abe and I talk about that faked attack in the fall of 2022. Today Abe runs construction teams for a company with several worksites in the Carolinas and Illinois. He's a grandfather now. I ask him if he still has the Amish hat that he brought to the *Sally Jessy Raphael* talk show and put on to great studio-audience applause. His Amish accent remains as pronounced as ever; his words come softly, with rounded edges. Though he feels differently today, at the time he was incensed about what happened to his cousin.

He saw Eli at the hospital that night of the attack.

Abe recalls that the wounds were razor clean. Not messy or jagged like one might expect from a sudden, violent act. Eli was inconsolable and erratic. He repeated over and over that he'd been the target of an orchestrated retaliation, one that even had been forewarned. Eli showed Abe letters that put him on notice that someone was coming after him. He was flopping around to such a degree that nurses tied down his arms and legs and pumped him full of tranquilizers.

Ed Stoll was livid about the attack. He confronted Jim Frost in the hospital.

"You assholes are supposed to be taking good care of him and this happened. You know what's going on."

Frost took a step back. "It's not what you think."

"I know what I think," Ed said.

The undercover drug operation and the bizarre events at Ed Stoll's farm are without question the prologue to Ida's death and the cover-up of her murder. This is not a red yarn line from one Post-it note to another on my cabin window; this is a connection made of steel.

A quid pro quo? A promise? Maybe just the fear of exposure. We can't ever truly know what's in the heart or mind of a killer and conspirator. Talking heads do it all the time on broadcast and cable TV. Reddit forums are laden, truly overflowing like a full diaper, with comments from observers who are absolutely sure they know the truth.

And they can copy and paste to prove it.

On the evening of November 20, 1974, Sheriff Frost interviewed Eli in a hospital room at Dunlap Memorial Hospital. The room had been cleared of doctors and visitors, and the former Amishman and sheriff met in private.

Frost noted Eli's injuries in his report:

> *The victim had [a] cut on his left arm[.] Also the victim had a large lump on the left side of his forehead[.] [T]hose were the only visible injuries that I could see[;] however he had blood all over his hands.*

What, if anything, he thought of the injuries being confined to Eli's left side and the fact that Eli was right-handed is unknown.

Next, Frost recorded the "facts" and "descriptions" of the perpetrators.

> *The first subject was a white male, brown hair, medium cut, who did most of the talking. [He was] five eight, 130 pounds, wearing a blue jean jacket and blue jean wide flare pants. The subject had a mustache and a little beard on his chin, age mid-20s roughly 24.*

The description is interesting in its detail. Eli, like many fabulists, overdoes and embellishes. More is, well, more. And more is better. False reporters often paint a picture of their assailant in vivid detail because they think added information will bolster the veracity of their account.

Others who report a fictitious crime sometimes offer the flip side. They have little to nothing to say. They take a broad brushstroke approach, which in its own way seems plausible given that they've just witnessed the unthinkable. Oregon child killer Diane Downs told me when I met her at the California women's prison near Chowchilla that a shaggy-haired stranger shot her three children on a remote country road. It was the best she could come up with given the "shock of what was happening to my kids."

Incidentally, Diane never blinked her cracked-marble blue eyes when she also told me that she didn't think Farrah Fawcett was pretty enough to portray her in the ABC miniseries made of Ann Rule's true crime classic *Small Sacrifices*.

Eli was never a broad brushstroker (at least in the sense of his lies). Frost wrote of the second assailant's appearance:

> *White male, blonde hair cut in a bang fashion down to his eyes, nasty temperament, stated he was going to kill Eli, 6 foot 180 pounds. The subject is the one that did the cutting, possibly wearing a bright red shirt. Subject was wearing corduroy jeans, either blue or green in color and a blue jean jacket.*

As presented in Frost's report, Eli spun a story about the lead-up to the attack. How the men questioned him about cooperating with the sheriff's department on the pot buy and turning on the Miller brothers. After that, the brawl began. Eli managed to strike the corduroy jeans–clad assailant in the knee with a pitchfork, but they got him down.

> *They searched him and found his pocketknife which was never recovered from the scene. They accused him of carrying the*

pocketknife for some other purpose, indicating he meant to protect himself.

Eli did some foreshadowing. Again, with the embellishment of detail.

He said the suspicious vehicle that was in the area at the time prior to the attack, that had two white males in it, a medium brown, Dodge Swinger. It had large wheels on the rear and looked like a souped-up vehicle. It had out-of-state plates which he thought were orange or yellow in color and [was] occupied by two subjects.

Frost noted how he'd ended the questioning because Eli was groggy from pain medication. He wrote how he'd gone to see the Miller brothers, "the people that Eli illegally [*sic*] informed on," and found all of the Millers at home.

The sheriff pressed his palms against the hoods of the Miller vehicles and wrote that all were cold to the touch. His report concludes with his take on the Miller brothers' involvement.

They said they knew nothing about it and wanted to keep changing this topic of discussion into the bad things the Sheriff's Department does in their opinion. It appears to this officer at this point that they did not directly assault Eli; however they could know who the assailants were.

Eli wrote out a statement the next day, for Detective Jim Board.

I was doing chores while someone threw a stone down from the second story. Following came a brown-haired guy, which started asking questions and throwing things. He asked why I was cooperating with the Sheriff's Department. He wanted to know why I gave them information on grass and drugs. As the second guy appeared, which had blonde hair, I tried to leave the barn but was caught and hit by the blonde-haired guy's sharp object. He swung the object against my stomach, and I try to dodge away so he hit my arm instead. So, I ran back to the other feed alley. In order to get through I hit the brown-haired guy with a silage fork. I was caught again by one of the guys and he pulled me back to the main alley where they hit me some more. From then on things are not clear to me.

A day later, Eli did an amazing about-face with another statement from his hospital bed. This time Jim Board wrote it out as a Q and A–style interview.

Question: Whose idea was it for you to write the two threatening letters to yourself and for you to make it look like someone assaulted you?

Answer: I feel it was Levi, Earl, and Lester Miller's idea because they told me to get screwing the Sheriff's Department.

Question: What did they tell you to do to screw up the Sheriff's Department?

Answer: Somehow make a front-page article against the Sheriff's Department. They suggested for me to stab myself and cut myself or to see a psychiatrist or physician, that I tell them I am going crazy to make it look real bad for the sheriff. They said it would have to be done soon. They told me to get my story to Bill Evans before you guys get to them.

Question: When did they tell you this?

Answer: They were up at the Stoll farm on Friday and Saturday after the raid and I went down to their place on Sunday because they told me to come down to cooperate. I actually figured this was my way out because I was afraid of them.

Question: Did anyone help you write the threatening letters?

Answer: No.

Question: Did anyone help you assault yourself?

Answer: No one knew I was going to do it. I just planned it within the last couple of days because I couldn't . . . sleep, and . . . because I was afraid.

Question: What did you think you would gain by the letters and assault?

Answer: I thought doing that what the Millers boys wanted me to do to get off my back. I just couldn't stand it. Lester said you better be careful. I said that I'll try to cooperate with them.

Question: Were you afraid of the Millers?

Answer: I really was . . . it was death not to cooperate.

"Eli did this to himself," Sheriff Frost announced to reporters from his office in downtown Wooster on November 22, seemingly satisfied in cracking a difficult case. "He even wrote the letters."

The type on the letters matched a typewriter found in Stutzman's bedroom.

"There was no assault," Frost said. "This is a completely false complaint and was confirmed by the victim that it was his own doing."

Dairy owner Ed Stoll refused to believe it when he heard that his hired hand Eli made it all up. "I said, 'No way he could have done that.' So, I go to the hospital. 'I'll have Eli tell me. That's the only way I'll believe it.' People told me what room Eli was in, and I went up. And I just asked him. He says, 'I did it all myself.'"

That truth shook everyone who had been sucked into Stutzman's carefully orchestrated tale of brutality.

The sheriff's department policy was to refrain from publicly commenting on self-inflicted injuries or suicide. Frost, however, made an unprecedented exception in the case involving the twenty-four-year-old former Amishman in Marshallville. Those in the department later wondered if it was because of Frost's concern about optics—putting an unstable Amishman in harm's way for an undercover operation was most definitely not a good look.

If Stutzman was ashamed or bothered by the whole business, it didn't seem that way to others. From the day he returned to the dairy, he acted as if nothing had happened.

This was serious stuff. Crazy stuff. Memorable too. But for some reason, Frost never brought up the incident again. Not once. And especially not on the night Ida died.

I have always been a believer in the value of a face-to-face interview. I almost never conduct a "real" interview over the phone. Body language is only a part of the reason. And just to be clear, Zoom is no replacement for actually sitting at someone's kitchen table, petting their dog, sharing the anguish found in the pages of a scrapbook recounting the life of someone gone too soon. I have stayed connected with people I've written about because I came to know them as people first, not as the friend of a killer or the mother of a murdered child.

Because I'm that guy who still prints out paper boarding passes, I ask Claudia to go online to book a flight to Columbus. She surprises me with a quasi upgrade with more legroom and free drinks. I'm in.

I sit next to a woman on her way for a cancer treatment. She tells me her whole life story, including her husband's affair. Her stalking of the other woman and the confrontation they had in person. It's good stuff. I have that kind of face. Or my manner. In any case, people tell me things that they have never told anyone. And I make the promise that I won't betray them.

I've kept those promises too.

The woman in the window seat is also an author. She writes sorcery romances or something along those lines. We talk about a tragic murder in her own family before we get to talking about Ida and Eli and all the things that bring me to Ohio.

"The Amish are so fascinating," she says.

I agree.

"And let's not get started on the Hutterites," I say, joking.

At least I think I am.

"Right," she says, "that's some serious strangeness there."

We talk about my quest for truth in a cold case, and I tell her that I'm going to turn over every stone I can find until there's nothing left because that's what you do when you are digging for the truth.

"After thirty years a lot of people are dead now," I say. "My first stop is a deputy who diagrammed the scene of the crime. I have a name and an address, and I'm sitting here with my fingers crossed that this guy is the right one."

PART TWO

Autumn 2022

CHAPTER TWELVE

As a writer of nonfiction, I miss the days of the door knock, the MO of interviews when there was no internet. No reverse phone directories. When you had to haul yourself to the library and try to find the address by actually poring through listings in old phone books.

And then the knock on a stranger's door to see what happens. A true "hold your breath" moment. It feels uncomfortable, and yes, intrusive. Of course, anything can happen. I mean *anything*. I've been bitten by a dog. I've had someone say they were going to "shank" me. More than once, I've been invited in for cake and coffee.

You stand there and wait.

As far as I know, Phil Carr is the only law enforcement officer still alive who worked the scene the night Ida died. Carr's name appears in some reports, as he was a Wayne County deputy sheriff at the time, and yet I'd never met him. Honestly, I didn't even try the first time around. I spoke to the neighbors on the scene, the young cousin who lived with the Stutzmans, and the fire department. I figured I had it covered.

The Carrs live east of Columbus in a town that no one at the airport had a clue existed. True crime readers, however, know Howard, Ohio, as the site of one of the most gruesome and bizarre murders in recent memory.

Actually, probably of all time.

I take a little detour to the Kokosing Lake Wildlife Area.

In November 2010, Matt Hoffman, then thirty, entered Tina Herrmann's home to rob it. When Tina and neighbor Stephanie Sprang surprised him there, he stabbed them to death and proceeded to dismember them in the bathtub. In the middle of all of that, Tina's son and daughter came home from school. The boy, eleven, was killed right away, but Hoffman had other plans for the thirteen-year-old girl. He took her to the basement of his home in nearby Mount Vernon and held her captive.

A quick search on my phone brings up the killer's confession:

> *I was back in the bedrooms when she entered the house and was unable to exit without breaking a window and trying to jump out. I had brought my knife for a certain amount of intimidation in case I ran into someone and needed to make an escape.*

> *I grabbed the knife that I had put down on the nightstand and stabbed the woman on the bed, through her back, twice. I chased the other woman down (Stephanie) and stabbed her a couple times in the chest. Instead of running out of the house, she had run into another bedroom. I could tell that both women were now dead.*

> *I stabbed the boy in the chest a couple times. I ran into the bedroom after the girl to make sure she was not on the phone for help . . . I saw the girl was not on the phone, and I could not bring myself to kill her.*

Instead, he took her to his home and held her captive.

All of that is gross and horrifying.

It suddenly moves from gruesome to horrifically strange.

Hoffman—an employed tree surgeon—had a bizarre obsession with trees. He took his victims' body parts and stuffed them into a hollow beech tree in a nature preserve. At his home, he made a bed for the girl out of leaves. Lots of them. His house had a number of huge mounds of leaves in various rooms. In fact, there were more than one hundred bags of leaves collected by investigators.

After confessing, the killer begged the state not to damage the hollow tree where he'd stuffed the bodies.

The tree, however, was cut down to stop it from becoming a dark tourist attraction.

Which is why I can't find it when I stop at the reserve.

The place is beautiful, in stark contrast to what Hoffman did there. I suppose that's how I look at the stories that I choose to write about. The pretty teacher who abused her student. The young nurse who suffocated her children. And yes, the killer Amishman who has brought me back to Ohio.

The lethal intentions hidden under the veneer of kindness, success, or beauty are essential elements of the kind of true crime that at once rivets and disturbs readers. The Green Beret physician who did—or didn't—kill his wife. The blonde schoolteacher who went to prison for the rape of her student. The billionaire who stole millions from his clients. No names are needed here. We know who they are because of what they presented to the world and how their façades were merely a cover, camo, a mirage.

Those who have it all. Those we wish we could be. Killers and criminals too.

Less than a half an hour from where the gruesome hollow tree once stood, the Carrs' residence couldn't be more lovely. More ideal. More tranquil. Their street is bordered by corn and soybean fields on one side and new one-level homes on the other. Pride of ownership abounds everywhere. Lawns with the slight indentations of a mower's wheels leave an argyle pattern. And the grass is flawlessly green too. Astroturf perfect, but real, of course. This isn't Stepford. It's Ohio.

I hear the sound of two little dogs in the background as Beth Carr answers the door. She looks at me warily through a slit in the door.

"I don't even know if I have the right address," I say, stepping back a little. "I'm looking for Chief Carr."

I call him that because after he left his post in Wayne County, he served as the chief of police in a small Ohio town.

Titles are important to law enforcement professionals. As they should be.

I tell her why I'm here and she calls for her husband, Phil.

A minute later, the three of us sit at their huge oak dining table. Sprinklers go off at the house next door and a mist fogs the air behind a large window, which brings the riot of green hues from an Ohio summer into the room.

"I suffer from amnesia," he says right away.

I tell him I'm sorry, but inside I am feeling selfish and disappointed. I'd come a long way for nothing.

"So sometimes recalling stuff is hard."

"Join the club, sir," I tell him.

It's true. When I looked through a copy of *Abandoned Prayers*, throughout which I used pseudonyms for privacy reasons, it took some doing to recall a person's real name. A few still elude me.

We talk about the night of the fire and, despite what he'd said, Carr doesn't struggle at all.

"I was on midnight shift and was heading from Kidron to Dalton when I heard the sirens. I started driving that way to help with traffic or whatever. I remember the lady. She was laying on the ground almost in the ditch. Someone told me she'd been pulled from the burning barn, and she had died."

Beth offers a bottle of water, and I play that distinctly American game of twisting the top off and on between each sip.

I refer to Eli's history of instability. "You didn't know about the other things he did before he returned to the Amish?"

Phil shakes his head. "Not until after."

"But someone knew it that night, right?"

"Yeah. Tim Brown did."

"He told you later?"

Phil nods.

I asked if he knew that Tim was gay.

He answers in the affirmative.

"What about Frost?"

This time it's a no.

"He was married, had girlfriends. Later I knew."

"Do you think Tim Brown and Jim Frost had something going?"

"Yeah," he says. "Yeah."

Tim has always been one that I'd hoped would tell me the truth.

If he knew, that is. So far, he's not returned any calls or emails. I type on my keyboard with my fingers perpetually crossed that he and a few others will come around eventually. Everyone connected to Eli has their own little piece of a puzzle.

Then Phil tells me something that quietly rocks my world. I can't know if it is a fact, or merely a thought emanating from a foggy memory.

"I didn't think it was right to have Tim Brown be the investigator on the case."

"Huh?"

"Frost put him in charge. That's what Tim told me. It wasn't my job, but I thought it was wrong."

Tim was no homicide investigator. It couldn't be right. I'm not sure what to do with that disclosure, so I switch gears.

"Did you know Tim and Eli lived together later?"

Beth pipes up. "He called him a roommate. Seems like it was more. Why not say you were renting a room, instead?"

The Carrs say that they'd seen Eli and Tim together—along with a very quiet Danny—at picnics and other gatherings with members of the sheriff's department.

"I watched them to see how they behaved together, and they were a little familiar, you know," Phil says.

"A couple, maybe?" I ask.

He nods. "Yeah, a couple."

I ask if he thinks the case was fully investigated.

He shakes his head and starts telling me the department was small and young in those days. Some things were less scrutinized. Amish cases, mostly. The language barrier was part of it, but also the understanding that the Amish live in their own world.

"Everyone thought back then that the Amish keep to themselves, don't talk much about their lifestyle."

Phil talks about the difficulty in working with the Amish, particularly back in the late seventies.

"The Amish didn't want our help. If there was an incident, they'd call sometimes, but they didn't want charges brought. They said they handled their own problems."

He concedes that while there are a lot of crime-fighting tools and programs and even awareness, back then it wasn't the case.

"We were pretty much reporters, you know. We reported what we saw on the surface, especially with the Amish."

I return to the case at hand. Retired detective and retired police chief Phil Carr doesn't have much more to add about what he saw the night of the fire. His description is a decent mental sketch of the scene.

The fire. The woman's body. The Amish. Eli Stutzman calmly describing what had happened. Sheriff Frost standing in the middle of it all in complete control.

And that was something no one would mess with. No one could argue that Frost wasn't decisive and commanding. Even a simple question came out like a drill sergeant's order.

Phil did his part that night and directed some traffic, helped anyone he could. He was a patrol deputy.

Case closed.

And fast.

He says he'd wondered about a couple things over the years, particularly after the Little Boy Blue news broke.

He sits across from me, quietly, searching his memory to see if there was something there that he might have missed, something that would hold some importance. There wasn't. He'd been to other fires before and since, and this one wasn't remarkable. One thing that concerns him still, though, is Ida Stutzman's body.

"Was she even autopsied?" he asks.

"Sort of," I say.

Beth, a former dispatcher with the Wayne County Sheriff's Office, speaks up. She wants me to know Tim Brown is a smart and buttoned-up guy. Under the surface he might have been pissed off about something, but he never showed it. A real pro. She praises him for his work with police dogs. They talked about the cruises he and his partner had taken. She loved cruises too. They had common ground.

Tim also had a tender side, she tells me. He was concerned about Danny's welfare.

"It was in the summer, I think of the same year of the fire, but I'm not sure. All the sheriff's department had a big outdoor party and Eli and Tim hosted it. Eli had goats and I was into goats, so I bought a goat from him. I just talked to Tim casually about goats; at that point I said something about the little boy. I remember him saying, 'You know, Eli doesn't treat him very well.'"

Beth's dates could be wrong, and honestly, who could blame her? Eli's farm was a revolving door of young men during that time.

"Anyway," she says, "it was just bizarre to me that this Amishman would host an English party. Just the whole thing was weird."

Lots of things are weird in this story.

I thank the Carrs for their time and promise to stay in touch.

As I back my car out of the driveway, I catch a glimpse of Phil walking his dog over to a perfect patch of green grass. I give him a wave and he nods in my direction. As far as a door knock interview goes, it wasn't my best. It's possible whatever he knew about the fire had been lost in his bout with amnesia. I had seen the wheels turn, a little creakily, as he'd told me what he could remember.

That evening finds me in my room at the Holiday Inn Express in Wooster, as I plan interviews. The key is flexibility. All of the scheduling in the world can be upended by a great interview that goes long or by one that can only be considered a dud. I know who I want to talk to, but I don't know if they will talk to me. And I have no idea if they hold information that will lead me somewhere else, or if they will be a disappointing dead end. Always at the forefront is the knowledge that my asking questions about a crime, murder in particular, is about as welcome as, well, holding shit in your hands.

I go to the LongHorn Steakhouse, a chain restaurant that I thought was like a Sizzler but is actually much better. I have the rib eye and a gin martini. The young woman behind the bar has a necklace-worth of ear piercings and a pretty gap-toothed smile. She's friendly in the way that Seattle used to be, chatty, and freely offering tips on what to see while I'm in town.

"Wooster can be a fun place," she says. "Just have to know where to go."

The line echoes one from Dr. Chilton to Clarice Starling, when he creeps her in *The Silence of the Lambs*: "Because this can be quite a fun town if you have the right guide."

Since I'm nowhere near Belvedere, Ohio, I return to my room. I set out my index cards with the names and addresses of the people I hope to see. I place them in rows and groups, organized by location and relationship. Five piles of cards stretch across the desk like a tarot display with more than one Death card.

The most important card belongs to Melinda Hershberger, Levi Levi Hershberger's sister-in-law.

I got her address from a friend with a current Amish directory, a truly indispensable book in Amish Country. Every name. Every generation. Every date. It's all there. The only challenge is the Amish's constant recycling of first names. The naming convention of a father's first name as every child's middle name is somewhat helpful. On the other hand, it also leaves you with names like Levi Levi, for example.

CHAPTER THIRTEEN

The drive to the Hershberger farm in West Salem doesn't take long at all. Not even long enough to finish my coffee from the breakfast room at the hotel. Without any way to call ahead, there's always the chance of coming up empty-handed. I've experienced that outcome multiple times when seeking an Amish meetup. In a few cases, I've wondered if they've seen my car and decided not to answer the door. I know never to come on a Sunday and that Saturdays aren't great either—they're visiting days for most.

Dan Gingerich calls while I'm driving and we talk about Eli's funeral in 2007, four years after his release from prison for murdering Glen Pritchett.

"I was surprised that you weren't there," he says.

"I didn't know about it."

"You didn't?"

I wonder then if I would have gone. I think I might have. Just to see the conclusion of the story, I suppose. Maybe I'd find out something. I didn't mourn Eli, and I'm not sure that most who attended the funeral truly mourned him either. Mourned the people who got in his way, maybe.

"Abe was there," he says, of Eli's cousin and my talk show buddy.

"Right," I say. "I texted him about it the other night. He's looking through his stuff to see what he can find."

Dan gives me the reason he rode a bus from Minnesota to Fort Worth, where Eli had been living after his release from prison.

"You know, I would love to all of a sudden see the end of this. I can live without it. But that's why I went to Eli's funeral. I thought after the funeral I could ask to go to his apartment. I was just longing for a confession note. I thought he would hide a little note someplace."

"You hoped he would, Dan."

"Yeah," he says. "I hoped. I went in there and I looked on the shelves all over the place and nothing there. There was one thing there that I recognized from him. Him and Ida when they were still in Ohio. I bet you can guess what that was."

"I heard Eli kept a Bible."

Dan says it was actually a little black prayer book written in German.

"And that's the only thing. I thought maybe I'd find a souvenir about Ida or something. Everything was gone. Her clothes, her everything."

The conversation goes where it did when we met a couple of weeks prior.

Justice for Ida.

"I'm not smart enough to tell you how to put this to bed," he says.

"Well, what if the county did something?" I ask. "Like, if they would just declare it was a homicide, you know what I mean? Instead of just acting like nothing, like an accident. That would be something, right?"

He is unsure about the impact of an outcome like that.

"I don't want to see all the folks in Ohio get riled up about it. You know, in a lot of people's minds, they don't want to talk about it. It's history. And it is. But I meet people like Eli's nephews, the next generation, and they're curious. And I met one of Eli's brothers and his boys one time, in Chicago, on the train station. And he said, 'I can't get anything out of my dad, but I know why. They were embarrassed. Hurt. They had a rough life. They wouldn't even go to the little town for like sales and stuff because they were afraid that somebody would ask them, "Are you Eli's brother?"'"

Dan doesn't want the Stutzmans to suffer all over again.

I understand completely.

"But it would be nice if, you know, if we could get to a conclusion," he says. "But I guess we don't have to."

"And Eli gets away with what he did because Ida was Amish and maybe the sheriff didn't want to do anything."

Dan knows where I'm going and expands on it.

"Well, probably it's why Dr. Lehman didn't do anything, because she was Amish. I think the police knew that if they do something about it, they'll uncover themselves."

"And find Sheriff Frost right in the middle of it all."

"Yeah."

I don't tell Dan I'm about to turn into Melinda Hershberger's driveway. I'd promised not to use his support as a kind of calling card to get others to talk. I say goodbye and that I'll call later.

The Hershberger place is nestled up against a hill with a big white barn dominating the scene. There are two houses next to each other, very typical. The smaller "Daddi house" and the main house are a testament to lives that were lived with all generations together. No ice floe for the elderly. No old folks home. No warehousing of the infirm.

The Amish don't do any of that.

I'm met by a woman with one of her daughters in tow, both barefoot and dressed in the Amish version of Mommy and Me. A breeze shifts dark clothing on the line behind them. I hear the noise of a horse pulling a buggy on the road, the clip-clop sound getting louder as the buggy comes closer.

It turns out Melinda and her husband, Andy, are in Kentucky and will return on Monday.

I tell the young woman that I'm there on a mission to find out the truth of Ida Stutzman's death.

She knows the story.

Everyone does.

Her husband looks at me through gold wire-frame glasses as he comes over from the buggy carrying a lunch pail.

They believe Ida was murdered and the barn had been set on fire to cover up the crime.

"The young boy, the hired boy," she says, "was threatened. Told to keep his mouth shut about what he'd seen that night."

I learn that she's related to Chris Swartzentruber, a cousin or something along those lines. Chris and his wife, Dianna, are old friends with names and numbers written out on one of the index cards back in my hotel room.

They tell me to go over to John Yoder's place. John is Melinda's brother.

"He's a real talker," the husband says. "Might know something."

I use Amish directions—just turns and no road names to speak of—with no GPS assurance that I'll ever find the place.

"Look for the big white house," the young woman says, "with the big tree in front."

✕

Unbraiding who is related to whom in Amish Country is challenging—with or without that directory. Everyone is an offshoot of the same family tree, which I think is more of a mangrove with connections running from one settlement to the next than a mighty oak.

I find the house partially obscured by a gigantic maple tree. A woman emerges as the family dog checks me out. A second or two later, a couple of kids join us. The kids don't say a word. They stand quietly behind their mother, dressed in shades of blue.

The couple has eight children, seven boys and a girl. They live on the farm with Melinda's brother and his wife.

I learn the Yoders are not home.

I'm batting zero today.

I tell her that I wrote a book about Eli Stutzman and have been wrestling with the truth about his wife's death ever since.

"I was a young man then," I say. "It was thirty years ago."

"Looks like you've got some age on you," she says with a pleasant smile.

"Thanks for the reminder," I say back.

Also with a smile.

She is outgoing, confident. She says without hesitation that a "dark cloud" had hung over Levi Levi's life.

"Everyone suspected that he was involved in her murder or knew something about it," she says.

I pick up a few little things as we talk. Having suffered a stroke, Levi was unable to speak at the end of his life. He passed in 2015. Sammy Miller, who lived briefly with Eli in Austin during the time Glen Pritchett was killed, is the woman's uncle. Miller testified at the trial. I doubt he'd see me. In the book, someone was quoted as saying that he wasn't the brightest bulb in the chandelier or something like that.

While we talk, her husband and oldest son arrive in a buggy pulled by a beautiful dappled horse. He carries a briefcase and an Igloo brand lunch box. *An Amish executive,* I think.

He's friendly but doesn't add much to the conversation.

"You could write a letter to John," she says, referring to Melinda's brother, her father-in-law. "He's a good letter writer."

Good talker. Good letter writer. Two "goods" bring a lot of hope.

I have a little time, so I drive over to Dalton and park in front of Eli's old place on Moser Road. Property records tell me the Kratzers, who bought the farm from Eli, still live there. I'd met Mr. Kratzer years ago, but unless he holds a Guinness World Record, he's long gone by now. He must have passed the house on to a son. I knock, but nobody answers. A dog runs around the yard with a half of a pizza in its mouth and wanting to be friendly. I call over to the barn to see if someone is there—again, no response. I take photos and decide to come back later.

As I'm leaving, I run into a woman getting mail from the box across the road. A sour expression takes over her face when I tell her who I am and that I wanted to walk the property.

"That chapter is closed," she tells me. Her tone is harsh, abrasive. "You are free to write about whatever you want, but I don't want you to set one foot on my property."

So much for midwestern hospitality, I think. I don't tell her I've already been on the property, knocked on the front door and, oh yeah, took some photos.

So there.

Back at the Holiday Inn, I write out cards to brother and sister John Yoder and Melinda Hershberger. I reiterate what I told their families. I am searching for the truth about Ida. I know that Levi confessed to something before he died. I know this is all very painful, but I need help.

The next day is an important one. I'm going south to Hillsboro to meet the only remaining witness to the start of the fire.

When I can't sleep, I binge three episodes of a Netflix series about a dangerous, devil-worshipping, *Children of the Corn*-ish cult in Ohio. Research, I tell myself. Next to what happened to Ida, Danny, Glen, and others, however, the series is child's play. I shut it off when the cult leader shows up wearing a getup that looks like Moira Rose in the ill-fated eastern European production *The Crows Have Eyes III*.

CHAPTER FOURTEEN

It's, I think, an ungodly hour.

Not quite day. Not night.

I'm groggy and in search of a Starbucks. When I don't find one, I make do with a big cup of McDonald's famous scalding coffee. A thunderstorm darkens the sky in front of me as I drive south to see the Stutzmans' hired boy, now a man, in a place called Sinking Spring, Ohio. The weather feels as though God is mocking me or reminding me of the tale Eli Stutzman told of a lightning strike. The sun rises behind me, sending a glow over my shoulder as the black curtain of the storm fills my windshield. Jagged lines of lightning scribble over the hilly landscape.

Eli insisted he'd seen the lightning hit the barn as he drove the buggy home on July 11, 1977. I'd taken a test drive myself down Moser Road to his farm more than three decades ago, and I've done it again several more times over the years. I don't see how he could have seen lightning strike the barn. In July the broad leaves of chestnuts and maples are impenetrable view blockers.

The terrain doesn't help either. Yes, the road dips down as it winds its way to the Stutzman farm, but at no point is there any kind of overlook or vantage point where anyone could see such a thing as Eli described.

It took him a day to round up the information, then Abe Stutzman texted his younger brother's address to me—an actual address, by the way. Not the Amish version, which is usually along the lines of "turn at the red barn, go past a mill, take the fork to the right, and look for the white house."

Most houses are white. Barns are red. Forks in the road are aplenty.

Abe and I, along with others, appeared on the *Sally Jessy Raphael* show in an episode made memorable because at that time Amish people were a supreme curiosity. It was twenty years before the explosion of Amish romance books and reality shows like *Breaking Amish* or *Amish Mafia*. Abe, who left the Swartzentrubers when he was a teen, brought his black hat and put it on to the delight of the mostly female audience.

He's often wondered what his little brother had seen that night at the fire. If there was something more.

"He was spooked by Eli," he told me when we caught up on the phone recently. "A lot of Amish were. They knew Eli was capable of anything. And speaking against him wasn't something anyone was willing to do."

"That was a long time ago," I said.

"A lot of time to live with something," Abe said.

Eli Stutzman's cousin, the hired boy at the time of the fire, who was also named Eli Stutzman, is now fifty-seven. He and his wife, Mattie, were married in 1989 and eventually settled on a farm.

That's where the thunderstorm that's been taunting me finally breaks.

Mattie is gathering eggs for a customer when I arrive unannounced in my Kia rental car. She is friendly. Eli, she says, is visiting their daughter at a farm not too far away. I tell her that I was there about Eli and Ida. That I wrote a book about them. She's heard of it but says she hasn't read it. She tells me that her husband and many of those close to Ida have been troubled over the years, wondering what really happened.

"It is like a circle," she says, echoing Dan Gingerich's metaphor. "One thing people say leads to another, then it comes back again. It is like there is really no end. Nothing final."

I tell her that I'd been on the story a long time. I started writing the book when I was in my early thirties, and it has been in my thoughts since then.

"There can't be any real legal justice in the sense of a trial," I say, thinking of Dan's concerns about how the Amish would feel about a reinvestigation. "But if it had been your sister, child, mother, wouldn't knowing whatever the truth is give you some peace of mind?"

"I believe it would," she says.

When I ask where I could find her husband, she calls over in the direction of the egg buyer.

"How can I give him the way there?"

The man puts three cartons of brown eggs in his red pickup truck and instructs me to follow. Just before we leave, Mattie calls over to me.

"Come back here and I'll give you a loaf of bread."

The truck barrels down the narrow roads and I recall Mr. Toad's Wild Ride. Fast and twisted. My Kia can barely keep up. A newspaper headline comes to mind: "Obsessed Author Dies Before Learning the Truth."

When I get to the farm down a long and bumpy dirt lane, and ask for Eli Stutzman once again, I'm provided with further proof that this is a group of people in need of a baby name book. I ask a boy for Eli Stutzman and a man emerges from a building under construction. He's way too young.

"You want my father-in-law," he says. "He's also Eli Stutzman."

A minute later a stocky, solid man wearing shades of blue greets me. I tell him that I saw him for only a few minutes at a sawmill near Kidron a long time ago. That I wrote a book about Ida, Danny, and Eli. He is friendly, but reluctant to talk.

Finally, he says he will. He looks at my phone.

"You can't record me."

I toss the phone on the passenger seat and hold up my empty hands while he recounts how a New York producer secretly filmed him for a TV show at the height of the Little Boy Blue story. I know the woman and the show. It was FOX TV's version of *Hard Copy* or *A Current Affair*. The video shot by *The Reporters* was blurry and required captioning because of his accent. And to be fair, they were the only show that did the story any justice. Dan Rather and other network big shots covered Eli Stutzman's story but focused solely on Little Boy Blue—and not on the other deaths associated with his father.

We cross the rutted lane and go into the barn. His feet are bare but steady over the lumpy terrain. Inside, a giant Jenga of hay bales separates us from six horses. Eli sits on a white Lowe's bucket, and I perch on a stack of rough-hewn lumber. He fishes a mason jar of milk from an insulated cooler. His beard, red when I met him decades ago, is now white. He's balding on top with a wispy fringe of long hair dropping over his protruding ears. Not a comb-over, but the Amish opposite of such a thing.

I have no idea how long he'll talk, so I bring up the night of the fire right away.

Eli looks directly at me as he speaks.

"I was picking apples and Ida told me to come inside. Lightning is dangerous. She was concerned. Later when Eli came home, he immediately ran upstairs to look out the window, then he came back down to where me and Ida and Danny were. He said that he'd seen the lightning strike the barn, like a big fireball. He saw it when he was coming home."

I ask if he'd heard the strike or if Ida had.

He shakes his head.

"Eli was concerned about going upstairs to look, but we didn't go out to the barn right away. We went later to put some straw in bags for the sows that had pigs. He didn't bring up the lightning right then. After we were working in there, he told me he smelled smoke. He was up in the hay mow. I didn't smell anything. I think I told him I did, because maybe the suggestion of it made me think I did."

Eli remembers how his older cousin made a show of dousing the supposedly smoldering straw with a bucket of water. Maybe two buckets.

It was theater, I know. Seeing the strike. Smelling the smoke. Pouring water on the straw. Each was a seed planted by a devious gardener to provide credence to a false narrative.

At twelve years of age, Eli would find this night to be the most traumatic of his life.

Awakened by the orange and yellow of the flames outside the open window, he dressed, hurried outside, and ran into his older cousin Eli by the porch. Eli told him to get to the neighbor's place to call the fire department. He was terrified. Not only about the fire, but about the prospect of going to the English neighbor.

"I was young. It was important for me to do what he said, but I was scared. I climbed over the wire fence, and I saw Ida next to the barn. I crawled back under the fence to help her. She was not moving. I called out to her. The side of her face was hot from the fire. And then Eli saw me and told me why didn't I go to get the fire department? I told him Ida is hurt. Then he said to get the rescue squad. I was so scared that I didn't really think about it right then. Later I thought, *Why didn't he tell me Ida was hurt?*"

He ran down to the Gerbers and stood on the doorstep. He was afraid to knock. It was late. They were English. Finally, he did, and right away, the fire department was notified.

"When I got back, Ida had been moved away from the fire."

So much of what happened that night is unforgettable but still locked away in the memory of an Amish boy, now a man, who knows something sinister, something evil, was lurking there. He says without hesitation that he feels Eli killed Ida, but he didn't see it happen.

At Dunlap Memorial, where Ida's body and Eli were brought that night, family members, including Amos and Lizzie Gingerich, arrived. As did Levi Levi Hershberger, Sheriff Jim Frost, and J. T. Questel, the coroner.

Young Eli was there also.

"At the hospital Eli was crying and crying," he tells me. "I remember they gave him a paper bag to put around his mouth and nose to breathe into. Was that to get the smoke out of his lungs?"

"He was hyperventilating," I say. "The paper bag helps put carbon dioxide back into your lungs and evens oxygen flow."

"Oh."

Eli told everyone Ida woke him after an explosion or "loud pop" came from the barn. He also said she had probably had a heart attack in the milk house. It had been too much work for her and "too much smoke."

Eli tells me one more thing about the night of the fire that I'd never heard before. He says the kerosene lamps on the main floor were lit. Someone had taken the time to light them in the middle of a fire that had sent a shower of bright light through the windows.

※

The truth of this story has always, sadly, been that Ida as a victim is a lot like one of those faceless dolls the Amish make for their daughters. She was pretty, blonde, had a nice smile. That description sounds bland because the Amish aren't braggarts. They don't revel in pride about personal accomplishments and attributes. Obviously, they don't pose for endless selfies to prove how amazing they are. In fact, the only photos that likely exist of Ida Stutzman are the pair of Polaroids Dr. Questel took when he examined her body.

"Tell me about Ida," I say.

Eli doesn't answer right away. Instead, his pale-blue eyes glisten, and he pulls out a crumpled bandanna.

"Ida was good," he answers. "She cared about everyone and was always doing nice things."

He can't come up with much more about her. Not because she wasn't wonderful. Of course, she loved her baby. Of course, she was kind. Of course, she wanted nothing more than to serve God's purpose and to be a wife to her husband. When people die tragically, it is often the case that those who remember them glorify them to some degree. A chronic drunk might be "fun-loving and unpredictable," while a person who is decent and kind often comes across as beatific but dull.

Ida was so much more than any description that anyone could provide. I find myself wishing that I could have known her. If like her brother, she and I could have been friends. I admired everyone that I'd met from her family. If she was anything like them, she was, indeed, a wonderful woman. And now, as I revisit her story, I think about how her life might have been, or rather should have been.

Danny, another child, or more.

Grandchildren, maybe even great-grandchildren, by now.

Happy.

Back in the car for the return to Wooster, I turn on my recorder and start talking.

"While we're sitting in the cool, dark barn, a big furry spider scurried across the floor in front of us. Eli gave it a look and said to me, 'Maybe that one's a little like Eli.' We both laughed a little. Not because it was funny, but because it is an apt analogy. He said he was always afraid of Eli after that night. 'If Eli could kill Ida, that maybe he could kill me too? Like if I said the wrong thing?'"

As I drive, I think about two things. First the questions I didn't ask. Had he ever heard Eli and Ida argue? Did she tell him she was unhappy? Did he see Eli do anything against God? Did Eli hurt him in a way that he cannot say? I didn't ask any of those things because he was so quietly emotional over Ida's death. I liked him. I had empathy for what he'd gone through. I respected his boundaries as an Amish person.

Maybe others had done the same thing during the investigation. Maybe that's the reason Eli Stutzman wasn't stopped that night when he should have been.

The other thing that occupies my thoughts is that he said the lamps were lit when he woke up and went outside. It seems like such a small thing to wonder about, but I can't make sense of it. A fire is burning outside and there are livestock and equipment to be saved and either Ida or Eli takes the time to light the lamps.

I don't think so.

CHAPTER FIFTEEN

I open a soda from the Holiday Inn's little cubby of a store ("We have some Stouffer's if you're hungry"), plop onto my unmade bed, and fire up my Mac. The day has been long and mostly uneventful. I could call home to Claudia, but it is late and she's likely under a heap of dachshunds. I shuffle through index cards of Ohio contacts, culling dead ends and placing those "still possible" in what I think might make the most sense geographically.

One has nothing to do with Stutzman: *"Dahmer house, side trip?"*

The new multipart documentary on Jeffrey Dahmer has been going gangbusters for Netflix and, of course, I watch another episode. Maybe two. Before my trip to Ohio, I checked the local crime scenes within the area and saw that Dahmer's boyhood home was about thirty miles from Wooster. I put on episode 3, "Doin' a Dahmer," and despite its frivolous title, it's as chilling as anything I've ever seen.

My eyes stay glued to my laptop as the actor playing Dahmer offers a ride to an eighteen-year-old from Akron heading to a music festival (Michael Stanley Band headlined) at Chippewa Lake Park. It was in June 1978. It's that benign moment that we all know will lead to tragedy. Dahmer promises Steven Hicks some beer and partying at his place not far away in Bath Township, a suburb of Akron. Steve accepts. I could call Hicks a hitchhiker like everyone else does. It was, after all, what he was doing with his thumb out on the highway. The word, however, is loaded. Judgmental.

I grew up when people still thumbed for a ride, but they were considered stupid and careless to risk getting into some stranger's car. In those days, "hitchhiker" went along with the word "prostitute," as in "He was just a hitchhiker . . . She was just a prostitute." It was a cruel and dismissive shorthand for "They should have been smarter and more careful. Whatever happened to them was their own damned fault."

Steven Hicks was a sensitive soul who cried when hunting. He had just graduated from high school and was making plans. His mother said he had a big smile that could get him out of any little skirmish. A good kid enjoying that last summer before adulthood kicked in. His hair was long and wavy, and his mom was right about his smile.

I lean back a little. This series troubles me more than any other true crime show I've ever seen. As I take in the train wreck that was Jeffrey's life, I can't help but feel a twinge of sympathy for players on both sides of the drama. As acted by Evan Peters with a decidedly flat midwestern accent and a kind of blank-eyed visage that camouflages what's really going on inside his head, Jeffrey is frightening as hell. From the very beginning, he is kind of an all-American tragedy in the making. He's stolen the lives of young men as though they were nothing, only mere objects of his desire.

What I find unsettlingly tragic is that Dahmer was aware that he was a monster and understood his actions were evil. He knew full well that each and every time he brought some unsuspecting young man or boy to his Milwaukee apartment for a drug-induced Polaroid session, they were going to die.

It was a compulsion. Something that he couldn't stop.

The episode is over, and before Netflix can force-feed me the next one, I search online for the address of Dahmer's old house. When the results come into view, I learn that the current owner is a local music legend who formed the band the Waitresses. The group's big hit was

"I Know What Boys Like." And while that slice of New Wave is rarely heard on the airwaves anymore, the band's "Christmas Wrapping" is a holiday staple. A holiday antidote to the bombastic and relentless cheerleading performed each season by Mariah, Brenda, and even Burl.

I hide my laptop under my pillow. Moments later I find myself behind the wheel, heat on full blast, not-so-bad coffee in the cup holder. The thirty-mile drive takes me from one highway to the next, past exits with gardens of restaurant signage rising high to meet my eye.

When I arrive at the address on Bath Road, I inch past the three-bedroom, midcentury modern home two or three times before I park. I know being there is stupid. At that time of night, or really, anytime. The house faces a wooded ravine, and a pair of windows are lit like big eyes looking over the drop. I take a few pictures and then walk to the driveway. Signage there reminds me—and other lookie-loos—that trespassing is verboten. A camera stands guard just in case someone ignores the sign.

Not even the sound of the wind nor a dog barking impedes the silence. A whisper from across the road could be heard. I stand still, scanning the ravine, then the hillside behind the house. I think about the boy who became a killer. I think about the parents who raised a monster. About the brother who changed his name after Jeffrey's arrest in Milwaukee. It's here in this quiet place that a boy became a killer, and a killer took the lives of seventeen men and boys. A heaviness in the air just then. It is my own doing.

I wouldn't feel it if I didn't know what happened here.

As the darkness retreats, I think about the investigators coming here to search. It must have been the proverbial needle in a haystack—the ground spongy with fallen leaves, and the killer had said that whatever they'd find wouldn't be large.

No one can know for sure if what Jeffrey confessed to was completely true, but this part I believe: Steven, his first victim, had a few beers in that house but wanted a ride back to Akron or maybe just the highway. He wanted to leave. Jeffrey wanted him to stay.

That seems about right.

The rest is conjecture based on what Jeffrey said and how we try to knit the story together. The why, remember? We want to know the trigger that led to the act of murder. Did Jeffrey come on to Steve? Did they argue? Did Jeffrey lose control? Or did he simply take a ten-pound dumbbell and strike Steve over the head from behind?

We don't know. We *can't* know.

Jeffrey told investigators that after Steve slumped to the floor, he hauled him to the basement where he could have sex with him. Or was it a corpse? He said he dismembered the body, pulverized the bones with a sledgehammer, and scattered pieces throughout the wooded property.

Done with my macabre look-see, I return to my car, wondering how many others are stashed around the woods in Ohio. Why wouldn't there be? No one knew what happened in the house on Bath Road for more than a dozen years. And it was known only because the killer confessed. And unlike Ted Bundy and others who started to talk, he did so not to stay alive, not to bargain with his sentence, but because he'd known that his compulsion to kill was a sickness. That kind of truth-telling is an extremely rare occurrence in the annals of crime. Points for self-awareness, I guess. Also, a measure of decency from a monster. Is that even possible?

Just before an intersection to the main road, I come across something I'd missed on the way in.

A dead opossum.

It's almost comical, like a Road Runner bit from a Saturday morning cartoon. Whoever ran over it severed the roadkill into halves. The head, with a protruding fuck-you tongue, is taxidermy ready, the middle is as flat as the proverbial pancake, and the back end is a stretched-out tail curling at the tip.

Something Jeffrey would have brought home to dissolve, dissect, and in his own hideous way, covet.

The next morning, I review my notes about the purchase of the Stutzman farm. I'm going to see Chris and Dianna Swartzentruber for lunch. It was Chris's brother who sold the farm on Moser Road to Eli and Ida. The first week of May 1977, Eli and Ida met with loan officer Richard Armstrong in the offices of the Federal Land Bank in Wooster to go over the terms of a farm loan. The Stutzmans sought the loan to pay off the contract with Daniel and Sarah Swartzentruber for the Moser Road farm.

On July 7, the loan was approved and a check for $55,000 was cut for the Stutzmans.

Daniel Swartzentruber had no idea Eli got all that money then. He and his wife continued to receive regular payments until Eli sold the farm and left for Colorado years later. Further, Ida would never have signed a loan application perpetuating a fraud. The money she signed off on had been for the singular purpose of paying off Dan and Sarah. Not five years later, but upon the disbursal of those funds into their bank account on July 7.

That didn't happen.

Just five days after the check arrived, she was dead.

CHAPTER SIXTEEN

At lunchtime after Dahmer, I find Chris and Dianna Swartzentruber sitting side by side at a table in the restaurant in the basement of Town and Country, a store in the heart of Kidron. Even from across the room, Dianna's eyes hold the same fiery spark as when we appeared on the *Sally Jessy Raphael* show in 1991. She was among the first to draw the connection between Little Boy Blue in *Reader's Digest* and Danny Stutzman. She worked the phone like an old-school telemarketer, telling the authorities in Ohio and Nebraska to get their act together and throw the book at Eli.

"He killed Ida, and he killed his little boy! You cops know it. Do your damn job!"

Chris grew up with Eli and left the Swartzentrubers around the same time. When he stands to greet me, I go to his side of the table and give him and Dianna a hug. We haven't talked in thirty years, but the connection between us is strong.

While others on my return to the story are people I hope will be more forthcoming this time around, I know these two have always been right there with me.

Chris orders a burger, and Dianna and I opt for the BLT. We catch up on family stuff. The last time I saw their daughter, Amy, she was in a playpen. She's now grown with children of her own. We all agree that there is nothing better than being a grandparent.

An Amish family of five takes a table on the other side of the restaurant. Only the tourists pay them any mind. A girl in a tie-dye T-shirt thinks she's being sly taking a photo with her phone. I give her a look and she sets down the phone.

"We all know Eli killed Ida and Danny," Dianna says while the waitress fills our cups.

"Knowing it and proving it are different things," I say.

Dianna steals a french fry from her husband's plate.

"I knew he was lying when he told me about the fire," he says.

At the time, Chris was living in Greenville, Ohio, adjusting to life away from the Amish, when his buddy Eli came for a visit. Eli told him of seeing the lightning strike.

"I didn't know anything about the fire, but when he told me that, I knew something smelled. There was a tree line; you couldn't even see the barn. I mean, that's not right. And I did not argue nothing to him about it. I just thought that to myself. It's not possible."

"You didn't think he killed her back then, right?" I ask.

"I didn't really think much about it at that point, you know, till later on, I started putting things together."

Dianna pipes up. "And other people would say, 'Well, this is what he told me.' Right. Everybody had a different story."

Chris is sure that Ida's murder was premeditated.

And longer than others might imagine.

"I think he planned this whole thing out, about 'How can I go back to the Amish? How can I?' You know, he figured all this out . . . get married to Ida. And when you go back to the Amish, they're going to do everything they can to help you. And he just took advantage of it."

"He still had his driver's license," Dianna interjects. "What about that? After Ida died, he drove to see you."

Chris nods. "Yeah, he came out to my house and I just had to scratch my head. To have kept his driver's license and, you know, he had something planned."

Dianna bolsters the point.

"Look," she says, "by keeping his driver's license, he is saying that he's not going to be Amish for long. How does he know that? Because he knows his wife is going to be dead!"

Chris jumps back in. "He sold that farm right out from under the Amish and made a lot of money. And if he had insurance, he was not staying Amish."

Insurance.

How did I miss that the first time around? I knew Amish people didn't buy insurance. Doing so was betting against God. It was the same reason the Amish didn't install lightning rods on the peaks of their barns.

God's will was never to be tampered with.

I drive back to the hotel, thinking of the money and how much Eli might have had.

Howard Runck, the rancher Eli moved in with in Colorado after he left the Amish, would be getting a call from me.

CHAPTER SEVENTEEN

At seventy, Greg Ferrell radiates the same youthful energy he had when he submitted a long-distance application from Orange County, California, for a deputy's position with the Wayne County Sheriff's Office in the spring of 1976. For Ferrell, it was a way to return home. He'd been raised in the county. His father ran a small farm market that catered to the Amish.

"I went to a little township school; we had Amish in our class. It always amazed me how well they played softball and ran in their bare feet," he tells me as we sit in his den, a room filled with memories of his years in law enforcement and love of all things western.

At five eight on a "good day," it was his height that kept him from securing police work in California, a much more competitive job market. He had a degree in criminal justice and experience working for a private security firm. The twenty-two-year-old flew out for a round of interviews on his own dime to vie for a job that paid about two dollars an hour.

Sheriff Frost was impressive. Ferrell saw him as a kind of old-school cowboy figure with a bolo tie, boots, and a truck with a big star decal. He carried his .357 around like an accessory. He was smart, unabashedly particular, and completely full of himself.

Greg and his wife, Sherry, had been married only a year when he got the job and was told he was needed right away. That was in June 1976. He started unpaid peace officer training for twenty hours a week, plus his full-time job at the department. It was exhausting, but that's the way things were done.

Jim's temper tantrums were legendary.

"I remember one time we were working the fair, and one of the officers had a Stetson and he hooked it on his gun, and he was out there directing traffic and Jim saw it and reamed him, went into the dispatch center, and called everybody into this little dinky room, you know, and everybody that was working that day had to come in. And he proceeded to scream at us about the appearance and how that looks. He would do things like that often. Just throw these fits."

He even demoted a deputy over something that was clearly an accident.

"So, one day he came in, and I can't remember if he opened his car door and knocked over the sheriff's motorcycle or if he bumped it, parking, and set it back up. There was no damage to it. The sheriff just went berserk, demoted the guy."

"Deputies and staff on edge a little?" I ask.

"Yeah," Greg says. "Whenever Frost felt slighted by someone, that person—deputy, secretary, or dispatcher—became a target."

When a sergeant's position was posted, Frost made it known he wanted Greg to apply. Greg considered the job, but he didn't think he was ready. Besides, the pay increase of around twenty-five cents an hour didn't pencil out with the increased hours.

"So, I come in, they said, 'Sheriff wants to see you.' I go upstairs and he says he's got the list and saw that I didn't sign up for the sergeant consideration. Ever since that day, I couldn't do anything right."

Frost, it seemed, couldn't hang on to staff. The City of Wooster paid a lot more than the county, so there was an exodus from the sheriff's department to the city.

"Was it just money or morale that caused so many to leave?" I ask. Greg thinks about it for a moment.

"I think it was both. I mean, I think they all fed each other. First you had the sheriff who's just getting progressively worse, right," he says.

Frost was demanding and there was a lot to admire about what he wanted to do, but his personality and personal choices began to wear on the department.

"This thing with Ken Kerr irritated a lot of people," I say.

A very likeable guy, Ken was twenty-three, handsome, and self-deprecating. He joined the Wayne County Sheriff's Office in August 1976 and was promoted in May 1977 to sergeant.

"You could see he and Frost were friends right away. There was favoritism. There was no question about it. You know, he lived with Frost," Greg says.

"I did, but what did you all think about it back then? That something was going on between them?"

"Oh, yeah," he says. "Ken would drive Frost's Corvette. And we were all like shocked because his Corvette was like his baby."

"Special privileges?" I ask.

"Seemed like it at the time."

Every person in law enforcement in the county knew Jim Frost and Ken Kerr had a special relationship. Most didn't consider it a love affair. Though the two of them shared a house in Orrville, they didn't go out to restaurants or other public places and show that they were a couple. Roommates, yes. Good buddies, absolutely.

Lovers? Well, that might have been the subject of some Justice Center whispers in Wooster, but rarely even considered by the general public. A gay sheriff? That didn't seem even remotely possible.

And then it was over. Not by a breakup, but by a terrible accident.

The accident in question had a sole survivor, Darlene Croskey.

When I try to catch her at work, the manager at the busy Orrville Ford dealership informs me that I just missed her. She's at lunch. I find her ten minutes later in a booth in the deli section of Buehler's, a local chain that serves as a variant of Whole Foods for the region. She and her friend Becky, a friendly blonde, are waiting for their matching orders of BLTs.

With fries.

And ketchup.

Darlene wears her hair dark and spiky. Her eyes are accented by a generous helping of mascara, and they truly sparkle when she speaks. This is a woman who never met a stranger and doesn't like to speak ill of anyone. I like her at first sight. I expect most feel the same.

I want to talk about Ken Kerr, the good-looking young man Frost plucked from a criminology class at the community college where he taught.

Darlene is flabbergasted and those pretty dark eyes pop when I mention they'd been lovers.

"I only dated him three times," she says while a waitress sets down a decent-looking BLT. "He never appeared to be that way. Yeah, he hugged me, but I was never involved with him sexually."

She takes a breath and tells me the story I've come to hear.

Darlene was on a motorcycle dinner date with Kerr on the night of August 25, 1977. All she has to do is close her eyes, and she still sees the beauty of the evening and feels the sadness of what happened that day. They had dinner at the Geisen Haus in North Canton. On their way back to Orrville, Ken lost control going around a curve in Stark County.

It was their third date.

"It was like right before midnight, no alcohol was involved or anything, but he had never been on that road before. There was a curve, and we went off the road and hit all these fence posts with barbed wire and a huge utility pole. And Ken was, I think, probably killed instantly. I was in Massillon Community Hospital for two months."

After the accident, James Frost took Darlene to Parma, Ohio, for a dinner with Ken's family.

"I felt bad because here I am alive, talking to his parents," Darlene said. "And, you know, it was hard for me, but I did go. His parents had a big meal for us and that was tough. I met them and, you know, their son's gone and I'm alive."

I ask Darlene if there might have been something else going on at that dinner.

"Do you think he was presenting you as kind of a love interest of their son?" I ask her. "You know, Frost and Kerr had been roommates."

She dips a fry in ketchup.

"Maybe. Possibly. We only had three dates. Maybe that's why he invited me. I don't know. I just felt bad. Their son died and they had this big Greek Orthodox spread and were so nice. They loved Ken so much."

Before I leave, she lets me know that Frost was a very good lawman.

"He would have arrested his own father if he caught him speeding on Main Street."

"That I don't doubt," I say. "He's a very complicated guy."

Something strange happened not long after Ken Kerr died. Frost announced that the young sergeant was to be promoted posthumously, and not only that, but he was also honored with something called the White Star Award.

Greg Ferrell put it this way: "And then we're all looking at each other like, wow, what's that about? That whole thing of him being promoted was strange. I don't want to speak ill of the dead, you know, but it was like everybody was like, you know, if he would have died for a deputy-related death, would be one thing. Yeah, it was weird."

"Why do you think he did it?"

"I think that was just his way of dealing with his, you know, his sorrow and his loss."

Frost was struggling and it showed.

"I would go out of my way to try to be nice to him after I left. I walked up to him one time he was in front, still at the old jail. And I went over there, and I said, 'Hey, Sheriff, how's it going?' And he just looked past me, turned around, walked away without even speaking because I quit the department. That's just an insight into his personality, right? I mean, it's obvious he really needed some professional counseling. I mean, it is a shame; he had such emotional issues and personality disorders. He needed help."

Frost was never the same after Kerr's death, an incident that caused a downward spiral. He lost the next election and went on to serve as police chief in Orrville for a while. After that, he vanished from everyone's radar.

Until an incident brought him back into the news and clarified what many close to him had suspected.

A secret that he couldn't divulge.

CHAPTER EIGHTEEN

Former Wayne County sheriff Jim Frost, then thirty-nine, made head-lines of the humiliating kind in the *Miami Herald* and other South Florida papers on October 12, 1983: "Off-Duty Officer Is Stabbed in Beach Restroom."

Initially Frost said that he was robbed by three men who wanted to steal a ring he was wearing.

"I should have given it to them," he said.

Over the next forty-eight hours, however, his story changed. It's likely that the detectives investigating the violent assault of one of their own were skeptical right away. The area where Frost was accosted was in the heart of Miami Beach's gay district, a distinction it holds today.

Frost, injured from a chest wound, parked his brand-new Trans Am on the sidewalk and staggered into a Burger King for help. He was bloody and in a weakened condition.

Witnesses to the incident said that they saw two men arguing in a parking lot near a beachside public restroom. Police followed up and found blood in the restroom.

Around that time, a Wayne County sheriff's investigator named Jim Gasser took a call from a Broward County sheriff's detective investigating the case involving his old boss.

Recently Jim recounted his memory of the conversation.

"He said Frost was involved in a love triangle down there and got stabbed. He asked me if I ever saw any homosexual tendencies with him, and I said that I'd worked many late nights with him, long hours, and he never tried anything with me. I then told him that he had been involved in relationships with several deputies in the department and I left it at that."

"So, by the content of their inquiry," I said, "I take it that Frost wasn't truthful about what he was doing in that part of town."

"Yeah," Jim answered. "That's a fair assumption."

After the initial report ran in the Miami paper, a follow-up indicated that the hunt was still on for Frost's attacker.

"We've got a story with a lot of holes in it," a Broward County sheriff's spokesperson said at the time. "It's going to be up to him to fill in the blanks."

I guess he never did fill in those blanks.

No one was ever charged in the attack.

And the drip, drip, drip of Jim Frost's once-promising career was on its way to becoming a deluge.

CHAPTER NINETEEN

When researching a book, information doesn't come in a linear fashion. It's more like dribs and drabs. In some ways that kind of cadence was especially appropriate for the way Jim Frost's life had gone since losing his bid for a third term as sheriff, and working in Orrville as police chief, then dropping even lower to hotel security in Cleveland before moving to Broward County, Florida.

The dribs and drabs were fed by his increasingly dangerous abuse of alcohol. Each step downward was fueled by a drinking problem that turned the law enforcer into a lawbreaker.

On April 20, 1987, an officer was notified by a citizen that a driver appeared to be intoxicated in the area of Twenty-First Street and Collins Avenue in Miami Beach, just next to the restroom where Jim Frost was stabbed four years prior. When the officer arrived, he found Frost in a blue Chevy with the engine still running. The officer asked Frost to step out of the vehicle and upon doing so, the officer could smell alcohol. When Frost tried to answer the officer's questions, his speech was slurred and his eyes were bloodshot. When the officer ran his information, he learned that Frost's license had been suspended in February of that year. He was arrested and taken into custody.

On October 7, 1995, just two days after his fifty-first birthday, Frost was arrested for driving under the influence in Fort Lauderdale.

It was only two thirty in the afternoon when he was stopped near the 800 block of SE Seventeenth Avenue, just blocks away from Broward Boulevard and Las Olas Boulevard, popular stomping grounds for gay men.

Two years later, on August 24, 1997, around 8:00 p.m., Frost was arrested again for driving under the influence at SE Fifteenth Street and Miami Road. Just three blocks north of where he was arrested for DUI in 1995.

Frost was drowning himself with booze. He was running away from failure and drinking heavily to convince himself that his best years were not behind him at all. Those closest to him felt that he'd shoved himself deep into the bottle in an effort to forget that the love of his life was really gone.

"I don't think he was ever the same after Ken died," a friend of his said years later. "He didn't want to lose his standing because of his homosexuality. But if he had to in order to make a life with Ken, that's what he would have done. He never got the chance. Losing Ken was bigger than losing the election. With an election he could run again. With Ken dead and gone, Jim was just lost."

Frost lived at a time when society likely would have shunned him as a gay elected official. That's an understatement for the ages. Harvey Milk was elected to the San Francisco Board of Supervisors the same year Ida died in the fire. He'd been the first openly gay man ever elected to office—and despite his win in liberal San Francisco, his life and career ended tragically. I feel sorry for Frost. I really do. I think of him as a doorman in Cleveland, a beat cop in Florida, a man who held such promise and possessed such brilliance and ambition.

I have to draw a line somewhere. He was an alcoholic, and that's a disease. He was gay and had all of that to deal with at a time when it was far different from today. Again, not his fault. However, he was also a liar and a conspirator. What he did and chose not to do the night Ida died cannot be forgiven. It just can't. He decided to save his own reputation over doing his sworn duty.

And when he made that deal with himself, he let a monster loose.

My blood is boiling now because all I can think about is Danny, clad in that blanket sleeper with the feet, frozen in a ditch on Christmas Eve. He will forever be nine. And Glen Pritchett tossed like garbage into a ditch in Travis County, Texas. I see his kids on Facebook, where we are friends and have exchanged a few messages over the years.

Look what you did, Jim Frost. You not only destroyed your own life; you had a hand in the ruin of others.

Not harsh. Just honest.

I open a fresh pack of old-school index cards and start making notations. Every line is information gleaned from a law enforcement record or an interview. I know that each card by itself won't be enough to send Wayne County officials for a meetup at the prosecutor's office to amend Ida's death certificate from natural causes to homicide and draft some face-saving way of conceding corruption and cover-up.

"Mistakes were made . . . blah blah blah."

The coroner has been less than responsive, and the former prosecutor told Robbin to take a hike when she contacted him. So I'm counting on Sheriff Travis Hutchinson. Former deputies like Greg Ferrell are unequivocal in their support and admiration of the current sheriff. He is the real deal. Hutchinson not only has a firm grasp on ethics but also knows that cops are people. People make mistakes. A badge doesn't provide a protective bubble against corruption.

Robbin schedules a preliminary interview with the sheriff.

"Great," I tell her. "He's our guy. I know he's a member of the Jim Frost fan club, but that's because he doesn't know what we know."

"Right," she says. "I'll call him and set things up for the big reveal."

I smile.

The big reveal.

I know the number of scrawled-on cards will grow and in time assume the heft of a set of flash cards.

House of cards, more accurately, I think.

Justice, I hope.

CHAPTER TWENTY

It's spitting rain when I drive up to see Ed and Bonnie Stoll, the dairy farmer and his wife who hired Eli, essentially through a referral from Abe Stutzman, Eli's cousin. They had three hundred head of dairy cows when the cousins worked there, and their business would grow to three thousand head before they sold it to live a retired life that means *only* eight hours a day of work managing one thousand acres of farmland, and rental property.

Ed and Bonnie are a classic door knock interview. They've never returned any calls, and Bonnie once hung up, saying that they didn't want any telemarketing calls, before we even had the opportunity to chat about why it was that I'd been calling. They live across from the mammoth dairy farm that had been a huge source of pride for the family and, indeed, all of Marshallville, Ohio.

My theory of the entire debacle of the barn fire and Ida's death investigation hinges on what happened across the road from the Stolls' ranch house.

We've never met in person, but Bonnie invites me inside right away and points to a bookshelf that has the original edition of *Abandoned Prayers*. She plants herself in a comfortable chair in the family room off the kitchen. She's flanked by family photos and mementos that speak to a farm life. It isn't a Joanna Gaines aesthetic of black-and-white "Modern Farmhouse," but the real deal.

Authenticity rules the day in the Stoll home.

A few minutes later, Ed comes into the kitchen. He stays there for the most part, resting his palms against the counter pass-through that separates the two rooms.

The Stolls are "America First," unabashedly so. They are deeply concerned about where the country is headed, and quite honestly, they have a lot more skin in the game than those who blather endlessly on cable TV or social media. They ran a huge dairy operation, provided hundreds of jobs, and managed to make a living out of it all. No easy undertaking. Ask any farmer. It's more than a full-time effort. It's up early every day. No day off. It's a constant worrying endeavor when it comes to the pricing of dairy-related commodities. It's barely ever having a vacation.

Ed is second generation, having taken over the dairy from his father, Walter. While it might have been a dream that his three children would do the same, it was not to be.

"It was not the kind of life they wanted for themselves," he says. "And that's fine. It's not a life for everyone."

"Eli never should have been believed the night of the fire because of what happened on your property," I say.

They don't disagree.

Eli is a sore spot, a kind of scab that never really crusted over. I see that right away. The name still stings, and their heads still shake in disappointment over the young Amishman who played them. Honest people seem to think that being fooled by someone is a mark against their own character, when really it is the opposite. Good people want to believe in good. They assume others are truthful because that's how they live their own lives.

They tell me about one night in 1974. Eli had dinner at the Stolls, with Liz and Leroy Chupp also in attendance. This wasn't an unusual occurrence. Eli was polite and on the shy side. Liz and Leroy were nearly like family. One time stands out to Ed and Bonnie.

"He told us that there are ways to kill people without it showing," Bonnie says with a headshake.

"Eli worked at Dunlap Memorial serving time as a conscientious objector during the Vietnam War," Ed adds from the pass-through. "I think that's where he learned that."

"He said that?" I ask, just to be sure.

"He sat right there at our table and said it," Bonnie says. "And we just looked at each other. What? It didn't surprise Liz and Leroy because he lived with them, and he probably had said it to them before."

Eli lived at the dairy during the week, and Ed drove him down to Apple Creek on Friday nights and picked him up Monday morning. Ed learned more about Eli's life—some experiences as a teacher at Cherry Ridge, some mentions of how things were at home.

"His dad was really rough on Eli," Ed says.

Bonnie gives her husband a look. "Wasn't rough enough."

For as long as they live, the Stolls will never forget November 19, 1974. Ed had spent the day hauling corn to a storage building nearby. He left Stutzman in the barn doing chores just after 5:00 p.m., when he took the last load. That load took about an hour, instead of the usual half hour. Stoll returned at dusk and found that the barn had been ransacked and blood stained the walls. Eli was curled up on the floor among bloodied rocks, bricks, and scattered bales of hay.

"What took you so long?" Eli said, barely getting the words out.

Eli muttered something about having been jumped by two guys. He said he had seen a strange car with West Virginia plates driving up and down the road near the farm. Later, when he was in the barn, someone hiding in the hayloft threw a rock, hitting him on the head. Another man jumped from behind and slashed him with a knife. Stutzman said that in the struggle he had stabbed one of his attackers with a pitchfork, but they had overpowered him.

"He had told us before when he turned those guys in for the dope, he was afraid for his life," Ed says. "And he told us the sheriff's department said, 'Well, we'll take care of you. Don't worry.' And he says, 'Well, they didn't protect me.' He says they didn't show up, you know, nothing. And this is what happened."

The Stolls and I connect on Liz and Leroy Chupp, whom Eli lived with on the farm when he took a job at the dairy. When I was working on *Abandoned Prayers*, my family stayed with Liz and Leroy on their new farm near Lake Erie. My girls were fascinated by some of the simplest things. When Liz needed carrots for a soup she was making, her daughters went out and pulled some from the frozen soil. My girls were astounded. I'm not sure they knew carrots came from the ground. Liz made the best pillowy donuts we'd ever had. In our home, donuts were from a bakery or a grocery store.

Marie, the Chupps' oldest, took our girls into a bedroom to show them something "so beautiful and amazing."

It was a battery-powered fiber-optic floral arrangement. She turned it on, but only for a minute.

The next day, our families loaded into a van and went to see Niagara Falls, which, by the way, was beautiful and amazing too.

I hadn't talked to Leroy since hearing that Liz passed in 2005. I ask Bonnie if she knows how it was that Liz had died so young.

"Marie said it was cancer," she says. "They took her to the doctor, and they just brushed it off. They knew it was cancer but because she was Amish, they brushed it off."

Liz was Amish. They brushed it off.

The Stolls went to Liz's viewing in Pennsylvania.

"Eli had gotten out of jail by then and we said we were concerned," Bonnie says. "They said, oh, no, don't worry, they put the word out. They didn't want him around. And so, he did not show up."

We talk more about America, politics, the way things are, and before I leave, I state the obvious.

"What Eli did on your property was calculated, devious, and ugly. But you took him back, you let him stay here after that because you wanted to help him."

Bonnie answers. "Ed's mom said he's a Christian. Mom says, you know, he just needs to repent."

"And he wasn't here very long after that," I say.

"He just disappeared all the time," Bonnie goes on. "Mom had such good intentions. He really took advantage of her."

"He took advantage of everyone."

"You know," Bonnie says, "that's probably true."

I mention the letters, not the faked ones, but ones that Eli received at the farm until the time he left in early 1975. Ed's mother, who put the mail in his desk, once found some items so strange that she didn't even know exactly what they were. She did know, however, that they had to do with sex.

Later, Ed's mother found a cache of magazines tucked under Stutzman's mattress. She was so shocked by their content, she burned them.

"Eli had some troubles," Ed says now. "Some things he needed to work out."

Understatement, I think.

I drive over to the massive barns that are the old Stoll dairy and take in the view. It happened here. The particular pairing of Eli Stutzman and Jim Frost would lead to so much subterfuge, so much hurt, later. Frost was no dummy; that can't be disputed by anyone who knew him. And yet he found himself hitched to a maniac like Eli for the rest of his life.

CHAPTER
TWENTY-ONE

Harley Gerber's name had been mentioned by Cousin Eli, the former hired boy, when I'd met up with him. He thought he might know something and directed me to the feed mill at the bottom of the hill from the Stutzman place in Dalton.

Gerber Feed is an impressive operation. More than twenty grain silos are clustered into a steampunk skyline on the opposite side of the property from the office. Trucks laden with corn and grain roll in with the raw materials for swine, dairy, poultry, and beef, and feed the rumble of a business that started when Harley was in his early twenties in 1964. I go inside and introduce myself. One of Harley's grandsons tells me that he'd been talking about *Abandoned Prayers* a week or two ago. His grandfather is retired and lives in a Kidron condo complex. We try to figure out the name of the place but come up empty.

"You can't miss it," he says. "It's on the right just before town and it's the only one."

He gives me his grandfather's phone number and off I go.

✕

Heritage Green is indeed easy to find. It's right off Kidron Road less than a mile from the center of town, which includes Amish tourist hot spot Lehman's and the Kidron auction where Amish gather in black-hatted droves to bid on cattle and other livestock. It's a circle of about twenty color-coordinated homes with cathedral ceilings and private, smallish patios. It's suburbia in the middle of the country. Harley, now in his early eighties, is sharp. Very. His snow-white hair creeps from under a ball cap. His glasses are wire framed. When Harley says that he doesn't recall many details, it isn't because his memory is failing. It's because out of the time the Stutzmans and Gerbers were neighbors, with the exception of a couple of instances, there had been nothing remarkable to make note of. "The Amish are private," he says, "and live their lives for the most part in their own private world."

Cue "Weird Al" Yankovic's "Amish Paradise."

Harley recalls a knock on the door in the middle of a July night and finding the Stutzmans' hired boy standing at the front door.

"Barn is on fire," the boy said urgently. "I want to call the fire department."

Harley made the call and went up the hill.

"Howard Snavely and I both got up there about the same time," he says. "So, we picked Mrs. Stutzman up and carried her across the road into the pasture. I was not aware that she was dead at that time."

He pauses and pulls up the memory.

"Soon as the fire department got there and some of their men were working, you know, somebody said she's dead. Oh, hell, I was not aware of that. It was a terrible night," he says.

"Right," I say. "It was more terrible than you knew at the time."

Harley is every bit of an honest midwestern man. It isn't part of his ethical makeup to repeat gossip or say something that he doesn't believe to be 100 percent true. He thinks before continuing.

"The fire was intentionally set," he says now. "He made it so she suffocated in the smoke."

He takes another moment, thinking it all through.

"That's pretty well what happened, I think," he says.

"And after the fire," I go on, "things changed drastically."

Harley remembers when Eli Stutzman returned from a trip he'd made to Florida. Harley and his wife had been watching Danny. "It was no trouble," he says. That's what neighbors do in Wayne County.

"When he came to the back door and knocked, we almost didn't know him. He wasn't Amish anymore. You know, the beard was gone, the clothes. He looked like a different person."

The change hadn't really come out of the blue.

The Gerbers saw things going on up at the Stutzman farm, but they didn't know what to make of it. Harley didn't compare notes with Howard Snavely, for example, about the fire. And he never contacted the authorities about the rumors.

"I just really didn't care to talk about it much," he says. "Still don't."

If he knows more, Harley's not going to give it up. It's a dark chapter. Like others who were caught up in Stutzman's wake, it's that feeling that whatever could have been done, should have been done nearly fifty years ago. Nothing could be done for Ida or her little boy now.

It weighs on him even now.

It weighs on everyone.

Making some noise in 1977 might have changed things for other victims for whom Eli Stutzman was the last person they saw.

"Eventually Eli went out west with Danny," Harley says. "Danny never came back."

CHAPTER
TWENTY-TWO

The afternoon that I talk with Harley, my assistant Robbin and I play a version of West Salem parcel bingo as we go over the lives and deaths of neighbors related to the candy murder. I'm drawn to investigate because of James Frost's audacious and curious move of announcing that a cold case murder was solved yet refusing to point the finger at anyone.

"Frost is a big liar," Robbin says in her cut-to-the-quick manner.

"He's a lot of things. Liar is definitely on the list," I shoot back. "The flip side is he was a meticulous investigator."

"Right," she says. "So much so that he annoyed the fuck out of everyone he worked with."

I smile just then. Robbin holds nothing back. I've spent my life writing about people with the balance I think is required to be fair. At times, probably more than fair.

But yes, Frost was a liar. And yes, he was fucking annoying.

Here's the nutshell version of the murder.

Upon returning from errands the morning of March 15, 1971, sheep farmer Clifford Badger, fifty-nine, retrieved a package from his West Salem mailbox. The package containing homemade chocolates was wrapped in brown paper and came with a note: *"To Our Good Neighbor."*

No name. No return address.

Moments later, after both Helen Badger and her husband ate the candy, Helen, fifty-seven, called the fire department, telling dispatchers Cliff had suddenly collapsed and she felt ill. By the time rescuers arrived, Cliff was dead, and Helen was found convulsing on the kitchen floor.

Helen was rushed to the hospital, where she eventually recovered.

At that time, Glenn Rike was Wayne County sheriff with Dr. Questel serving as coroner. Lab tests of the candy concluded that the couple had been poisoned by strychnine. Who would do such a thing? There were theories, of course. The one that got the most traction was that Cliff had a habit of killing dogs that attacked his herd of sheep and a dog-owning neighbor sought payback. It might be unfair to say, but it appeared through reading about the case that Mr. Badger was actually not a "Good Neighbor" and had a reputation as a hard-ass and a bully.

Try as he might, Rike was unable to solve the case. He even posted a $500 reward out of his own pocket. Limited resources were but one of a host of factors.

Something else was at play here. West Salem is a close-knit farming community with secrets impossible for outsiders to unlock.

Very Wayne County, Ohio. And a little *Devil in Ohio* too.

So the case sat there. Meat-locker cold until June 1974, when a puffed-up Sheriff Frost announced at a press conference that it was solved. He said the killer had been identified through a handwriting sample that had been submitted to his office anonymously. The sample was compared with the "Good Neighbor" note at the Ohio Bureau of Criminal Investigation (BCI) crime lab. They matched.

And here's the part that interests me the most. Frost refused to release the identity of the suspect or the motive for the poisoning, saying the killer was deceased and to do so would sully the reputation of his or her family. He also said that the Badgers agreed with his plan.

Seriously?

In what universe is that okay? Case closed? The public had a right to know the name of the poisoner. It was a murder, for God's sake, not some low-level infraction. Indeed, is there a more nefarious crime than poisoned candy? Anyone could have consumed it. A grandchild of the Badgers, perhaps?

And without naming the killer and his or her motives, how would anyone know if she or he had acted alone?

My use of the female pronoun has nothing to do with inclusivity. While the female poisoner is a favorite trope of writers (guilty!) and Hollywood, real crime statistics put it in the myth category. Men and women commit murders by poisoning nearly equally in terms of raw numbers of actual homicides. Women, however, are seven times more likely to use poison as a vehicle to murder.

After dozens of calls made by me and Robbin, and overnighted letters, it seems no one from the family wants to go on the record.

A former wife of one of the five Badger sons sends an email response:

"I received your letter and would have nothing to add to the information you have apparently already researched. Therefore, there is no point in meeting to discuss the matter further. Please make no further contact with me."

I sit there dumbfounded. I can't imagine having a family member murdered and just letting it go unanswered. It makes me think that all the crappy things people said about Badger were more than true. He was a jerk, a bully, a man who shot his neighbor's dogs.

I make a Zoom call to Robbin, who's into her second glass of wine and is sequestered in her master bedroom while her husband and daughters watch a video.

"Badger's former daughter-in-law is out," I say.

"What?"

"Right."

"She seemed like she'd help. She made us listen to that podcast."

She's referring to an *Ohio Mysteries* podcast that relied on press accounts, somewhat witty banter, and a call-in feature in which a listener speculated with the hosts about the crime. The family member said to take a listen and then call back if we had any questions.

"Change of heart, I guess."

"The grandson's wife told me to never call back," Robbin says.

"Jeesh. These people," I say. "Sure like keeping a secret."

"If my grandpa had been offed by someone, I'd like to know who did it."

"You wouldn't," I say, holding my thoughts for a second, "if someone in the family did it."

"Mrs. Badger?"

"I don't know. Someone. Look up the death records. Get the autopsy reports on anyone who died in the months prior to Jim Frost's out-of-nowhere announcements."

"You got it," she says.

CHAPTER TWENTY-THREE

Jim and Marianne Gasser have been a part of my life since my visit to Ohio. When my family planned a trip to see friends in Cincinnati, I brought our girls, then four, on a research trip. Claudia joined us a few days later. To be completely candid, almost all of our family vacations have involved a side trip to the scene of one crime or another.

Even Disneyland.

That's another story.

At thirty-one, though I was employed at a resort camping magazine, money was tight. The Gassers invited us to stay at their place in Wooster, and I was grateful. And lucky. It was the beginning of a long friendship that included a few visits between that time and my return this year. Marianne, a fabulous Italian cook, made pizzelles and biscotti—both recipes from her father. "Daddy's Pizzelles" became a Christmas tradition in our home. And now my daughters have incorporated the recipe into their own family's holidays.

Doubtful that the next generation—four grandsons and a granddaughter—will know that the recipe came from a search for the truth about an Amish boy and his mother's death.

Marianne is making another of her father's dishes for dinner, and the aroma reminds me that the best Italian food I've ever had comes out of her kitchen. This time it's a skillet zucchini dish made with sausage and mozzarella. And of course, her better-than-you'll-ever-have-in-a-restaurant homemade tomato sauce. Jim is now retired from the sheriff's department, and Marianne, who used to dispatch there, retired from her job in retail. Her black hair is silver now, and his, which is as thick and wavy as ever, looks like the color of sun-bleached barnwood. Jim is a big strong man, barrel chested, forearms like Popeye. He could probably be scary if he wanted to, but it would be a big act. His manner is kind and thoughtful. Even gentle.

When I was researching in Ohio the first time, Jim gave me the names of those still around who had some knowledge of Ida and Eli's life together. He was working for the sheriff's department then, so I understood he could tell me only so much. I'd always felt that Jim was carefully, diplomatically, urging me on in my search.

Thirty years ago, he thought Ida's death was suspicious, but he didn't know of any proof. After all, he didn't work the case. In addition, Jim wasn't the type to disparage a friend's character or sully the reputation of the sheriff's office. Yet he helped me whenever I visited in person or called.

We talk about my day out trying to interview the Amish in New Salem and about their amazing garden. The sweet corn that Marianne picked that afternoon is akin to gnawing on honeycomb. Jim's not much of a traveler, but Marianne and I convince him that a train trip to the Pacific Northwest would be well worth the effort.

"Plus," I say, "I have a place for you to stay."

"I'll cook," Marianne says.

"Deal."

Jim gives in. He promises someday "soon" they'll come.

The conversation turns to the barn fire. Jim thinks that it is entirely possible that a right could be wronged, even after all these years. That support fuels this entire endeavor.

"What's your gut tell you as a law enforcement officer about what happened that night? What do you really think?"

Jim is a careful thinker, but this time he doesn't hesitate.

"I think he killed her."

Marianne looks in my direction, nodding.

"And have you thought that all these years?"

Another nod from both.

Jim discloses something that he hadn't all those years ago. I consider it a bombshell, which is a thing most crime writers can relate to—that moment when you hear something that, well, like the best flap copy says, changes everything.

Jim tells me he was on the scene the night of the fire.

Flames from the barn lit the sky as a channel of wood smoke worked its way through the tree canopy. The fire department was still on the scene, though it was winding down and the house was no longer in danger of catching fire. Neighbors and onlookers from the area lined the fence along the road. Jim Gasser pulled up to get to work. He'd heard that an Amish wife had died in the blaze.

Jim Frost, who was directing Phil Carr and at least one other deputy to manage the traffic on Moser Road, appeared at the driver's side window.

His car was barely in park, and he hadn't even set a foot on the ground.

"I don't need you here," Frost said. "Got this handled."

"Huh? What about the victim? The wife?"

Frost was dismissive. "Accident. You go home."

Perplexing as it was, Jim took it as an order. In fact, everything that came out of Sheriff Frost's mouth was pitched in the same cocksure and strident manner. Even telling someone to have a good day. Or see you tomorrow.

Frost, at least according to Jim for the past three decades, was a good officer. By the book. Trustworthy. Yet something was wrong that night.

"A cover-up?" I ask.

Jim takes a beat to think.

"When I was driving home from the scene, I thought that. Why else would I get shoved away from a crime scene? That was my job in the detective bureau. And I got shoved away. And that never happened before."

I push for more.

"When you got shoved away, you didn't know all the things that you would later learn. Not all of them. So did there come a time when you started putting the pieces together?"

"Oh, it was pretty much right away, yeah. Like I could just tell. I could just tell anyhow, a feeling I had."

I bring up Undercover Eli and the incident at Stoll Farms.

Jim wasn't involved in the case, and his knowledge on the subject is vague. He does, however, know the character of Jim Taylor, the deputy Frost enlisted on the sting against the Miller brothers. Jim Taylor was a young deputy at the time.

"What could they have had on Eli to coerce him to do such a thing?" I ask. "I mean, we know he clearly didn't want to make the buy—considering what happened later when he tried to get out of it."

"Well, in the first place, Jim Taylor would never have done anything like that. He was a good deputy. He was not aggressive at all. He was reactive. Not proactive."

"No secrets to hide?"

"No. And he probably didn't even know about Frost or Eli. The only thing he knew is what people would tell him, you know. Every morning when I go to work, we go out on the porch, say, give me a cigarette. I'd say, 'What are you hearing?' And that's how he found stuff out about it. Talking to people in a department."

"Not involved in setting up the sting?"

"No, he was involved as an investigator of it, but not the instigator."

"I'm thinking about the night of the fire."

"That's good because that's one thing that really troubles me—that Frost knew about the incident at Ed Stoll's dairy barn. How in the world could a man who cut himself up and admitted to it later be believed the night his wife dies in a fire? How could that not even have been mentioned?"

Deputy Carr didn't know about Marshallville. Frost never brought it up. Not to members of the Wayne County sheriff's department. Not to the fire department. Not to the coroner. Not to Ida's family.

"He didn't tell anyone," Jim continues. "I would bet everything on that."

"Why the cover-up? What was it all about?"

"Honestly, I think it was because Frost was gay," Jim says. "He and Eli probably knew each other. It played on Frost's mind a lot, I'm sure. Not wanting it known. Honestly, that's what I think."

There were several gay men in the department back then. One was Tim Brown, the deputy who later lived with Eli at the farm in Dalton. He didn't broadcast it, but Tim didn't hide it either. The other two? Sheriff Frost and a deputy named Ken Kerr.

Jim Gasser nearly got fired when he found out.

The department hosted an appreciation event at Dragway 42, a racetrack north of Wooster, for the deputies and other staff who rode motorcycles. Most went home at night, but Frost brought his camper to the track.

Before leaving for home that afternoon, Jim kidded his boss.

"Don't go wandering around at night. One of those guys will get you."

"We'll be all right," the sheriff said.

The next morning Jim banged on the camper door. It was early, but not that early. It took Frost a little while to answer.

When he did, Jim noticed "sucker bites" all over his boss's neck. Again, he made a joke.

"Looks like you found one of those guys last night."

Frost was none too happy with the remark, and he let Jim know it.

"That's none of your business."

His tone was the usual, emphatic and concrete.

"Yes, sir," Jim said, catching a glimpse of Ken Kerr through the doorway. The young deputy was half naked. *Okay,* Jim thought, *I get it.* He left without saying another word. He never brought up what he'd seen or what he thought about the encounter. He didn't care whether Frost was gay, but fraternizing with deputies was not a smart move.

"I thought that part of it was wrong," Jim says. "But I'd been through too many things with Frost by then. To push it, I would have lost my job. He was the sheriff and he told me what to do. And that's what I did."

X

Marianne started working as a sheriff's dispatcher in 1977, the same year of the Stutzman barn fire. She didn't have any real handle on that case, other than what she read in the papers and things her husband told her later.

Despite that, she was pretty adamant about what happened.

"It doesn't take a lot to figure out that the man was guilty of murdering his wife," she says over dinner. "She's a pregnant woman out there, fighting the fire. Give me a break."

Ida's pregnancy is a valid point. Murder, I know, is the cause in some 5 percent of the deaths involving pregnant women. Famous true crime cases with that storyline abound. Californian Scott Peterson, who was convicted of murdering his wife and unborn son; Coloradan Chris

Watts, who strangled his wife and two little girls; and most recently, in a lesser-known case, a St. Louis man named Beau Rothwell are poster boys for such crimes.

"Ida was in the way," I say. "Just as his little boy would be years later."

All three of us are in total agreement there.

Marianne goes back to the night of the fire, things that she's struggled with over the years. "Nobody did anything to stop it. He didn't make any effort to make the flames stop. Go get the hose!"

Ever the investigator, Jim speaks next. "Well, I don't know that he could do that."

"Well," Marianne goes on, "you could do something until the fire department got there if it was accident."

There is a huge difference between theories and facts. I know too many things were ignored when they should have been reviewed by someone like Jim Gasser.

"Way more conspiracy going on than we ever thought," I say. "I mean, everybody that Eli was involved with had a secret life. Many had something to lose."

Jim doesn't disagree.

"Well, because back then," he says, "nobody talked about that."

I take another serving of the zucchini dish and remind myself to get the recipe.

Marianne speaks up after going quiet for a bit, taking this all in. "The only way out of a marriage with the Amish community is through death."

"Right," I say.

"I was sitting here thinking while you guys talked that maybe he was planning this for a long time, trying to get out of that lifestyle so he could pursue the one he wanted. Like when he cut his wrists or whatever, he might have been planning all of this all along doing what he did on purpose. He was mental."

She's not far off. Eli was a manipulator of the highest order. Cunning too.

"Get married. Get the farm. Kill Ida," I say. "And then be free to do what he'd only been able to do in secret."

We talk about the things we know now, that were unknown then. Or things that were ignored. Intentionally. I wonder out loud if a case could have been made if someone had stepped up and spoke for Ida back in 1977.

"And today, could a case be made today?"

Jim has no doubts about convicting Stutzman back in the day but seems uncertain if there would be any point to doing so now. While cold case detectives do amazing things with DNA testing and other modern forensic tools, none of that comes into play in the Stutzman fire.

"Was there an autopsy?" Marianne asks.

I think a little before I speak. Jim was very close to Doc, as everyone called J. T. Questel.

"Not really," I finally say. "When I interviewed Dr. Questel, Ida's death was a touchy subject. All the stuff about Eli, Danny, and Glen was making big news and opening up a lot of questions about the fire. He conceded—a little defensively, which I understood—that he might have missed something."

Jim hands his plate to Marianne as she clears the table, and then she brings some dessert.

It's getting dark now, and the sounds of cicadas are making a TV test-pattern type of humming sound. Michael, their son, and his wife, Becky, come home. Michael was a kid when I first met him. He's now in his forties. Amiable and warm. Becky grew up on a farm in the Dakotas. Both are employed in the health and medical industry. Their arms are inked in an array of intricate and beautifully done tattoos.

They join us as our talk about murder among the Amish winds down.

"It's a shame," Jim says. "There should have been an extensive exam-ination of the body, because I've been on too many calls similar to that with Doc. I mean, he's thorough, okay? Why he wasn't on this one was always a puzzle to me. And I didn't challenge it. And I'm probably ashamed because I didn't. I didn't. He taught me so much over the years about investigating right at the death scene, you know."

I do. A pained look overtakes Jim's face. Dr. Questel was the Gasser family doctor. Both of their children went to him. He and the coroner were close, with a bond built on trust, respect, and admiration.

"I just feel bad about Doc being drawn into this," Jim says.

"He was a decent man," I say.

"He wouldn't have done this for just anybody."

"Maybe an agreement?" I suggest. "A forced agreement between Frost and Doc?"

Jim stays mute, and I go a little further.

"It could have gone down something like this, Frost telling him that I need you to do this for me. Let's get her in the ground. You gotta help me out on this."

"I firmly believe that's what happened," Jim says. "He put Doc on the spot real hard."

"Questel knew he messed up," I say.

Jim nods. "He knew."

The man across the table has devoted his life to serving the public. He is loyal to the department. Respectful of the people he's encountered on the job. Devoted to his family and friends.

And he's telling me something that hurts him on every level.

"You know, he knew he messed up. And why did he mess up? Because somebody told him to. Or made him."

"Yeah," Jim says.

"Or lied to him."

"Yeah."

Marianne wonders if Ida was murdered so that Eli and Frost could carry on a relationship.

I say I don't think so.

"I don't think the cover-up was about clearing the way for a specific love affair but was something else."

Jim offers what I consider a likely scenario.

"Frost didn't want all his personal information to get out to anybody in the public."

I agree. "Eli had something over Frost, and he cashed in his chips the night of the fire."

"Yeah, he did."

CHAPTER
TWENTY-FOUR

Back home for a couple of weeks, I turn the key to box 7, and there it is, a response to my letter asking Levi Levi Hershberger's sister-in-law, Melinda Hershberger, to confirm or deny the story that I'd heard about Levi's deathbed confession. The envelope is thin, and I actually hold it up to the light. Maybe hoping that a kind of X-ray vision would kick in and I'd see right away everything I was looking for—the truth. I return to my car in the post office parking lot and read it.

Dear Sir,

We received your letter, but although there was some con-versation on the table—my bro-in-law is in his grave and I'm afraid, in God's eyes it is not right to publicize another soul's weaknesses. I rarely speak about this matter, and I just don't feel [right] to have it written in a book for the world to read. What if someone would write a book of what I did wrong—Oh No—how terrible—and for the sake of my beloved favorite sister I could N-O-T.
 Sincerely,

M. Hershberger
Not meant for evil! But out of love, for everyone involved.

I show Melinda's letter to Claudia when I get home.

"That's too bad," she says. "She said no."

I give my wife a good look. "No? I see it as a yes."

She gives me a look back. "How exactly is this a yes?"

"A couple of things. She says right here that there was 'some conversation on the table.'"

"Right."

"That means someone there wanted to talk to me."

I get the same look she's given to me since Ted Bundy sent a letter to our house from death row. It's quizzical, disbelieving, and something else. Possibly the look of someone who can't understand my fascination with crime because it is the opposite of her interests.

"The second thing?" she asks. "You said two things."

I nod. "Right. She sent the letter. That cracks open the door. I'm going to go back to Ohio."

Again, the look. "Of course, you are," she says.

Less than a week later, I'm back at the Columbus airport and in a rental car.

⋊

Melinda Hershberger is my best bet, best hope. She'd answered my letter in a way that confirmed she knew something but didn't want to talk about whatever it was that she'd held inside.

I stand on her West Salem porch for the second time. I have wondered for a generation about Ida and what happened to her that night. I don't doubt she'd been murdered. I don't doubt that law enforcement

147

had applied a soft touch on a case that should have been pushed like a bulldozer. Believing that doesn't change a thing.

Only the truth can.

I knock.

A woman my age opens the door.

"Are you Melinda? I'm Gregg. May I come in?"

She looks me over, but I don't think she has a clue who I am.

"You wrote to me," I go on. "I sent you a letter about Eli Stutzman, your sister, and Levi Levi?"

"Oh."

"I've been working on this for a long time. I was thirty-one when I wrote about Danny Stutzman. I'm sixty-four now. Lizzie and Amos Gingerich were friends of mine. They've passed, you know. Recently, a family member gave me the chance to look at some letters that had been written over the years about Eli and what happened when Ida died."

I have no way of knowing if she's going to shut the door or invite me inside. She is listening and that's good.

"I know how you feel by your letter back to me, but I'm hoping you'll help me anyway. I feel like it's important to try to find out what happened. Some in Ida's family feel it's important to find out the truth of what happened. We all kind of think we know."

"Well, I don't know," she says. "Eli is gone. My brother-in-law's gone. I don't know, but we have our impressions."

"What's your impression?" I ask right away.

She hesitates. "I don't know if I'm correct. And I shouldn't put my feelings from my thoughts into a book for the world to read. That's the way I feel."

She opens the door a little more, and just like that I'm inside. The kitchen is spotless with a row of jars of fruits and vegetables. An arrow of light through the window hits the jars, igniting the beans, corn, and tomatoes to near luminescence.

Melinda, like most in the Stutzman circle, is Swartzentruber Amish. Some refer to the sect as Low Amish, the type for whom a simple life is completely devoid of pride, hence their yards are not as tidy, their clothing may be worn a day or two longer without washing. Not Melinda. Her home is impeccable. She leads me to a sitting room with hickory rockers, a woodstove, and a calendar on the wall as its only artwork.

She says some of my information is wrong. That her sister, Lydiann, who was married to her husband's brother, had not been present at the confession from Levi Levi.

It was someone else.

I go on with what I'd heard, hoping that she will tell me more.

"That Levi Levi had confessed that he knew Ida was going to die ahead of time, but there was nothing he could do to stop it."

She leans back in a hickory rocker. She is struggling, but in a measured way. This burden has been heavy, but she's dealt with everything life has thrown at her. Her first husband's death from cancer. Marrying her brother-in-law Andy after Lydiann died. Other illnesses. All are a part of God's plan.

"Is the person who told you truthful?" I ask.

She nods. "The bishop told my father."

Hearsay, I know. Yet as I look at her, I can't think of any reason why she would lie. Or why her father would. Or the bishop for that matter. What we are talking about is a terrible sin.

"And my father is gone."

"Right."

"So, everybody's gone." She leans back in the rocker. "Was my brother-in-law involved? It just hurts me."

"I know it hurts you," I say. "But it wasn't anything your family did."

"It was," she says.

"It's not on you."

"But if I tell somebody that's going to write a book, that hurt is on me. Should I say that for the world to read? Suppose I'm wrong?"

"You know your father is not going to lie to you about what the bishop told him."

Melinda doesn't push back. Her father was, indeed, an honest man. The bishop was a man of integrity, the kind needed for his role in the community. Regardless, she's fearful. Nervous. Unsure.

"What are you afraid of?" I ask.

"Who knows who killed the woman?"

"You know someone killed Ida. It wasn't an accident."

"I don't know who did it. Who admitted to doing it? Did Eli?"

I shake my head. "No, he's never confessed. To the day he killed himself, he never confessed to anything that he had done."

"Then how do we know?"

"He is a killer. He shot his roommate. I was at the trial. They proved it."

"They proved he did," she repeated.

"Yes, evidence did."

"He killed like thirteen people. Like a chain killer?"

I tell Melinda that I think he might have killed five people.

"But he never confessed?" she asks.

"Never."

"I thought he did. I didn't go to the trial. I didn't ask him. I just know that my brother-in-law confessed to the occasion that he said he didn't report it right."

"Levi was there that night. You know that."

"Yes," she says. "It's such a strange case. And if Eli doesn't come in and confess, how can we know?"

She is struggling and I feel for her. Melinda's torn between the truth and her loyalty to her sister and, by extension, to her brother-in-law. This battle inside has nothing to do with her faith, which is absolute.

"And I'm not the one to say that I knew Ida had died before the fire, even though I'm very suspicious," she says. "All I know is what he said.

And I don't want to put it in the book and say that I know just because of what he said; he told the bishop he knew what was going to happen."

She stops the rocker.

"But why was he there?" she asks me.

"He was there that night," I say.

She nods.

Again, she sits there looking at me, and I try to give her some peace.

"Melinda, that he confessed to somebody like your bishop means that he had a conscience. Maybe Levi Levi got involved with something that got out of hand, out of control. And you've lived with it a long time. And it's eaten at you. Maybe Levi Levi, you know, it isn't so bad because he was able to confess."

"I hope so," she says. "You know, I really, truly hope that he confessed the truth."

I change the subject to Eli.

"Why do you think Eli would have wanted Ida dead?"

Melinda looks past me and shares how Ida was isolated in Dalton, far from her home farm in Fredericksburg. She'd dropped hints that something wasn't right with Eli, that she didn't think he loved her.

"Is it because something was going to come out on him that he didn't want anybody to know? That Ida was going to tell something?"

Melinda gives me a quick nod.

"She was censored," she says. Her eyes dampen. "She had such a good nature that to be around her, I was almost ashamed of my personality compared to her. She was that kind of a person."

I ask what she means.

"I'm not worthy of being there around her. She was just such a good-natured person. Why did he want her dead? I knew her from girl up, and I ran into her because she lived with my sister at the house when they first got married."

"Gideon Gingerich's farm?"

She nods. "I just felt like she was such a wonderful person that I was almost ashamed to be around her because of her personality compared to mine. I just felt . . . I just felt like I'm not good enough to be there."

I have never heard anyone say anything like that about another person. Her respect for Ida is huge. It gives me hope that it will be enough to override all of the reasons why she wouldn't disclose what she knows about what happened.

"Why would you want to kill a person like that?" she asks.

"Maybe he didn't want another child," I suggest. "He'd be trapped if he had more kids."

She doesn't feel that's right.

"I think there were other issues, but I don't know. How could he have killed her so he wouldn't have had a baby? That's not enough. That's not reasoning."

We talk about other theories. Maybe she caught him doing or saying something. It could have been about sex, or it could have been about finding his driver's license. Or that he was consorting with unsavory types in the horse business.

The conversation is upsetting her.

"I wouldn't want anybody to write a bad book about me. I made all these failures myself. I told my brother, you know, we all have."

"We all have made terrible mistakes and things we wish we hadn't done," I say. "Some are big and some are small. And they all weigh on us, right?"

"And that's probably why Eli never confessed," she says. "Because it was just too terrible to confess, I bet."

"But Levi Levi did confess to the bishop that he was there. That he knew it was not an accident. That there was nothing he could do about it."

She stays quiet.

"Doesn't that confession to the bishop say something good about your brother-in-law?"

She accepts the premise of my question. "He was definitely tired of this way of living, the way he was running his life."

"You never asked him directly?"

"No. He had a stroke."

"Right. He couldn't answer?"

"That was a part of the puzzle," she says. "Why can't you speak now? Maybe it's better not even to say it anyway. I hope he made everything right with God."

"I understand," I say. "It is a puzzle."

She reflects and chooses her words carefully. "Well, if he didn't help the killer. I really hope so."

I ask if God could forgive Levi Levi if he had an actual hand in Ida's death, more than mere knowledge that she would die.

"I'm not the one to say," she says. "God is the only one."

Melinda tells me that she still wonders why her father disclosed the confession only to her ears.

"My brothers didn't know. I have seven of them. John and I talked about it, and he didn't know anything about it. Why didn't my father tell my brother? We live together. Am I thinking things that I shouldn't be?"

Melinda sees her brother-in-law Levi Levi as living a life wasted, a life that could have been so much more.

"He just had problems. He could have been such a good man. Yeah, because he tried, bringing up his family. And then the one thing, that my sister was patient. She had to stand in her line. She had a lot of patience. Levi didn't turn out to be what she thought he was. Some people do change once they get married. Some don't. The days were not always the sunshiny days, but he was just a nice person to be around. Instead of taking this cleverness and doing good, he did some things that weren't so good, right? I hope he wasn't involved in killing the woman. But how can I know?"

"There were two sides to him," I say. "I wonder what leads people astray?"

"When everyone around them can say good advice? I don't know."
She mentions the letter she sent to me.

"I am glad you wrote to me, Melinda."

"Well, I don't want to be unfriendly. I just hate to do that to my brother-in-law and to see my own life like I wrote. It's kind of a sarcastic letter."

"Not at all," I say. "I see the conflict. I also see that the way you wrote the letter let me know that mostly what I'd heard was true. Otherwise, you would have said, 'I don't know anything about that.' But you just said, 'I don't want to talk about it.'"

"I didn't want to lie, and I didn't want to say something about him that makes the world gasp. How can this be true? And as far as I know, there was only one person that had done it. But why was Levi there?"

To help Eli, I think, *kill her? Cover the crime? Make sure that no one would find out what it was that had troubled Ida. Money? Sex?*

"Eli must have felt something horrible," she says. "Or he wouldn't have committed suicide himself. He had a troubled conscience."

I don't tell her that psychopaths don't have a conscience.

"We won't ever know that."

"There's a lot of questions. And even if somebody tells, do we know? Even if we think we have the answers, do we know?"

"I think we know, Melinda."

She takes a breath. "Well, we know that he killed her."

Melinda's husband enters the room just then. Andy Hershberger has a genuine Santa beard and a friendly smile. He takes a seat as I introduce myself and tell him that I'm sorry about his brother's illness, the reason for their recent travels.

He says things like that are "going around" these days.

"Now, you know, a year ago yesterday, I had a stroke. So, I am pretty well recuperating and recovering all together."

"You look good," I say, because he does. I wouldn't have noticed the little stiffness on his right side. "Did it affect your speech?"

Melinda interjects that it did, and he still tires more easily.

"I could move my arm like this," Andy says, raising his arm. "But I couldn't hold a pen or make any strokes."

It turns out his right hand is more important than most people's. Andy lost most of his left fingers in an accident when he was thirteen.

"I was playing with a dynamite cap. Didn't know what it was. I went outside. My brother followed, of course, and I held this thing. And so, I lit this match. That time we didn't have lighters. And the first match didn't work."

"The second did?" I ask, thinking of the stupid things my brothers and I did at that age. Some involving fire. Caps. Cherry bombs. Anything we could touch with a lighted match.

"Oh, yeah," he goes on, "I was back against the wall. And I was splattered with blood, and I ran around the shop. My first instinct was I got to explain this to my parents when they get home. Then I realized, oh, this thing is just hanging. This was gone. There was nothing to hide."

We talk about telephones, his walking regimen to get his mobility back, and other things about Amish life. About his life. He's easy to talk to. When I move the subject back toward Ida and Eli, he tells me that Amos Gingerich and his mother were brother and sister, making Ida his first cousin. That doesn't surprise me. The Amish world is a small one.

As it turns out, he and first wife, Lydiann, were in Ida and Eli's wedding.

"So, we were young, married the second day of December. And they got married right around Christmas Eve and moved into our church district."

While they were connected, Andy never had good feelings about Eli.

"We went to visit him after the funeral. After the fire and all that. And here he was so innocent. He was seeming like he was very broken."

"It seemed believable and real?" I ask.

"Yeah, it did. He turned out to be a liar, and I was too dumb to think otherwise. But Ida's family was there; they noticed things before I did."

Andy, Lydiann, and her folks rode together to Ida's viewing in a double buggy. They came into the bedroom to pay their respects to Andy's cousin, and the first thing he noticed was the way her hand had formed a stiff hook or claw.

No one had ever seen anything like that.

"We didn't say anything to anyone, but we among ourselves talked about it."

From the other side of the room, Melinda addresses me.

"What did it mean?"

I tell her I don't know.

Andy continues. "I remember somebody told us that somebody tried to bend the finger down, but there was no way he could do that. And I think they had to break her finger to get it back."

We talk about Eli after the fire. Andy, along with other members of the Swartzentruber church, came to help him whenever they could.

Another thing happened after Eli became a widower, Andy says. It was about Ida's sister Susie and what she discovered hidden in the bedroom where Danny and Eli slept.

When I met with Susie in Michigan all those years ago, she wouldn't come right out and say what it was that she'd found. It was so terrible.

"She found a camera," Andy tells me.

A camera? I had thought it was porn or something. Maybe a sex toy. Susie was so upset about what she found that she couldn't bring herself to say it.

A camera. Now I get it. It was such a violation of the Ordnung that he would possess a camera, that while Susie couldn't tell me, neither could she keep quiet about it to the members of the church. As Andy tells it, Susie had hoped, in the way that people often do, that somehow the device had "accidentally" ended up in the house. She confronted Eli and he admitted it belonged to him.

"Eli confessed to the church," Andy says, "but it didn't add up to me. He was sorry, you know, and said the reason he had this camera was because he was a widower and he got lonesome, and he had it to help him pass the time. Well, when I was a kid, I played with a radio. Listened to music. How did a camera help him pass the time?"

It wasn't that Eli was out shooting scenic Wayne County farm vistas and then running off to a drugstore in Kidron to get them developed. He was Amish. Swartzentruber Amish at that. He wasn't an Old Order Ansel Adams. He wasn't developing his own film in a darkroom. He wasn't risking being called out by taking it to a drugstore and getting the film processed there.

The camera, I think, must have been a Polaroid.

Andy resurfaces a memory. He shakes his head and scrunches up his brow. He wonders out loud if he has another clue to the depths of Stutzman's manipulation. Eli told Andy that a week or so before the fire, Eli and Ida had been visiting her grandparents in Fredericksburg. As the buggy approached a graveyard, Ida became quiet and fixed her eyes on the cemetery.

"He said she had a longing in her eyes, like she had a longing to be there."

Andy thought back then that what Eli had said made sense.

"He was trying to impress on me that this was all God's plan."

"He was playing you," I say. "Because of your good nature. And he's a wolf. He's a pretender."

"Yeah, I think so. Oh, another thing I remember," Andy says as I get up to leave, "he wore shorts. I remember telling the preachers about that. I don't know what they did about it. What was he doing then? We heard this Amish kid is living down there. Then he started attending a different church. That was like his first step out of the Amish."

I nod.

"And then Eli sold the farm, packed up Danny, and was gone."

Andy stands and Melinda follows me to the door as I thank them for their time. I tell her that I might have more questions and I'll write another letter.

She gives me a smile. "I'll send you another sarcastic one."

I smile back.

"I'll look forward to every bit of sarcasm."

As I drive to the next unscheduled interview, I consider the lengths Eli would go to and the lies he told about what happened before, after, and during the barn fire.

Ida had a longing to be in that graveyard.

I know that Andy's story was just another one of Eli's manipulations. How did he convince so many people? Was he "mental," as the Amish believed, or simply a good actor?

Decent actor, I guess. Most of the Amish fell for it. And Eli had a genuine flair for drama. I'll give him that. Andy and the others didn't know they'd been had because they couldn't imagine one of their own would lie right to their faces.

On the one-year anniversary of Ida's death, Eli did what he thought he had to do to get rid of the do-gooder Amish who kept showing up at the farm to help him. He feigned another breakdown by exhibiting erratic behavior. Whenever he spoke, his words were incomprehensible. He was out of control, over the top, and desperately in need of intervention. Family members called the authorities and had Eli admitted to a psychiatric ward. Released a week later, he continued to appear emotionally unstable. There seemed no fixing him.

And still they tried. They'd been trying since the fire, though it never seemed to help.

Late summer the year Ida died, Eli's brothers took him to the Amish-approved Ortman Clinic in tiny Canistota, South Dakota. I look up information about the clinic and learn that many Amish view going to Ortman as akin to visiting Disneyland, a vacation spot. A spa. Eli checked in for a round of chiropractic treatments, purportedly for sleep issues. The planned treatments were to take about a week. Eli, it seems, didn't have the patience to be a patient. He was back home after a couple of days.

$$\text{\Large \ensuremath{\text{\textbf{X}}}}$$

Two broken porch lights hang limply on either side of the door, reminders that this house is now Amish. No longer electrified. John Yoder, seventy-two, and his wife, Ada, seventy-three, are home and let me inside right away. John has been recovering from shingles for the past ten days. He's using vitamin E as a topical treatment. He sits a little uncomfortably in a rocker while his wife cuts up apples into pieces of equal size to dry them for the "young ones."

Melinda is John's sister, and she told me he's fully aware of Levi Levi's confession to the bishop. He thinks it might have been made on his deathbed but isn't sure about that.

"There has been a lot of talk about Eli and Ida over the years," he says. "I think all of the Amish believe he killed her."

Mrs. Yoder says it was suspicious that the hired boy was not awakened.

"Why didn't they? The hired boy was there to help."

John also thought it was highly suspicious that the authorities, who knew that Eli was "mental," would believe him when he said Ida had a bad heart.

John says he knew Eli growing up.

"He was a little bit raw," he says, "and a little bit untrustworthy."

We talk more about the Swartzentruber community in West Salem, now three hundred strong. I hate to go; the coziness of their living room, as spartan as it is, is so comfortable. Such nice people.

CHAPTER
TWENTY-FIVE

I can't get over the obvious loyalty Melinda had for her sister and her former brother-in-law Levi Levi. How hard she wrestled with telling me what I wanted to know. Both parties are dead, but Melinda struggled over recounting the confession. I think about how loose-lipped everyone in the English world seems to be. There isn't a day that goes by that someone doesn't release ugly, hidden information. Private stuff. Much of it not true. Some of it might be, but I ask myself if someone's need to share is more legitimate than someone's privacy.

The difference is that in our current world, we traffic in disclosing things that, say, even twenty years ago might have been private.

Melinda says that Levi only knew about the plot to kill Ida and had not been a participant. That very well might be true.

I dig through my Dropbox folders and retrieve a sheriff's report from 1998 with additional insight about Levi Levi Hershberger.

As small as he was, at only five three and 140 pounds, Levi Levi, or Little Levi as some called him, was, quite ironically, big trouble. Several calls—one involving an arson fire in one of his corn fields—were dispatched to the Hershberger farm over the years. The one occurring on

November 26, 1989, however, was the most consequential and, frankly, the most disturbing.

Lydiann Hershberger had flagged down a neighbor to get help.

"It is my husband," she said.

She was terrified. From the road, the man who stopped saw the front windows of the Hershberger farmhouse had been shattered. Levi, Lydiann said, had been drinking and had become out of control and violent. By the time a sheriff's deputy arrived a little later, the house was empty. Eventually, he found the family in the barn. Their heads were down and they were busy milking.

No one looked up.

From the deputy's report:

> *Hershberger refused to stop milking and would not talk with us until he was done. He would not tell us how long that would be. He began to argue and then stated he wanted to go to jail. He also told the complainant earlier that if he did not go to jail, he would continue breaking stuff at the house. At that time, he stood up and started charging out of the barn toward the police cars yelling that he wanted to go to jail. At that point he was arrested for disorderly conduct and placed in the back seat of deputy [Wood's] vehicle at that time, he was still arguing and stating he was used to jail and that he would enjoy being there. He was also kicking the inside of Deputy Wood's patrol car.*

Lydiann said Levi not only had a drinking problem but also had been taking a Valium-type medication.

From the report:

> *She advised that he was taking them and had been drinking and that they had got into an argument over the chores,*

and he began to throw blocks of wood through the windows. She advised that she was not assaulted, however she was very afraid. She also advised that in the past he had talked about shooting her with a gun. She stated that he gets these ideas from reading western novels. She and her children were in fear for their lives.

Levi was arrested on the spot. Lydiann retrieved the medication, diazepam, from under the bed and asked the authorities to destroy it. She also gave the Good Samaritan neighbor all the weapons in the house—a Jennings semiautomatic .22-caliber pistol, a High Standard .22-caliber revolver, a 9-millimeter AMT semiautomatic pistol, and a JCPenney .410 shotgun—for safekeeping.

At booking, deputies confiscated a bottle of diazepam with six pills from Levi.

The little Amishman with the big attitude pled guilty, paid an eighty-one-dollar fine, and was released the next day.

CHAPTER
TWENTY-SIX

Time heals everything.

That phrase, that little bit of hopeful thinking, comes to mind as I find a spot in the Sugarcreek parking lot of the *Budget*, the newspaper the Amish have been using as a kind of printed Facebook since 1890. The last time I was there, the paper helmed by a spectacled, white-haired editor, George R. Smith, was marking its centennial. No celebration, of course. Just a plain acknowledgment that the milestone had been reached printed in the paper. Balloons and streamers wouldn't be appropriate, considering the readership. Too fancy. Not plain.

I'm here on a mission, the same one as before. This time, I'm all about Ida. Melinda, Dan, and others that I've reconnected with seem to feel that as difficult as it is, the time to speak out about Ida Stutzman is now.

Or never.

And as formidable as the Amish grapevine is, I need to get the word out in every way that I can. I've reached out to several Ohio weekly papers, but they are short-staffed and suggest that I send in a press release. I strike that idea. I need action. I need a direct route to the Amish community at large.

That's where the *Budget* comes in.

Thirty years ago, getting into the *Budget* was easy—until it wasn't. Things started out on a positive note, as they often do. Scribes, those volunteers (free notepads and postage!) who fill the pages of the *Budget* with newsy bits (weather, visitors, deaths, and more weather), mentioned me in the paper, and how I was researching Eli Stutzman's life as I trekked through Amish communities. I even met legendary editor George R. Smith, already an old man with thin white hair scraped back and finger-smudged glasses. We chatted about the story of Little Boy Blue and about his career at the weekly—it started in 1920 when he was a kid. He was pleasant and interested in what I was doing.

Until *Abandoned Prayers* was published.

George wrote a short piece in the November 28, 1990, issue, saying the book was out and it was graphic, but it was out there, nevertheless. In that same issue, Warner Books ran an ad promoting the book. It was a smart move on the part of the publisher. Lehman's hardware store in Kidron was on a perpetual reorder, selling thousands of copies.

To the Amish, of course.

Then on December 12, the backlash. It hit hard. As a subscriber to the *Budget*, I read the notices from a few scribes objecting to the book. I also received some letters from a few of the people I'd interviewed. Most felt I had gone too far in describing how Eli lived, and they offered prayers and support.

I think of Danny Gingerich's line: "I'd rather hold shit in my hands than do what you do." But at the same time, he was glad that I'd taken up the cause.

Most had been.

On December 19, George R. Smith (he never went anywhere without that initial) published another editorial.

We have received a number of comments on the book
Abandoned Prayers by Gregg Olsen. The comments ranged

from shocking and horrifying to just plain disgusting. Last week we published a letter from S.D. Miller which stated that the author's intent appeared to be to promote homosexualism.

Mr. Olsen objected to that interpretation and sent us the following note:

As a journalist, I reported the truth of what happened to Eli E. and Danny Stutzman (Little Boy Blue). I certainly do not condone the boy's father's actions in any way. I was horrified at what I learned through my interviews and research. It is important to remember that this is a true story, to the best of my ability as a human being I have sought to maintain accuracy when relating what people told me about the case. As shocking and disgusting as many will find parts of the book, it is unfortunately the reality of what went on in the Stutzmans' lives. The book is explicit because it is the truth of what happened.

As has been stated in a previous issue, this book is not—ABSOLUTELY NOT—family reading. Though it is about a child, it is not for children. I have been taken to task by some of my Amish friends for the language appearing in the book. I apologize to those who have been offended. I have the highest personal regard for the Amish people and their lifestyle. I simply reported what was being told to me. Finally, S.D. Miller suggests prayer might be in order. I agree. I hope that he will join me in praying that people witnessing a child in distress will come forward—no matter the risk to themselves. Looking the other way or denying what is happening will lead to further tragedies. Danny Stutzman is gone but he is but one of thousands of abused and neglected children. The fact that other children need our help is the real message of *Abandoned Prayers*.

We now prefer to make no further mention of Abandoned Prayers. We believe our readers have been sufficiently warned that this book has no place in the family library. We feel the four-letter words and explicit homosexual language were not needed to get across the message of the book and we see no need to further publicize it by carrying on a controversy in the columns of The Budget.

There's no denying that the content was explicit. I didn't make any judgments on what the men who knew Eli told me about their time with him. Sure, it was about sex. It was also about being a lonely gay man in rural America. Eli was a dream in faded Wrangler jeans and a pearl-snap-button shirt. He was soft-spoken. Polite. And since nearly every man I talked to brought it up, he was exceedingly well endowed. Best of all, I think in terms of his appeal, was that he was Amish. The "Plain People," as they were sometimes called, were a romantic mystery in the seventies and early eighties. *Witness*—with Kelly McGillis and Harrison Ford and its haunting score and gauzy imagery of undulating fields and fluttering laundry on a line—wouldn't premiere until the year Danny Stutzman died.

I included things that I'd never heard mentioned before, words that evoke an action—fisting, rimming, and such. I wrote about a mortician who met truckers on his CB radio using the handle Wienie Washer. About hookups. Orgies. I wrote about places where Eli and his friends would meet up for sex. HIV/AIDS hadn't been on anyone's radar in the very early part of Eli's reckless sojourn from one country boy to the next. It was a different time.

When my girls were in school, one of them asked if she could read *Abandoned Prayers*. I was firm in my answer.

"Not until you are twenty-one."

She cornered me when she finally read it. "Dad, I can't believe you wrote this stuff."

I took the book from her hands and looked at the page she was pointing to.

"Wow," I said. "I guess I did."

Much to his chagrin, I expect, George R. Smith found himself in the position of revisiting *Abandoned Prayers* in the December 28, 1990, edition of his paper. I'd left messages for George, but I never heard back, so I can't really know how bad things were at the *Budget* as they relate to the complaints received. I bet it was substantial. By then, I'd heard that an Amish bishop in Apple Creek had banned the book and told members of his church district to burn it.

George wrote:

> *Last week we said we would prefer not to make any more mention of the book, Abandoned Prayers. However, we have been accused of recommending and promoting the book, so I would like to set the record straight.*

> *The day before we went to press with the November 28th issue, I received a copy of Abandoned Prayers. I skimmed through the book and noticed some passages that I considered objectionable. I had no intention of mentioning it in this column until I noticed an advertisement for the book was to appear in that issue.*

> *Fearing that some of our readers would buy the book, expecting that it would be suitable for family reading, I hurriedly wrote some comments, warning the readers of its content and stating very plainly that we did not recommend it.*

Had I read the book I would have made the warning much stronger and would have asked that the ad be cancelled. Our advertising department had no knowledge of the content of the book, so they are completely blameless.

I still have not read the entire book and probably never will. I don't know how to say it more plainly—unless you are willing to accept a lot of filthy language and accounts of homosexual activities, don't buy the book!

It has been more than thirty years and George had died at ninety-three in 2000, so I open the front door of the Amish newspaper with a teeny bit of hope that all had been forgiven.

Or at least forgotten.

A woman named Loretta lights up from behind the front counter when I tell her I want to buy an advertisement and a subscription. She is about my age with a nice smile.

I wonder how long until that smile fades.

I'd had the sinking feeling since I thought of buying an ad that I'd be met by opposition. Even before arriving on this research trip, I had Robbin call for information on advertising and was met with a question about the product.

I didn't want to say I was digging into the past.

"What should I tell them?" Robbin asked.

"Butter" was the best I could come up with.

Butter? What a dumb idea! Anyway, we stuck with it.

Loretta's smile doesn't fade when I give her my credit card. She tells me six months, at forty-two dollars, is the minimum subscription price for the national edition.

"And you want an ad too?"

"Right."

She says that she'll get someone from production. As she turns to do so, she asks what I'm advertising.

I can't say butter.

"It's about a book that I wrote thirty years ago. I'm trying to solve a murder."

The smile flatlines.

"Oh."

I fill the awkwardness suddenly between us by telling her about Little Boy Blue and that I was now investigating the death of his mother in a barn fire.

"We'll need to run it by the publisher," she says.

"There's nothing inflammatory in it. Just asking for help. George," I say, indicating the legendary publisher, "put notices in the paper." My eyes land on a little shrine in his memory. A closer look indicates his actual length of service was seventy-seven years.

"But times have changed," she says. "People get offended really easy nowadays."

Cancel culture has arrived in Amish Country.

"When will you be able to get an answer?"

She's not sure. "Tomorrow or Wednesday."

"All right," I say. "Everyone gets offended, I know. But the Amish really want me to solve this."

She gets the production manager, and a less smiley woman named Kim joins us at the front counter. She gives me her email address and I forward the ad copy.

Who Will Help Bring Justice for Ida Stutzman?

In July 1977 Ida Stutzman died in a barn fire in Dalton, Ohio. She was 26 years old and expecting her second child. Her husband Eli Stutzman said his wife died

because of a bad heart—a lie among many he said that
night and in subsequent years. Eli and Ida's son Danny
gained nationwide attention as "Little Boy Blue" when
his body was found on Christmas Eve 1985 in Chester,
Nebraska. Although never charged with murder for
the deaths of his wife or son, Eli Stutzman was convicted of killing his roommate in Texas. Someone in the
community knows what happened the night Ida died.
Please help right a wrong by sharing any information
you might have.

Circulation Loretta tries to close the deal while we wait for copy
approval.

"Let's do it all at once," I say. "I won't need a subscription if I can't
buy the ad."

Kim returns with my proposed copy.

"I did swing into my publisher's office," she says. "And he said when
the book came out, we fielded probably between fifty and eighty calls.
Most people didn't like the book."

"Well, they all read it," I say. "They wanted to know what happened
to Danny and to his mother."

"I understand that," Kim says. "But then our readers contact us,
upset that we included something that upset them."

"They care about Ida and Danny."

"Well, I mean, they heard about the book, and they got mad at us
because somehow word of the book was in our paper."

"Because people that I had visited back then mentioned me and
what I was doing in a nice way."

Kim's trying to be nice as she dismisses me. "Yeah, yeah. And that's
fine. But then they come after us because we put it in our paper, and
it isn't because there's anything wrong with the book and because the
incident is so fresh in people's mind."

I remind her that it's been more than thirty years.

"What if I changed the wording?" I ask.

"No, I'm sorry."

"People really want her case solved," I say. "The Amish want it."

Kim puts it on their unsophisticated readership.

"The way they see it is when we talk in our paper, we did it. They don't see it as somebody else put that in our paper. They see it as us. They don't always comprehend the difference."

"Oh," I say.

"And then they attack us," Loretta adds.

Seems like the whole world is like that now on just about every little thing.

Kim keeps going. "But, you know, not that we don't appreciate what you're trying to do. We can't be disrespectful to our readers. We have to try to make sure that things don't come back on us. And it's just been a really tough couple of years trying not to offend anybody."

Tell me about it. But the Amish don't even have Twitter.

"Like what?" I ask.

"Just the littlest things," she says. "It doesn't even matter. I mean, one of our writers wrote a funny story about how he had a fart gun and he just pulled the trigger on this fart gun in the store, right behind his wife, you know, as a joke. I mean, and this really happened, and we probably got twenty-five calls on that. They thought it was offensive and they didn't feel it was appropriate for a paper. Yeah. I mean, just innocent things like that, right?"

"Just somebody having fun," I say.

"So, yeah, it's crazy what our world is coming to. So, I do apologize."

"It's not your fault. I'm disappointed because I just know that the missing piece is out there."

"Yeah," Kim says, "I'm sorry that we couldn't help."

"And then you're probably not interested in a subscription," Loretta says.

I shake my head and congratulate her for her sales efforts.

She should be employee of the month.

And now I'm thinking billboards might be the only way to get my message out. It worked for Frances McDormand in *Three Billboards Outside Ebbing, Missouri.*

CHAPTER TWENTY-SEVEN

A buggy makes the slow climb up a hill, and I find myself slowing to about ten miles an hour as I make my way back from Sugarcreek to the hotel in Wooster. I'm not annoyed. And neither are the cars behind me. This is the uphill pace out here. After the crest, when it is safe to do so, we'll all file past, checking out the driver and passenger as they fade from the view of our rearview mirrors. An Amish girl with Olympic-athlete calves actually bicycles past me. It flashes through my mind that I haven't seen any fat Amish children. Adults too. It makes perfect sense, naturally. They are either working or working. No one is TikToking or flopped in front of a TV with a bag of chips.

It isn't that they don't have the bag of chips.

It's the TV part.

My phone rings. It's one of Dr. Questel's sons, Kelvin. At this point, it's been a big no from Questel's progeny—his daughter and his two other sons. Kelvin's my last chance to find out what the coroner might have said about Ida's death in the years since I interviewed him. My instincts tell me Questel helped cover up the murder in one way or another. I believe 100 percent that he gave Frost a pass because of their close relationship. Maybe he saw the need and just helped. Or maybe it was more overt. Maybe Frost called upon the coroner to assist in a more direct way. I obsess over it. It keeps me up at night. How it might have gone between the two of them.

"Just this one time."

"No one will question it."

"I'm in trouble here."

"You gotta help me."

If Ida's cause of death was natural causes due to a bad heart, how could that have been determined without a full autopsy? Questel made that ruling based upon the word of a known liar, and that statement was relayed by the sheriff who had covered for him.

Kelvin Questel's phone skills aren't exactly warm and fuzzy. Seriously, he seems a little stiff. I plead that I'm only in town for the rest of the day. Reluctantly, he agrees that I can stop by his place of employment—the Wooster Cemetery.

Stiff is about right.

The cemetery is on a hill off Madison Avenue. It's impressive in the way that cemeteries in the Midwest often are. No edicts or covenants that require a headstone to be sunk into the grass, flat for easy mowing. Markers here are grand, tall, and uneven on the hillsides. I park by the brick office building, and though he said he'd be there, no one's there. I wander up to a guy working on containing the massive deluge of leaves that come with the season. He stops his leaf blower and tells me that Kelvin drives a white pickup, and if it's not there, then he's gone.

"I just talked to him on the phone."

"Did he say he was going to be here?"

"Yeah."

"He's in and out all day."

"What's his job?"

"He runs things, caretaker. So technically he's in charge."

The leaf guy doesn't need to say much more about how he feels about Kelvin. I get it. He goes on anyway, telling me that he and another coworker have been there thirty years.

"Technically," I repeat.

"Yeah, we run it ourselves."

On my way to the office door, I step around an array of loose head-stones that appear to have been sitting there a while. Maybe rejects. A typo or wrong color of stone and just waiting for the body that goes under them.

The office is small. There's an oak table and chairs to the left, where I'm sure grieving families gather to review plans, location, and cost. And cry. To the left of that area is a step down to the office, where Kelvin sits behind a drift of paperwork. He barely looks up through his glasses. He is decidedly cool. His hair is wiry gray, and his complexion is ashen. His frame, it passes through my mind, is cadaver-like, though that's probably just the milieu of the place driving my perceptions. Rail thin would work too.

I try to get him to come up to the crying table where we can talk. Hovering on that step to his office is weird. I'm neither here nor there.

I take a seat, and he finally gets up from behind his desk.

"I wrote a book thirty years ago," I start. "I interviewed your dad about a murder case he worked on."

He stands still like one of the stone figures outside.

"Won't you sit down so we can talk?"

He doesn't.

This is nothing short of painfully awkward. At least for me. Kelvin Questel's face exhibits zero emotion.

I start to brief him about the story, thinking he doesn't know what I'm talking about. He cuts me off right away.

"I've heard of it," he says somewhat curtly. "But I don't know any details about it."

Okay, fine, I think. *This is how it's going to go.*

"I just want you to know that, later when I talked to your dad and then when the newspeople talked to him, he felt bad about what had happened. He had a regret about that case. Did he ever express that to you?"

"No," he says.

"Did he ever speak about the case? Do you know what I'm talking about? The Amish woman who died in the fire?"

"Yeah. Yeah, I know that there was a lot to do with it, but he never really spoke to me and never seemed troubled about it."

"Really?"

"Never mentioned it."

He's glued his feet to the floor, but his body language indicates that he's already done with me. I know for a fact that his father was bothered by it. I know that he had a mostly solid reputation among law enforcement.

The silence from his children is strange.

"Why don't your siblings want to talk? What's that about?"

"I have no idea," he says. "I can't speak for them."

I pivot, thinking maybe there is some other reason.

"Did all of you grow up with your dad? I mean, it's not like you were all out of the house."

He nods.

"You don't know anything, but you were around. Strange. That's what I'm getting at."

"Yeah, they probably did the same thing," he says. "They were around, but they don't know anything."

"Your sister, though, was real upset about an interview."

He doesn't even blink.

"Yeah, well, I don't know."

"What about Frost?" I ask, switching the subject. "What do you know about him?"

"He was sheriff. Right now, I really don't know anything."

"Was he a family friend?"

"No."

"You never saw him come around the house or anything?"

Again, no, with the possibility that he'd been by on official business a time or two.

I stay at the table.

He wants me to leave.

"Did you ever see your dad on TV?"

"No."

"I can send you the link."

He passes on the offer. Never saw his dad on TV and doesn't want to watch him now. Seems weird to me.

"Were you close with your dad?"

"Off and on."

And just like that, it's over. Worst interview in a long, long time. Reminds me of the times when you get an interview that's important to the story and the person offers one-word answers, and probing for more gets only another single word.

"Well, I'm sorry to bother you," I say, getting up to leave.

The door shuts behind me. I wonder about the Questel siblings and the wall built around their father's memory. I didn't get the impression from Kelvin that it was because they revered their dad or that they had wanted to protect his memory. Of course, it could be that. The truth is that I'll never know. And yet I wonder how it was that Jim Gasser and James Frost saw J. T. Questel as a mentor, maybe even a father figure, when at least one of his sons didn't seem to register much love or admiration. Any interest about him one way or another. It's curious, and I don't know how to reconcile that at all. The connection, however, between the coroner and the sheriff was deep enough to make them lie about what happened in July 1977.

I know that to be 100 percent true.

Robbin asked me the other night if I thought Questel and Frost had been lovers.

"Seriously," I say, "this is not a story about some gay conspiracy."

"Right," she says. "But it could be."

"It isn't."

Sharing a secret is the only thing that binds people together and twists ethics into impossible knots. Sometimes people just want to help someone out of a jam, and that help becomes the knotted ethics. A secretary sees his boss cheat on an expense account. A man looks the other way when his son skips school, because he'd done the same. The boss loses his job. The boy drops out of school. No one said a thing when they should have.

No one thought anyone would get hurt.

CHAPTER
TWENTY-EIGHT

It's lunchtime and I take a break for lunch at an Amish restaurant. It's a buffet. I particularly hate buffets, but I figure when in Amish land . . . Amish food is hearty. Lots of macaroni salads and fried this and that. It's as humble as it is delicious. Farmhand food. Rib-sticking. I sit by myself next to a window and carb load while I take a break from Ida overload and look over the latest information I'd collected on the candy murder.

It's messed up and James Frost is in the middle of it, so there's a thread, like those red strings in my cabin, connecting it from Ida's murder but to a different wall.

Ohio BCI partnered with the Wayne County Sheriff's Office and the Wooster Police Department to identify a suspect in the killing of Clifford Badger. As they would in any homicide, they first looked at the people closest to Clifford: his five sons, David, James, Carl, Phillip, and John; and his wife, Helen. In the months after Clifford's death, all were given polygraphs to exclude them as suspects. Clifford's five sons passed their examinations, but Helen's initial test was deemed inconclusive. To determine she had nothing to do with her husband's death, another polygraph had to be administered.

On December 9, 1971, nine months after her husband's murder, Helen Badger was given a second polygraph. Helen arrived at the Wooster

Police Department around 10:00 a.m. on her own free will. Prior to the test being administered, the police gave her legal forms to sign that consisted of boilerplate legal jargon. *"You have the right to remain silent. Anything you say can be used against you in court."* Helen freely signed the forms and headed to the room where the polygraph examiner was waiting for her. She was politely greeted by the examiner, who asked her questions about her health, which was procedure. Helen informed the examiner that her health was good. As she continued, she told the examiner that she had taken a pill before she arrived. The pill had been prescribed by a physician, but Helen failed to remember its name or why it was prescribed to her.

Before the examiner could ask any questions about Cliff's death, he needed to set a baseline. He asked Helen fourteen simple questions that ranged from what her name was to if she was born in the USA. After the baseline was established, the examiner asked about her husband, married life, and his untimely death.

The report does not indicate what yes or no answers Helen gave the examiner. The only real clues as to what might have happened are found in the questions themselves. An examiner's questions are not some willy-nilly Magic 8 Ball affair. Each query is crafted based on content already gathered by the investigators.

"In your lifetime, have you ever contemplated suicide?"

"Do you have knowledge of Clifford Badger ever contemplating suicide?"

"Did you or your husband plan suicide in advance before eating the candy?"

"Did you love your husband?"

Those questions suggest that a murder-suicide pact might have been on the minds of the investigators. Maybe a history of depression or discord had infiltrated the marriage. We don't know. We likely never will, but the questions are telling.

"Do you have any knowledge of any strychnine ever being on your farm?"

"Since the death of your husband, did you destroy the strychnine?"

"Did you destroy the bottle of strychnine in the wooded area you pointed out to Carl Yund?"

Ah. The poison itself. Yund was Wooster's chief of police at the time. The question suggests something crucial. Chief Yund had been a part of the investigation and had spoken to Helen. There is no record of what that conversation was about, because like everything else associated with the "closed case," there is no file in the records centers at Wayne County, Wooster Police Department, the Village of West Salem, or any other jurisdiction involved.

The questions come at me like a punch in the face.

Make that three punches.

"Was your reason for destroying the strychnine to eliminate you as a suspect in your husband's death?"

"Did you poison your husband?"

"Was the reason you destroyed the strychnine to cover up for someone else as being a suspect in your husband's death?"

That final question brings me back to what I'd thought at the beginning, that another family member had been on the radar. All the Badger boys had passed their polys, yet passing such an exam doesn't proclaim innocence. It is a tool an investigator employs to rattle a suspect into doing something.

Slip up.

Lie.

Confess.

If Helen was protecting one of her boys, she wouldn't have been the first mother to do so.

The examiner asked Helen forty questions regarding the death and murder of her husband, Clifford Badger. It seemed the BCI's focus on Helen was due to the peculiarities surrounding her actions. Why did she bury and hide the strychnine on her property after his death? If they both ate the poisoned candy, and Clifford died, why did she survive? There was no antidote for strychnine. How did the suspect know that Cliff was going to eat the candy and not another member of the Badger family?

After Helen's examination, the BCI, Wayne County Sheriff's Office, and Wooster Police Department were no closer to catching the killer. It was the opinion of the examiner that Mrs. Badger was truthful in her answers to the questions.

All right, I think, *that's what the examiner says.* But those questions? They were so specific, so accusatory.

Why did they ask her if she'd destroyed the poison? Or if she'd shown where she'd buried it?

Unless she had.

I find Eli's one-time roommate on Moser Road, Levi Swartzentruber, on Facebook. This older version of him looks about the same as he did when we first met. Sure, grayer, and all of that. The same facial hair, same haircut, same oversize brown eyes. After speaking on the phone, he—as he did back then—agrees to help. No longer married to Connie, whom I remember screamed at me on the phone that she'd sue if I mentioned Levi's name in my book. Levi is married to another woman now and has a bunch of grandkids—some he's raising in Wadsworth, where he lives now.

While Levi had been a huge help the first time around, taking me to Amish sources that would have been difficult for me to find on my own, I always felt he had held things back, but it didn't matter then. I had more material than I could use anyway.

We meet in the parking lot of a cabinet shop near Wooster, where he's been working for some time. Sawdust coats his eyebrows, and he apologizes about the mess when he eases into the passenger seat.

"No problem," I say, indicating the coffee cups on the floor and the oily fast-food wrappers that tell the tale of my diet on this trip. "This car's a mess already."

He only has a few minutes, he says, or his boss will get on him. I tell him that I've come from an interview with an Amish family and found out something new.

"Ida's sister found a camera when she was helping Eli after the fire."

"What would he be taking pictures of?" he asks.

"Right. So, let's think about those days. There weren't selfies. You're not taking a picture of yourself."

"Okay," he says. "So, he has to have someone taking the pictures."

Of course, that's what I want to know. Levi lived on the farm with Eli, and while he says he moved away because things got weird, I don't think he's been entirely forthcoming. That's fine. He's helped me in other ways, and if the whole truth is something he wants to keep to himself, that's okay. I've never even asked him point-blank if he and Eli had any kind of intimate relations.

"I've seen the one naked picture of him," I say. "He's just focused on his junk. Somebody else had to take that photo. Who? Who was around there early on?"

"The only people I can think of is like Levi Levi," he says.

"Did he take the pictures?"

"Well, I mean, I was there later, '81."

"Right."

"And that was before."

"Sammy Miller?" I ask.

"I'm going to discard him," Levi says. "He was all about the women. I don't think he would."

I bring up Frost and Brown, but Levi doesn't have a bead on them. He thought they came later. I don't remind him that Frost and Eli were connected long before with the marijuana sting in Marshallville.

We settle on Levi Levi. It was his family that told me Levi Levi had confessed to the church. He was there at the fire and after. It was also his family that told me it was a camera that Susie found.

We talk about a few random things that I'd found out. I tell him about the story of Ida's supposed longing for the graveyard.

Levi gives his head a shake.

"That's another trick," he says. "He's playing on someone, on their emotions, on what they want to believe."

"Another mind game."

"Yeah, a mind game."

We lament how so many people are dead now and that the time to solve the case might have come and gone.

"I'm not quitting," I say.

Levi tugs on the car door handle.

"Maybe I can find out more about who was hanging around there back then."

"Anything you can do. Who took the photo? The photos were made around the time of Ida's death. Whoever took them knows something."

I like this guy. He's earnest and helpful. He just never gets to the finish line. He lived with Eli at the same time as other young men, guys who told me they knew Eli was into things that were against the Swartzentruber Order.

Levi Swartzentruber is always vague about those things.

"I heard he was having parties with all men around there. I don't know what they were doing."

"You lived there, Levi," I wanted to say. I just couldn't. I don't feel right about saying something along the lines of *"How stupid could you be? They were having orgies in the barn! You fucking lived there, Levi. You never saw anything firsthand? Get real with me."*

I could take another approach, I guess.

"I can change your name. No one needs to know it was you. I don't care one bit what you did or didn't do. I need to know about Eli, Danny, and Ida. I know you care. Help me."

The tactic feels a little desperate. Maybe even a little mean. I am torn because I know this is my last chance.

CHAPTER
TWENTY-NINE

Whenever Robbin calls me after being silent for more than five hours, I know where she's been.

The rabbit hole.

That's the scourge of true crime writing and research. You dig into a subject and find a juicy little bit of information that leads you on a path that, while fascinating, doesn't do a damn thing for the story you are writing at the moment.

"Look," I tell her when she calls me from a hallway in a library at Washington State University, "focus on Ohio, Nebraska, Florida, Texas, and Colorado."

The library is the only place in the country with the *Advocate* on microfilm. She's looking through every issue for advertisements from Stutzman, Frost, or a few others on my radar who might have published for sex in the personals section.

"I found some other ads we might want to run down," she says. "Horse and farmer types."

"If they aren't in the states of interest, then you're jumping into a rabbit hole."

"All right, boss. All right. I get it."

I'm one to talk, I think. The candy murder might turn out to be a rabbit hole of my own digging. I keep coming back to it because of Frost's bizarre actions associated with it. I can hear Robbin saying something about Frost and Badger being lovers and that we should look into that.

Help me.

I want to pound my head with both palms.

Enough.

Rabbit hole or not, I try my hand at posting a message on the West Salem community Facebook page:

"I'm an author looking into a 1970s West Salem homicide case and I need your help. If you know anything about the Clifford Badger 'candy murder' or individuals involved, please contact me. Thank you in advance. No lead is too small. For more on the case see my website."

My post gets just seven likes—one of which is my assistant Robbin's. On the other hand, it gets a heaping amount of hate among the forty-seven comments. Most people tell me to buzz off and forget about the murder of Cliff Badger. A couple of people were interested in the story, and I expect they've already been banned from the page or run out of town by now.

My favorite:

"Leave this alone. What are you going to prove. These people are long gone. Let well enough alone. Put your nose back where it belongs. And it's not around here."

CHAPTER THIRTY

I'm not only crushed but also a little gun-shy after the *Budget* shot down my ad. I worry that an outdoor signage company will also take offense, that what I want to do is insulting to the Amish and something that can never be done. The *Budget* folks were more concerned about losing subscriptions than helping to solve a murder of an Amish woman and, by extension, her son.

I contact four outdoor advertising companies serving the region, and I explain what I'm doing and that my billboards will be "classy" and "inoffensive"—along the lines of the missing persons and unsolved crimes billboards that are often placed by family members or victims' advocacy groups.

I'm not a family member. I'm a one-person victims' advocacy group.

I settle on Lamar with offices in Columbus, not only because of their reach in Amish Country but because they are the only company that seems to want my business. I tell salesman Josh that I want to start with five billboards placed in Wayne and Holmes Counties in locations that would be visible to both car and buggy traffic. He says that he can put together a plan for a two-part series.

The first will have an image of a burning barn with this headline: "Who Killed Ida Stutzman in 1977? Tell What You Know."

That billboard will run starting just after Thanksgiving. After the four-week cycle, three of those five will be replaced in favor of one with a photo of Danny taken at Gerry Thomas Moore's house in Akron with the words "Who Killed Little Boy Blue's Mother? Tell What You Know."

The call to action for both is to visit JusticeForIda.com, a website for anonymous tips and comments.

The media buy was spendy, costing about $5,000. But with the *Budget*'s cold shoulder and the fact that there is no online presence for the people I need to reach, it is the only thing I can think to do.

Old wounds, I know, are about to be reopened.

At least I hope so.

CHAPTER
THIRTY-ONE

If you ask what one of my fictional characters did in a particular novel, I'd have to really think hard about it. When it is about someone in a nonfiction book, it's right there. I don't have to dig up a thought. I think about the real people I write about all the time. I'd thought of Indianan Tim Parr now and then after *Abandoned Prayers*. I liked Tim because he had no guile. He told me whatever I needed to know wrapped in an earnest, very slight midwestern accent.

He was a young Nautilus instructor back when he answered this *Advocate* ad in the fall of 1982.

"Hndsm masc hairy W/M early 30's, 5'7", 140#, into ranching, construction. Seeks topman with same interests. Write with photo to Box 185, Bayfield, CO 81122."

It was Eli Stutzman, then living with Howard Runck on the ranch in Ignacio, Colorado, who had placed it.

At the time, Tim was twenty-four, married, and dealing with complexities and uncertainties about his sexuality. He loved his wife, but not in all the ways he knew she deserved. Eli was a few years older at thirty and was not only experienced but "out" in a time when many men, especially those in rural communities, were not.

When we connect by phone thirty years later—after Facebooking until my fingers hurt—I tell Tim what I'm up to with the new book, and he says he'll try to help.

"Before we get started," I say, "did you find love and happiness in life?"

Short pause.

I catch him a little off guard, but I had always hoped for the best for Tim. Many of the men I talked to for *Abandoned Prayers* had died either of old age or, sadly, at a young age because of the AIDS virus that was silently infecting the young men of his generation.

"I did," he tells me. "We've been married for ten years."

I offer congratulations when he says he's married to a wonderful guy, a guy who has never heard a word about Stutzman.

"So, he doesn't know you lost your virginity to a serial killer?"

He lets out a short laugh. "No."

It's the kind of grim laugh that eases tension.

Eli and Tim met for the first time when Tim drove from Indiana to pick him up at the Cleveland airport, and then they went down to the Stutzmans' farm after Christmas in 1982. The interstate was slick with freezing rain, and Tim's car did a one-eighty on the way down to Apple Creek. Eli, who had been away since leaving for Colorado, went inside the family home while Tim waited in the car for more than an hour, maybe as long as an hour and a half. Tim was just coming out at the time, and he was more than a little nervous. He liked Eli right away.

"He was very charming. Nice to me."

"You really liked him," I say.

"Yeah. I did."

"Were you thinking this could be a relationship?"

"Not really," Tim says. "We were friends. I had a crush on him. He wasn't the type to settle down, and I knew that too. He's very, very masculine," he says, starting to list Eli Stutzman's attributes like an old-school personal ad. "Very good-looking. Hung like a horse. Just everything any guy would want. He was a dream come true."

Until he started killing people, I think.

"Until he wasn't anymore," I say instead.

"Right," he says.

Tim and Eli were kindred spirits of sorts. Eli had been married too. In fact, just like Tim, he said he'd married his wife though he knew he was gay.

"I was struggling. I was in a marriage, and I was concerned about what I was doing, you know. And I was all curious about everything because I was very inexperienced."

While they spent four days together and had a good time, they didn't talk about much—and definitely not about whatever was going on in Eli's life at the time.

"You know," Tim says, "I think Eli was a very good actor. So, he didn't seem to be upset or worried. He didn't really talk about anything. Because that's the Amish—they keep stuff to themselves."

Tim mentions Danny, whom he saw when he was down in Austin for a visit in 1984.

"How was he?"

"Danny was polite. A nice boy. He was very aware of what was going on. You know, as far as guys sleeping together and having sex."

He says another roommate was there at the time.

"Glen?" I ask.

"Not Glen. He wasn't living there. I heard about him later, though."

Tim's reference is to a phone call on April 21, 1985, in which Eli said he wanted to come visit to get away from some trouble in Texas.

"He told me he was wanted for murder and said it involved gay sex or money."

The victim was Glen Albert Pritchett.

Tim picked him up at the bus station in Fort Wayne, Indiana. On the way to his place, Eli said he knew who the killer was. He didn't volunteer the name, nor did Tim ask. The whole idea of a murder investigation made his head spin, and over time he grew increasingly uneasy. The visit lasted a couple of weeks, with Eli making numerous phone calls to check on Danny, who he said was staying with friends out west.

"How did he act?" I ask. "Had his demeanor changed?"

Tim grows quiet.

"Calm," he says, taking his time. "Maybe not so much toward the end. I think he knew I wanted him to leave."

We turn to the subject that I'd spoken about with Charles Turner, Eli's last lover. How Eli was able to slip under the radar those months on the run from the Texas law. How no one from the gay community came forward to share what, if anything, they knew about Ida, Glen, David, Dennis, and Danny.

Tim is certain things would be different today, that gay men have found a voice they didn't have in the seventies and eighties, especially those living on farms and in small towns. To speak up was to threaten not only their jobs, friendships, and family relationships but also their personal safety.

And even with all that is known about Eli now, a fondness seeps into Tim's voice when he speaks of the man he knew. It's undeniably hard for people to reconcile what they personally know with what others have told them, or what they've read in the papers.

Or in books, for that matter.

The basis of the relationship might not have been sex but the fact that they'd both lived through similar experiences. Tim hadn't wanted to be gay. At that time, it wasn't rainbow-colored, championed, or even acknowledged in a positive way. He hated that part of who he was and tried his best to sweep it away by getting married.

Eli had been his guide, a seasoned one, out of the closet to the life that he wanted—not the life everyone had wanted for him.

"Basically, what he said was, you know, you got to be who you are. You got to live your life the way you want to live. He had been through it too. I kind of looked up to that. He influenced me, I guess, to continue with a divorce. Get on with my life."

"Your divorce was a good idea. Eli's way out, not so much."

Whenever Eli spoke of Ida, Tim noticed it was without any emotion. Just those haunting blue eyes staring off into space, capturing a memory and spinning it into a lie.

"I'm sure he killed her because she was pregnant," Tim says. "I know he was wanting to get out of the marriage, away from the Amish, so that was the only way he could do it."

He wants to know if Eli died in prison.

I tell him that Eli had been released and was living in Fort Worth, selling leather crafts as a vendor to the gay rodeo, when he died in 2007.

"AIDS?"

"No, not AIDS. Suicide."

"I guess everything caught up with him," he says.

CHAPTER
THIRTY-TWO

Eli never narrated his own life story as far as I know. Part of me doubts that he could with any accuracy because the most important moments of his life were obliterated by a convoluted and ever-changing string of lies.

I can only provide a glimpse through the eyes and recollections of those who knew him. And truly, we know how that goes. When someone is called out as a killer, friends and acquaintances quickly move from "seemed like a really nice guy" to "something was always off about him."

Versions of this are in the news almost daily.

Old Order Amishman Moses Keim has always been my most trusted guide into the time in Eli's life when the knot of his lies began to tighten.

When Eli was twenty-one, he moved from his parents' farm on Welty Road in Apple Creek to the one across the road owned by Moses and Ada Keim. The Keims knew that Eli was having problems with his father. The elder Eli, also nicknamed One-Hand Eli, came to the Keims' farm several times, seemingly very concerned about Eli. "My son is having more nerve problems. He is out of control. I don't know what to do to help him."

Others, including Keim, believed that it was a case of a father who could no longer control his son.

Amish people are first and foremost *people*. It seems silly to write that here, but the truth is a lot of people put the Amish on a pedestal. They live a godly life that is full of work and religion. And yes, they may conform in certain ways—dress, rules, philosophy of life—purposely striving to make no single person stand out more than another. And yet they do. They are seen as quaint and living a simple life unencumbered by all the bullshit that makes the modern world so exhausting, so hamster wheel. So, yes, empty at times.

Of all the Amish I have met over the years, there is no one quite like Mose Keim. He's as thoughtful, kind, and decent as anyone, but he also has a curious mind that allows him to stretch his views beyond others within his Old Order church district.

Mose doesn't like to say it, but when pressed he has no qualms in telling someone that Eli was a killer. Yet he also believes that redemption and forgiveness were possible for the man whom he took in when he was troubled and young, dealing with a controlling father in the strict Swartzentruber order.

What makes this man stand out is not only his compassion for Eli, but his drive to seek the truth. Other Amish might gossip and throw out an opinion here and there, but Mose didn't do that. He was, like Amos Gingerich and Elmer Miller, a detective of sorts.

Today, Mose still lives on Tater Ridge Road, where I interviewed him back in 1989. He was making bird feeders back then . . . and his family still does. The pandemic, incidentally, was a bumper year for the business, which now employs more than a dozen people, including a secretary. He greets me at his door. He's wearing a light-green shirt. His wife, Ada, is dressed in blue. She's at the stove making chicken noodle soup. He shows me his tiny office and produces my business card from thirty years ago.

At seventy-seven, Mose is the same weight as when he got married, a fit 165 pounds. He tells me that he's very careful in what he eats—farming organically all his life. Not long ago he walked up from the bottom of the Grand Canyon.

We talk about what I'm doing, and he agrees to help. He and Ada invite me to stay for lunch. The soup is delicious, and she lets me know right away the noodles are store-bought.

"So good," I say as she brushes away the compliment.

Ada and Mose are absolutely lovely people.

"It all started in my house," he says. "Eli had his nervous breakdown and kind of ruined his head is what you might say."

"Right," I say. "Also, I know you kept up with the story, Mose. I know you saw Eli in prison. You and I are alike, right? We both want to know the truth."

He doesn't disagree.

"I knew Eli really, really well when I visited him. You bet. And I read the story, and I read a lot. We're all different, but there's very few people that read stuff to be educated, to learn, to understand and to figure out."

He pauses.

"Does that make sense, what I said?"

"Oh, yeah, completely. I mean, you're right."

In early 1998, Mose made the trek to Texas to see Eli. Traveling with him was Eli's cousin Emery. Through the glass that separated them, Eli played the part of the misunderstood, a role he'd originated at Keim's farm. He kept his head low and spoke in those soft, familiar Eli tones. His voice, through a phone, carried with it a hint of regret or maybe wistfulness. As well as he knew Eli and what he'd done, Mose had a hard time pinpointing what Eli's regret was about.

Not about killing his wife.

Not about killing his roommate.

Not the two men in Durango.

Not Danny.

Mose tugs at his snowy beard. "I'm not a detective by any means," he says in a self-effacing manner that lets a listener know that he's likely an Amish Columbo. "That's not my life. But I like to kind of do some things that others probably won't do. So, when I went down to Texas and on the last time we visited at the last couple of minutes, I told Eli in a slow, plain way that he could understand."

Mose had said, "Eli, you already knew that Danny wasn't going to be with you when you wrote to your friend in Missouri," referring to the man Eli met up with that Christmas when Danny was dumped in Thayer County, Nebraska.

"Yeah," Eli had finally answered.

Mose pushed. Gently but deliberately. "Why did you write that, Eli?"

That moment became frozen in Mose Keim's memory.

He reflects on it even today.

"But, you know, human beings can be very smart," Mose goes on, "very evasive and whatever. But you should have seen his reaction to that question. It happened really quick. He went back and forth, sideways, back and forth. It took him about a minute to answer that. And he was the guiltiest person in the world."

Through the sheen of the thick glass, Eli had answered.

"Well," he'd said, "maybe if my plans had changed, huh?"

It was a feeble attempt to close the door on a question that couldn't be answered without incriminating himself. Mose didn't ask specifics about any of the deaths and misdeeds associated with Eli because he knew every word would be a lie wrapped in another lie. Mose refused to let Eli lie to his face.

"And I said, 'You know, I am not going to ask you what all you did, Eli. I'm going to tell you that we think we know. I think that you did some really, really bad things. And I really, really wish you could repent and acknowledge what you did.'"

A letter from Eli arrived at his place on Tater Ridge not long after the Texas visit.

"If I could do my life over again, I would want to do many, many, many things different."

Mose draws a breath. "I think that is probably the closest to a confession that he ever made to anybody. Do you agree?"

"Were you surprised Eli's father came to see his son in prison?"

"Well, I tell you what," Mose answers. "Yes and no. We are a people of our beliefs, right? Jesus makes us a people of love and forgiveness. You know what? Forgiveness is not automatic for human beings. Do you understand?"

"I do."

"If God is involved and we serve Him, that is the only way we can do it. And that's the only way I can see why he went then. Because of the relationship—father and son—and everything that's between them was bad. You know that, right? I think some of his children probably encouraged him to go."

"Three of his brothers and a cousin visited too."

Mose already knows all of this. The Amish grapevine remains a marvel of the not-so-modern world. He tells me what he'd heard from one of the brothers about how a prison official said that not too many people liked Eli and that maybe he believes his own lies.

We move to the fire and the night Ida died. Our feet are firmly planted on common ground on the subject. Have been since we first met. We both know Eli killed her. I tell Mose about my conversation with Cousin Eli, the hired boy, now a grown man making his home in Sinking Spring, not far from Tater Ridge.

"Cousin Eli told me he woke up on his own, and when he came downstairs not only were Eli and Ida gone, but the lights were on."

"Why didn't Eli call for him? Or Ida?" Mose asks, already knowing the answer.

"Ida couldn't," I say. "Because she was already dead."

"And the lights?" he asks.

"Kerosene lamps, right?"

Mose nods and I continue.

"If you have time to light lamps and fully dress as Ida did, you have time to call up the stairs to alert the hired boy."

Mose agrees wholeheartedly. "He was there to be a help to them."

The burning barn runs through my mind like it has a million times. The coincidences, especially. That it happened not long after lawyer Tim Blosser had gone. I wonder about how he'd said that Eli and Ida were so affectionate as he departed. How he'd made a point of saying how evident and unusual was the closeness that they shared. I know we can't know the truth of any given thing. That's why, as annoying and grandstanding as it is, when I hear the phrase "telling my truth" I no longer cringe. Truth is observed with the ears and eyes of a witness. It is that basic. Why had Blosser felt the need to paint that picture of Eli and Ida?

Was it the truth? Or was it an embellishment? Or even darker, was it a lie to convince me that Eli would never have hurt Ida?

He loved her.

I know that's not true. I know because in every interview I'd conducted with those who really knew her, they'd said Ida was tormented by her husband.

Eli did not love Ida.

Not at all.

Mose picks up on the night of the fire.

"Even if you had electric," says the man who never has had the utility, "would you really take the time to turn on all the lights?"

"Maybe a bedside light," I say, "but not all the lights in the house."

He nods. "Painting more of a picture of what happened there that night."

Next, I ask about the steel plate I'd seen referenced in Eli's autopsy report. I wonder if it was due to an injury suffered at the time of the nervous breakdown when, as Mose said, "something was wrong" with his brain.

Mose doesn't know a thing about it.

"Must have been later," he says. "He was still young and fresh when he was at my place."

I ask him to tell me the story of the breakdown Eli experienced at his place on a Saturday night in the winter of 1972.

He agrees, first prefacing the incident with some words about Eli's intelligence and how he, himself, isn't all that smart.

"I don't know anything about nervous breakdowns," he says.

I don't say it, but I know that Mose is smart. He knows about many, many things. The black hat he wears is not a dunce cap by any stretch.

"Eli collapsed on the bottom of the stairway when he was going to get ready to go see his girlfriend, Ida. And I don't even remember how me and Ada got him upstairs to his bed. From that Saturday evening he was one hundred percent unconscious until Sunday afternoon about four o'clock."

"You must have been deeply concerned."

"Ada and I were."

"What did you think caused it?"

"We had no idea then. We learned it later. You know, skulls are in four parts; right to the back part of his skull was drawn down tight against his spinal cord and slowed his blood flow to his brain. Not totally. Greatly, though. And that's what made him unconscious."

He thinks a bit more.

"And when you have lack of oxygen to your brain long enough, you have brain damage, or you might have brain change. You know who we are by our brain, right? Everything is in there.

"When I went up to get his dad, I told him on the way up the steps to Eli's room, I said, 'Eli, you guys are putting too much unnecessary pressure on him.' 'Oh,' he says, 'we don't put no pressure on him. There is nothing wrong.' I told Eli the next day that, you know, I said, 'You know, your father outright lied to me.' The Swartzentrubers are very secretive about their church. I'm not gonna say too much more."

An Amish woman, experienced in healing ways related to nerves, was summoned to the farm the next day. She was a self-taught practitioner of reflexology.

"When she came, we worked on him; the bottoms of his feet were as sore as a raw, raw wound. You couldn't even touch his feet. So that, yeah, it was terrible. He was damaged. And it went on."

Enter the doctor from Brewster.

"So we took him to Morton Bissell for treatment," Mose says. "Dr. Bissell was a huge man. Did you know that?"

"Yeah," I say.

"He probably weighed three and a half," Mose says. "And I can still see him pressing on Eli's skull on the table. He told me when I went in there that the plate of Eli's skull was pressing against his spine. That's what makes him pass out. So, Dr. Bissell put tremendous pressure on his forehead and worked on him about, I don't know, I'd say twenty minutes, thirty minutes. When Eli got home, it seemed as if he was as good as new. It was so awesome. Just great."

"Until it wasn't, right?" I ask.

Mose had told me this part of the story before too.

"One day," Mose starts, "soon after, he was out at the barn and he was crying and I said, 'What's wrong?' And he said, 'I have such a hard erection all the time and it's so terrible, painful, I can't take it anymore.' That went on for a long time. I don't know how long. We didn't talk a lot about it, but it was definitely there."

I ask if he thought maybe Eli was coming on to him, wanting some hands-on help with that never-ending erection.

Mose doesn't think so. "No. Not that."

"But did you know he was desiring of that?"

An admission here. Sometimes I start talking like my subjects when I'm interviewing them. Dropping the *g*'s when they have a southern accent. That sort of thing. This time, it was not so much an Amish affectation but more like Joaquin Phoenix's speech in *The Village*.

Mose dismisses the idea.

I don't tell him that I researched reasons behind the condition called priapism in the days before Viagra advertisements were on TV telling guys to get medical help for an erection lasting more than four hours.

Priapism can be caused by blood disorders like sickle cell anemia, an injury to the penis, or syphilis.

"It seemed to go on for months," Mose recalls. "Somehow that breakdown affected his sex."

As I sit there while a mantle from a gas lamp burns next to the table, I hold my thoughts inside. The collapse was a farce. It was a way to get out of a date with Ida while syphilis raged in his body.

And he sure as hell didn't get the disease from her.

So where did he get it?

$$)\!($$

Mose talks about a time when he and Eli were thrashing shocks of wheat at a neighbor's place in Apple Creek. Eli was sixteen. While he can't remember exactly what it was that caused Eli to become angry at someone, he clearly remembers the word Eli used.

"Cocksucker," Mose says. "He said that word and I wondered, *What in the world?* That's the first time, the last time, the only time I heard him say it. I never forgot it. So why am I telling you that? You know why."

I do.

"How do I know what all was in his head, right? We can't know it. The average person, even us Amish boys, would talk bad. But that is a word that very few people use."

Mose goes back to the brain damage as the cause of Eli's evil ways.

"How much brain damage? And that breakdown. I'm positive he had brain damage. They can't prove it."

"You want a reason for what he did, Mose. Don't you?"

He lowers his voice a little and cautions me.

"We have to be careful. You know, Jesus said, 'I will judge man.' The man doesn't decide. And that's what's going on today. But I can truthfully say that Eli had some damage. He must've had damage, right?"

"Maybe, but he was cunning. Always setting the stage for whatever thing he was going to do, Mose. Like the notes at your place."

Mose nods. During the time of his breakdown, Ada discovered several notes that Stutzman had written on scraps of paper and left in his bedroom. The words, written in English, included references to Satan and hell.

"And that was because of the brain damage," he says. "But, then, why didn't he write good notes? Why always bad? That was a devil working on him."

One morning Mose found Eli downstairs, dressed and standing in the kitchen, his long Swartzentruber hair crudely cut.

"Eli, what in the world did you do to yourself?" he asked.

Stutzman said he wanted to go to the Keims' Old Order church.

Mose, although a very careful talker, crinkles his eyebrows to his hairline as he ponders the right way to tell the story of Eli's trip to the mental institution in Cuyahoga Falls. He doesn't want to denigrate Eli's father or the Swartzentruber church. Even so, he says as far as he can tell, that's where Eli's mental problems came from. At least in part. Mose also knows that there is some mystery in everything we think we know.

He recalls watching a sheriff's car pulling up the lane and two deputies approaching him.

"Is Eli Stutzman working for you?" one of the deputies asked.

Mose nodded. "He is over in the field."

"We have to talk with him now."

The deputies left and a few minutes later returned with Eli, who was frantic.

"They're going to take me away!" Stutzman told Mose.

"Why?"

"We can't say, but we've got orders," one of the deputies replied.

With that, they put Eli into the back seat of the sheriff's car.

Mose, outraged, ran to the Stutzman farm and found Eli's mother, Susan, in the house.

"She was a huge woman and her heart was the same size. You get the message?" he asks.

"I do," I say.

"She was an extremely kind, well-liked person. So, I told her what happened and she says, 'Oh, my.' And I said, 'Where's Eli?' Well, she's not sure, but Eli and the boys went to Wooster. That's all she knew. Anyhow, so I knew right away what was going on. I went back home. I was discouraged. Disgusted. Eli's father had turned in his son."

Later that day, Keim learned that Stutzman had been taken to Fallsview Hospital, and One-Hand Eli had rushed up to Cuyahoga Falls on the bus with a suitcase of clean clothes.

Mose says Eli's father committed his son and then went to pick him up to bring him back home, where he could control him.

"What kind of father could do that to his son?" he asks. "They did tell him to go home and get out of there. But they released Eli the next day. So, what can you say? Eli called me and said, 'They released me.' I said, 'Are you kidding? I was told they got to keep you for three days.'"

Eli asked if he could come to the Keim farm and stay.

"'Eli, I am not going to tell you to come to my place, because if I do, your family is on me.' So I said, 'It's up to you. If you do come here on your own, I'm not going to run you away. It's totally up to you.'"

CHAPTER THIRTY-THREE

I follow Mose's handwritten map along Tater Ridge to the shop where Emery, also called Junior, Stutzman makes trusses. Emery's father and Eli's father were brothers. The directions are spot on.

"The only GPS I need," Mose says as I leave, "is God's Plan for Salvation."

Emery's connection to the story is more than shared DNA. Emery was one of a handful who visited Eli during his Texas incarceration for murder.

Inside the big red metal-sided building, a couple of Amishmen direct me to where Junior is working in the midst of a fragrant haze of sawdust. He's seventy-three, but with his red beard and smooth skin, he looks much younger.

Eli and Emery's contact was minimal in their growing-up years. Emery's family lived in Missouri before Emery and a brother took up residence at a farm in Holmes County.

He says he can spare a few minutes to talk about Eli and Ida, turns off the machinery, and leads me to the employee breakroom at the front of the shop.

"Of course, we heard the tragic story of the fire," he says right away. "That Ida passed away in that fire. My brother and I went to the funeral."

I ask what stands out about it all these years later.

"It was really warm. All the summers are warm. And one thing I feel, picture . . . or think of is that she was expecting, you know. And I was alone with her and the casket and her hand like this."

He makes a claw-like gesture.

"It was very unusual," he goes on. "I didn't think it was right."

The state of Ida's hand holds significance to those who saw it. Was she pointing at her killer? Was she pointing to God for help? What did it mean? It had to mean something. It was so strange. So remarkable. Unforgettable.

He tells me that he accompanied his father-in-law to help at the barn raising. Cousins, uncles, and other family members were there.

"I really remember that at noon, of course, everybody stopped for a big dinner. People are set up with tables and benches. And Eli was around everybody, you know, really pale-looking. It was really grief on him, you know."

"Devastated about Ida's death."

"I don't know," he says. "He looked like it."

This is the subtle Amish version of "he seemed so normal, but there was something I couldn't put my finger on at the time."

A month or so later, Emery's brother came with him to see Eli. Susie was there taking care of Danny. Eli was upstairs in a bedroom. Susie went to get him, and after a while Eli came downstairs and sullenly slid into a chair. He barely said a word.

"He answered what we asked and stuff like that, but he was really withdrawn."

"What did you think about what happened to Ida?" I ask.

"I didn't think much about that yet."

That changed, however, when he and his wife went to Harmony, Minnesota, along with his father to see Eli's brother Chris and sister Lydia. They stayed with other cousins.

"And I remember that morning we sat at the breakfast table. My cousin told me, he said, 'You know, Junior,' he said, 'Uncle John was up here.' His boy was the one working for Eli and Ida. And his story is that he thinks Eli killed Ida. He said when his son Eli came home, he told him about what he experienced that night. He woke up and everything was orange, and he found Ida by the milk house and told Eli, 'This is too hot.' And Eli told him to go for a phone. When he already came back, she was moved. It was so hot that his feet had blisters on them the day of the funeral."

When Emery came home from Minnesota, he wrote to Uncle John.

"'This is scary. You know, what happened don't match and everything.' And Uncle John wrote back that according to what his son says, it points that way."

"After the fire and the funeral and I think it was during the barn raising, Uncle John told his brother Eli that something's got to be done about his Eli, that he's really, you know, losing it," Emery says.

"And nothing was done, right?"

"I don't know. I don't think so."

Eli left the church and then left the community.

"It wasn't the end of the story."

"No."

After the *Reader's Digest* article hit Amish Country and opened the Pandora's box that was Eli's life, Emery's father and one of his brothers went to see Eli in Nebraska.

"Eli talks smooth enough that he had them convinced of his innocence," Emery says. "They come home and tell us, 'Don't worry, he didn't do anything.'"

Another brother also made the trip later.

"My brother talked to the filling station manager and to the sheriff. Well, by that time, you know, it was pretty obvious that he's not so innocent."

After the Texas trial and Eli was sent to prison, Emery decided that he ought to try his hand at seeing what he could get out of his wayward cousin.

CHAPTER
THIRTY-FOUR

Mose Keim and Emery Stutzman were on a mission to find the truth about Ida's and Danny's deaths when they went to visit Eli in the winter of 1998. They took the bus from Cincinnati to Houston to meet up with a Bible-study couple who had befriended Eli. The couple made the arrangements with the prison and drove the two Amishmen there the morning after their arrival.

Getting inside was intimidating. Lots of gates. Locks. Procedures. All things that couldn't have been further from the life experiences of two Amishmen. It goes without saying, I think, but neither Mose nor Emery has had so much as a traffic ticket in their lives.

Eli sat on the other side of a thick sheet of glass. He placed his palm against the barrier and Mose and Emery followed suit. Eli's hair was salt-and-pepper, but he looked, for the most part, the same. They spoke through a phone line in German. After a few minutes Eli requested they speak in English instead.

"I don't want the other guys here to think we are talking about them," he said.

The first twenty minutes were awkward. Emery felt uncomfortable because there were convicts on one side and distraught family members on the other. It was loud and the atmosphere was charged with emotions. A woman cried. A guard paced behind them.

Eli talked about prison life, the morals inside the walls, the hierarchy, and the rules that went along with everything.

They talked for a long time about family and where various members of the church were living before Emery brought up the death of their sons. It was common ground for both men.

Emery's son was about the same age as Danny when a truck slammed into the family's buggy as they returned home from a wedding in 1984. The boy was killed instantly, and the rest of the family were badly injured and taken to the hospital, some by helicopter.

"It was really hard to bury that boy, Eli. How did you lay Danny down in the middle of nowhere and then drive off?"

Eli twisted in his chair and fidgeted with the phone before answering.

"Well, I was just disoriented," he said, tearing up. "I didn't know what to do."

$$\chi$$

The phone in the truss-builder's breakroom, which I now know does double duty as the office, rings. Emery gets up and answers in German. When he returns, I ask if he thinks Ida's case didn't get the proper scrutiny of the county because she was Amish.

"I definitely do," he says. "Dr. Lehman and the others had a real respect for the Amish."

"So, that's the reason they didn't push or question?"

"Right."

"Not at all."

"They didn't investigate anything."

I bring up Cousin Eli, who had been the hired boy at the Stutzman fire. Emery's father and John were brothers. Cousin Eli lives nearby, and Emery tells me they spoke earlier in the day.

"Do you think he knows more?"

He doesn't hesitate. "I think he revealed some to his dad. There's something he don't want to come out."

I run through some scenarios that might have been the catalyst for Ida's murder. It was possible, as some suggested, that she'd caught Eli having sex with a man. The camera he had stashed away? Pornography? Maybe it was even worse. Not merely immoral, but an actual crime.

"Maybe Ida caught him in the act of molesting a child," I suggest.

Cousin Eli was twelve at the time.

"Something like that might be the reason why you might keep a secret," I say. "Being so ashamed though it wasn't your fault."

"He could be a victim," Emery says.

"He'd molested two of Ida's brothers. Did you hear that?"

"Yeah," he says, stopping and thinking. "I bet you he didn't reveal that to his dad, you know?"

"People keep secrets like that for a long time," I say. "They've been threatened. Made to feel dirty. And they don't let it out because nobody's going to believe them. Or worse, blame them."

He's listening intently.

"And then the unthinkable happens," I go on. "Eli kills Ida. And you think, holy crap. I should have told somebody. Because if I'd told somebody, she'd still be alive."

I get up from the table so he can get back to work.

"I'm glad you stopped here," Emery says. "Because you're the first person that I get to really, really talk to about this."

Emery asks to exchange information.

"You don't have a phone, do you?" I ask.

"We got our whole nine yards," he says, writing it all down for me.

On my drive away from Tater Ridge, I think of a twelve-year-old Amish boy. From what I've seen over the years, Amish children are younger in so many ways than outsiders of the same age. Exposed to far less of the world. Not corrupted by the media. Yet, they know what's right and what's wrong. It had never crossed my mind that this could be the reason for Cousin Eli's silence.

I understand. I really do. I had something like that happen to me too. I didn't mention it to anyone until I was in my forties. It didn't slip my mind. I didn't erase it from my memory bank.

I think about it all the time.

If it happened to him, then that's his secret to keep.

CHAPTER
THIRTY-FIVE

The air is freezing, and the ramp to the front door of David Amstutz's manufactured home is a luge. I grip the rail like my life depends on it. The door is ajar, and I rap a bruised knuckle against the frame of the storm door.

A little dog starts yapping and a voice calls for me to come inside. So I do.

The place is cluttered with boxes of things that someone is in the midst of organizing. A little of this here. Little of that there. It's a process that appears to have stalled for one reason or another, and by the looks of things, it's been a while.

David is on a recliner with a fleecy Christmas blanket pulled up over his chest and a big smile on his face. Under his neck is a maraschino-cherry red travel pillow. If only his recliner had wheels, he'd be ready to go. On the wall behind him is a gun rack made of upturned black-tail deer hooves.

I start to say who I am, but he cuts me off in midsentence.

"I recognized you the second I saw you," he tells me.

We chat about how much time has passed and why I'm here. David is eighty-eight now, with a full head of hair and a beard more Rip Van

Winkle than Santa Claus. He just got his driver's license renewed. He might be ensconced in a recliner, but he's sharp and ready to talk about Eli, Ida, and Levi Hershberger. David, a Mennonite, hauled everything from livestock to farm equipment to lumber for the Amish.

It was through Levi Levi Hershberger that he met Eli Stutzman.

Levi told him that Eli was obsessed with sex.

"Eli's hard all the time," he said.

He wasn't lying.

Eli offered David twenty dollars to let him give him a blow job not long after he married Ida, and the young couple was staying at the Hershberger farm. David refused the offer, which Eli tripled to sixty dollars. David gave him a harsh and definitive rebuke, pushing Stutzman out of his truck. Both had been drinking, but David saw Eli's play for what it was. He considered it a test, as though Eli was trying to see how far he could go.

"Were you shocked about that?" I ask. "I mean, like, did you know he was gay?"

David shakes his head. "I didn't know. I assumed he was."

"That offer of a blow job would be a good hint."

He smiles. "Yeah."

David is firing on all cylinders. There's no "not sure, can't remember, let me think" in our conversation. We talk about Levi's dubious business dealings and his penchant for booze. David says many of the Amish boys drank a lot, but Levi was a real standout in that regard. David would bring back liquor from one of his deliveries and Levi was always at the ready, his mouth open like a baby bird for a splash of alcohol. Some of the booze was kept in a spot at a local blacksmith's, and just about every Amish guy who drank knew it was there. Some could hold their drink.

"Levi?"

"Sloppy," David says.

I ask if he knew about the problems that Levi had at home related to his drinking. How his wife flagged down a neighbor.

"Doesn't surprise me," he says. "But I didn't know."

Whether it was the booze that was the cause or the effect of Levi being absent from church now and again, David couldn't say for sure.

"One time he had me come and get him at seven thirty in the morning and we started drinking then. I knew it was because he had a new preacher at church that day and he didn't want to face him."

"He had secrets?"

"Yeah, I think so."

David stirs and his dog, Snickers, looks up from the chair he's been sitting on.

"Levi wasn't always honest," he says. "I know that much. I also know he'd been in prison in Pennsylvania."

"Were he and Eli lovers?"

"Never thought that."

"What was their connection? The horses?"

"Right. I hauled horses for them. They were buying and selling."

"Anything illegal? Crooked about it?"

"I think it was all undercover. They were on the prowl."

"Meaning? A cash business without reporting income?"

"That's right. The money they made was all undercover."

The word "undercover" is a strange choice.

"You mean under the table?"

He smiles. "That's it."

Memories of the barn fire are vivid.

"I got a call about two o'clock in the morning. Got me out of bed with the news of the fire and Ida's death. I knew right then something was up."

"Really?"

He nods. "Yeah, because it didn't seem right. And everyone knew he didn't want to be Amish."

"Because of the blow job offer?" I ask.

"Yeah, that too. But also, he was running around with the horses and such."

"Right. So really, you thought it was a lie?"

"Oh, I knew. No question about it."

David recounts how he was asked to get Amos and Lizzie that night. David didn't have any of the details, other than he'd heard that Eli had seen lightning strike the barn earlier the day before.

"I knew it was a lie," he says.

"But that was later, right?"

"Then. And later I heard what the hired boy had seen."

"What was that?"

"He saw Eli drag Ida back into the milk house."

I let it sink in for a beat. "That's what you heard?"

"Right. I assume it is probably true."

I tell him that I saw the hired boy, now grown, and he never told me that.

"Afraid to probably," David says.

I'd heard over the years from several people that whatever it was that Cousin Eli saw that night was too terrible to repeat. Moreover, that Eli had threatened him if he said anything about the fire.

Snickers jumps on my lap, and I ask David about Levi being at the fire, but he doesn't have a memory of that. They stayed friends until Levi's death and while they talked about Eli, Levi never said he was there the night of the fire. Never confessed.

Our conversation is winding down. David catches my eyes land on a massive collection of salt and pepper shakers that fill a curio cabinet and counter space. Some of the boxes too.

He tells me his wife of almost sixty years, Amanda, is a collector.

"There's more back here," he says, getting up from his Christmas-themed cocoon. Relief washes over me. The walker next to his chair is not needed. *Good,* I think. *He's not a shut-in.*

I follow him through a minefield of boxes to a back bedroom. Cabinets line all the walls with thousands of salt and pepper shakers arranged. It's organized. It's a sight. I make a mental note of never to collect anything, except stories.

More than eighty thousand Amish call Ohio home, and the next guy on my list seems to know just about everyone. That might be true of all the Amish. In fact, just name someone, and after a verbal genealogy of the Amish kind, a connection is made.

"Is he married to Little Sam's Millie?"

"No, I think it's Daniel's Malinda you're thinking of."

"Yeah. Down in Newcomerstown."

Jake Weaver is one of those guys. He texts me to meet at the Dalton Wendy's parking lot after five when he gets off work. Right on the dot, a Kidron Electric van sidles up next to me and Jake gets out. He's a big guy, whiskered, but not Amish style. He's come from a repair job in Wooster and is dressed in his work clothes. This is our first face-to-face meeting. We first came in contact after Eli Stutzman's death in 2007 when he emailed me about a self-published booklet about his funeral, "Eli's Last Ride." I sent a check for ten dollars, which he never cashed, because, he said over the phone, it had my signature—in his view my autograph—on it.

If I could add an emoji here, it would be the eye-rolling one.

Jake is former Amish. His father was a preacher when the family transitioned from Old Order to New Order. He speaks German and includes many Amish as friends and—in the case of some New Order Amish—customers. He's deep into the Stutzman story, even making the trip to see Danny's grave in Chester.

He's agreed to be my guide.

We head down the road to see Henry Hershberger, "a good guy who knows a lot about everyone." On the way, we talk about *Abandoned Prayers*.

"I remember some of the people I talked with about the book; I know they always thought some of those salacious parts, you know, well they were like kind of taken aback by that. *'Why did he have to put that in?'*"

It's a fair question. I have thought about it over the years. Did I go too far on some of the sexual stuff?

"I was just treating it like any information that I thought was interesting," I say.

"And it was," he says.

"Everyone was touched by the humanity of the people in Nebraska. How they embraced and mourned a child found on Christmas Eve. The flip side of that was dark. Eli's life was dark, and of course so was Danny's. It needed to be in there."

Jake agrees. "And, you know, for some people it's so, well, 'this is getting interesting.' Yeah. But others, I think the Amish, would have just wished it wouldn't have had to say that stuff."

He tells me to turn into a farm with a sign offering brown eggs for sale. It's Henry and Esther Hershberger's place. The connection to the story is through Esther's sister, who is married to Eli Stutzman, the former hired boy at the fire.

Henry and Esther are finishing a meal when we arrive and Jake speaks to them, first in German, then later in English, when he introduces me. Henry sits at the head of the table with Esther seated by his side. He's friendly and doesn't mind my placing my phone closer to him so it can pick up everything he says.

Jake recounts most of the story of what people say Cousin Eli saw that night when Ida died. I'd have preferred less of a setup, but Jake is extremely enthusiastic. He informs them that I'm reinvestigating the case. Most of his gaze is directed solely at Henry.

"I remember you told me about a conversation you had with the guy and what he remembers," Jake says. "Did he wake up by himself?"

Henry answers in the affirmative.

And the whole cycle of questions and answers comes as Jake leads him through something that I would have preferred to have Henry share without an outline of prompts.

But again, Jake is very enthusiastic.

Besides, the ground centering around what Cousin Eli saw that night is well trodden. Everything Henry has to report aligns perfectly with what Cousin Eli told me.

Esther joins the conversation. She's a "double first cousin" of Ida's—on the Troyer (Lizzie) and Gingerich (Amos) sides.

"Tell me about Ida," I say. "Was she happy with Eli, do you think?"

Henry starts to answer but stops. Generalizing about people is seldom a good idea, but my experience in Amish Land is that speaking ill of anyone, no matter what they've done, is almost never done.

At least to outsiders.

I give them an open door.

"I heard things when I interviewed Amos and Lizzie, years ago when I went up to Michigan. And I talked to Susie too. So, I mean, I'd love to hear what you think."

Esther speaks. "She did say some things. He left her in the evening or things like that. She wasn't happy about it."

"Did she have suspicions about what he was doing?"

This time, Henry answers. "I don't know. I don't know."

I turn to Esther.

"I have a feeling she did," she says. "But what we don't know." She stops and thinks a little more.

I know this is difficult for her. I also know she cared about Ida and Danny and that the conversation we are having is important to her.

"What do you think?"

"She knew that he's into things that he shouldn't be."

"And he'd been doing bad things before they got married. She overlooked them, right?"

"Amos and Lizzie kind of wished she would just forget him," Esther tells me. "They probably told you that."

I nod.

"Yeah, they didn't like that," she says. "But she seemed like she just can't forget him, and she couldn't. And while he was around, he was nice, soft-spoken."

"Yeah, he was a good con," Henry says.

How Ida was clothed—fully dressed—brings Jake into the conversation.

"Your people wear a nightgown," he says. "Like my mom was Amish, you know, she always had a kind of bluish nightgown on, as I remember it. And that would still be the tradition."

Esther agrees it would.

"And so, for Ida to be found with a regular dress is strange, right?" I ask.

"Yeah," she says.

"And that Eli said she went out of the house first. Strange too."

Esther processes the scenario. Carefully.

I continue. "And would it take longer for you to dress in outside clothes than your husband?"

Henry answers for her.

"Yes."

I look over at Esther.

"Well, please. You're not going out there first, ahead of your husband."

"You know," she says. "No."

"And the lamps were lit. Remember this is all at midnight. Someone lit the lamps in the middle of a fire. Strange, right?"

Esther checks off the list. "Lamps? Get her dress on? Out there? No."

I tell them that it was only after the *Reader's Digest* and *People* magazine articles that anyone said a thing to the world about being suspicious of Ida's death.

Henry doesn't disagree. He adds that within the community, there had been talk long before Little Boy Blue.

Bill Garfield, who worked at Spidell Funeral Home and was a friend of Eli's father, said he was suspicious.

"He told my dad."

"At the time she died, or later?"

"At the time."

Eli's relationship with his father has been a point of discussion over the years. No one thought it was particularly close or loving. Rather, it was the opposite. His father was stern, deep into ensuring the Ordnung was followed to the letter. He didn't think his son should get a raise as a schoolteacher and pointedly told his son that repentance was the only way out of the never-ending fires of damnation.

"They were not close," I say.

"No," Henry answers, bringing up the time Eli's father got his hand caught in some farm equipment.

Esther nods. "Oh right. Yeah."

Henry describes a scene in which Eli's father was writhing in extreme pain, with his family all around trying to keep him from bleeding out before the rescue squad got there.

"But Eli went back behind the house and laughed about it," Henry says.

Esther speaks up. "Eli wished it would have killed him."

Henry nods. "Yeah, he did."

I bring up Levi Levi. Henry says he worked for him and that he was a good boss.

"But he . . ."

I complete his sentence. "Had a drinking problem."

"Yeah, he had a drinking problem."

"You know Levi Levi made a confession before he died."

"Yeah, I heard that."

"What was Eli's relationship with Levi?"

Both he and Esther say that was the horse connection, but I ask for more.

"I mean, was it about the horses or was it something else?"

I let the phrase sort of dangle. Though these folks are in my age range, I don't want to offend.

"You know what I mean?"

"I really can't say for sure," Henry says.

"How much he was into that," she adds.

"And the other stuff," I say. "What happened to Ida at the fire."

"Right," she says.

"It's possible because he was there a lot."

Henry answers. "Yeah, he was."

"Even the night of the fire?"

Henry goes on to say he remembers somebody telling him that Levi was there. Levi had seen the glow from the fire from his place and showed up at Eli's.

"They were out in the yard that evening at his place and saw the fire."

"Who was?"

"Levi and his hired hand."

I ask for the man's name.

"Was it John Miller, wasn't it?" he asks his wife.

Esther thinks so.

"He's not living yet," Henry says. "He's same age I am, and he had cancer."

Another literal dead end.

"Do you think seeing the fire was possible from Levi's place?" I ask.

Esther doesn't. "They were too far apart."

Levi's relationship with Eli continued after the fire.

"People didn't like seeing Levi there," Henry says.

"To see them together like that because," Esther starts to say, stopping herself short once more.

"Tell me why."

"Well, I don't know," she says.

I push gently and give her some room. She is not a person who likes to speak harshly about anyone. "Like a bad influence?"

"Kind of thing. Yeah."

We talk some more, and I ask which of Eli's siblings might speak to me.

"Andy," Henry says, giving directions that rely on all sorts of visual cues as well as road names.

As I wrap up, I ask if I can take a photo of their huge wood-fueled cooking stove.

Very *Little House*, I think.

"I bet you make some wonderful things in that oven," I say.

"Oh, I don't know," Esther says. While her modesty is cultural, I know that deep down she's got to be thinking, *Darn right, I do.*

As Jake and I head for the door, I leave them with a simple fact.

"When I come to interview people about a crime, I'm never afraid of coming to an Amish home. I know you won't shoot me. But those English guys, not so much. I have to watch out."

I think I cursed myself then and there.

I wasn't met by a man with a gun when I landed on the front steps of one of Eli's best friends the next morning, but it was a strange and unwelcome encounter. The address was on Church Road in Dalton—that alone should have portended a more welcoming situation.

The man who lived there with his husband was the same one that Indianan Tim Parr said he and Eli stayed with when he came to Ohio.

A thin man with uneven teeth opened the door.

I tell him who I am and why I'm there.

He doesn't say a word. Just looks at me and starts to close the door.

"I'm not here about you," I tell him, urgency in my voice. "I'm here about Danny and Ida."

He shakes his head.

A second later I stand there alone on the porch, knowing that my intrusion was an unwelcome one. Maybe a reminder of things he'd rather forget.

CHAPTER
THIRTY-SIX

The weather has shifted and it's colder. Really cold. I don't have a hat and my bald head is reminding me of my packing error. I pick up a beanie at the Millersburg Walmart, which is like every Walmart I've ever seen with a single exception. On one side of the parking lot is a row of stables and hitching posts for a certain segment of clientele.

I chat with Claudia about things at home (two of our four grandsons spent the day with her and she's beat) and with Robbin about things related to the case (she's still digging into the records search). I'm heading over to see Carl Badger at the convalescent center outside of Millersburg. He's agreed to meet. He wants the world to know who killed his father with that poisoned candy.

I want to know why Sheriff Frost acted so strangely when he closed the case.

I'd learned by then that Ida's case, Carl Badger's, and another shared the same DNA . . . all closed with zero disclosure. The other one was from October 24, 1975, and involved a crime at the Apple Creek Developmental Center.

Gary Allman, a mentally disabled man weighing only ninety-three pounds and standing four feet seven, was accused of the rape and murder of a staff member, but even Dr. Questel agreed that "secret" evidence the Wayne County Sheriff's Office collected was not sufficient to prosecute Allman. The Wooster *Daily Record* called out the whole debacle in an editorial.

"And we cannot help but wonder how the doubts of his guilt and the secrecy of the evidence against him will rest with the people of Wayne County."

I'm more of a word guy. Numbers have never been my strong suit. I can count, however. The Allman case, along with Badger and Stutzman, makes three cases in which there was no disclosure on what critical investigations uncovered.

The common denominator is James Frost.

Almost at once I decide that the red brick–faced convalescent center outside of Millersburg needs to engage the services of a wayfinding specialist. I park in an icy lot next to all the other cars, a visual cue that I was sure indicated the entrance. Not so. In fact, after wandering around a courtyard illuminated by windows from a dining hall, I find myself hopelessly lost. I get the attention of a woman pushing a cart by one of the back doors, and she tells me it is around the corner, so that's where I go. Inside, finally, I go to the front desk. The place is clean, though truth be told, there is that odor that I associate with old people. Grandma's house. Maybe a mothballed steamer trunk in a junk store?

The Mennonite girl at the front desk scans a laminated directory.

"Badger?" she asks, as her fingers do the walking across a plastic-covered sheet of names and room numbers.

"Carl Badger," I say.

Though it is late January, I notice that Christmas decorations are still up in the lobby. No rush, I guess, with the folks around here.

"Sorry," she looks up.

"But I talked to him last week."

"He's not here."

A thought comes over me and I almost hate to say it.

"Is he, maybe, dead? It must happen around here every now and then."

"All the time." Her tone is cheerful, and she adjusts her demeanor slightly to something closer to what is likely in the employee handbook.

"Old people are people too." I imagine the copy under a photo of white-haired people playing cards. *"Even if super-duper old, please show compassion. A sad face is always appropriate when a resident passes away."*

She's young and learning the ropes, I think.

I also think that being dead might not be a bad alternative. You know, over living here with a bunch of elderly people.

And yet, at sixty-four, I have both feet planted firmly in that demographic.

She sets the directory aside and offers what's meant to be an empathetic smile. "He might be up at our other residence," she says, turning her attention now to her cell phone. "It's the building right behind us."

She provides directions and off I go.

I park for the third time, and I still can't locate the entrance. As I get out of the Jeep, I spot a man making his way across the same sparse parking lot. His name is Reverend Caldwell. He's African American, which heightens the whiteness of his beautiful smile. As I press the intercom of the outside door, he offers to save me the trouble of freezing and lets me in.

We chat a little while walking through to the elevator, passing bins of prosthetic legs akimbo and dirty laundry. The smell turns my stomach, as he tells me about working first in the military as a chaplain and then later here. His godparents live in Seattle, and he's visited there a few times. We talk about it being a small world.

"Must be rewarding being a chaplain," I say as the elevator lifts us to the second floor.

Truthfully, that phrase doesn't have the meaning it probably once had. Now, I think, people say that when they are happy they don't have that kind of job. Or when they can't manifest a single reason why anyone should want to do that kind of work.

"I'll take you to the front desk," he says.

The odor in the hall is of a place like this. Lots of bodies. Corrugated skin, mishaps on the way to the toilet, maybe even the fish and chips served the night before—all are beyond the masking capability of any cleanser.

"God," I say to Reverend Caldwell, "I hope my wife kills me before I ever end up in a place like this."

"I know what you mean," he says, though I expect he doesn't. He also couldn't know that I've literally told Claudia at the first sign of dementia to put a pillow over my face.

Since then, I've amended it to the second sign. Just in case.

I spot Carl Badger's name next to an open door.

"Hey, here's his room."

The reverend goes inside, and I follow.

Carl is on a bed just to the left of the door. He's in a tangle of blankets and staring off into the blank space of the ceiling. The bed by the window is occupied by another gentleman, who is watching a World War II show at ear-splitting volume.

"Carl," Reverend Caldwell says, "this gentleman has come to talk to you. Came all the way from Seattle."

The wispy-white-haired man's eyes stay on the ceiling, slitted open about halfway.

Maybe he's dead?

"Carl?" the chaplain repeats.

His eyes open and go from vacant slits to sharp focus. Just like that. He looks at me.

"I came about your dad's murder."

Carl immediately sits and wriggles his feet into his shoes. He's wearing a T-shirt with the image of an eagle and these words: *"The pursuit of a dream can heal a broken soul."*

"I want to tell you everything," he announces, now upright and putting on a blue plaid button-down shirt, which he doesn't button.

Reverend Caldwell suggests going to the dining room or someplace quieter.

Which, I decide, would be just about anywhere other than his room.

Carl doesn't care where we go and says so. He just wants to talk. He adjusts the waistband of his jeans and out we go into the hall. The chaplain stays with us for the walk down the hall to freedom. Carl tells us he's been there only a while, about a year. Wherever he'd been before was much better than here. He is eager to tell me whatever I need to know about his father's murder.

Dreams come true, I think.

And that's just when things take a turn.

Dressed in a blue smock and capri pants, a woman whom I immediately consider to be a Nurse Ratched understudy (more Fletcher than Paulson) zips right over and demands to know what we're doing. I tell her I've come to see Carl.

"Is it approved?" she asks.

I say yes. So does Carl.

I give her my name, and she retreats into a fishbowl office and picks up the phone. Out of the corner of my eye I catch a dour expression on her face as her eyes pin themselves to me.

Uh-oh, I think.

A couple of men sit on hard plastic chairs facing the fishbowl. One is slumped over, picking at something on the floor, and another is frozen with his arms folded, actually unnaturally knotted, across his chest. He looks at me and bobbleheads for a second.

Something is wrong.

This interview isn't going to happen.

I hit the recorder app on my phone and hold it in front of Carl's face.

"Carl, who killed your father?" I ask right away.

"My brother," he says.

"You think? Why?"

"He wanted the farm. But he lost in the end. God took care of him. He got bone cancer. Blood cancer. Died from that."

"Now, who is this? Which brother?"

"My next-close brother, which is named James."

"How do you know that?"

"I know," he answers.

I repeat my question. "How do you know that he did it?"

"There are too many things that point to him. He was always bossy and a bully as a man and child. Then one time I said, 'You kind of think you're taking over. Don't you take over the farm.' And he says, 'You ain't seen nothing yet.'"

Just then Ratched-lite hurls herself out of the fishbowl.

"They said that they didn't hear about it being approved, so you can't."

"I called Carl. He approved it."

"But he can't," she says. "He has a guardian. He's not his own person. Legally, he cannot make his own decisions. He has a person that does that for him. He cannot receive any visits except for his guardian."

I ask for contact information.

"I can't tell you that. I'm supposed to walk you out of the building because they don't know how you got in here. But he is not supposed to have visits from anybody."

I turn to Carl.

"Did he blame a neighbor named Betty?"

Ratched interrupts. "Got to walk you outside," she says.

I stay on Carl. "Did he blame her?"

He nods. "Yeah."

She won't give up. "Sir, I got to walk you out."

I'm not about to give up either.

"I'm talking to him now." I look at her badge. "What's your name?" I read her name aloud, and she immediately flips her name tag over to the blank side like she's done some magic trick. "Are you an employee here? And you're telling me that I can't be here because of a guardianship rule?"

"You told me that this was approved."

"It was approved by Carl."

"But he can't," she says. "He's not in his right mind. You're in a psychiatric facility."

This is news. I thought it was some shithole rest home. It makes sense, though. I wonder now about the guy with the knotted arms across his chest. Was he wearing a straitjacket or was that pose a force of habit? Without a doubt, whoever was living there had to be mentally ill or victims of mega payback.

Carl, who clearly wants to spill everything he knows, starts speaking. And as I lean in to hear, Ratched talks over him.

Loudly.

"I have to walk you out of the building."

"What?" I ask.

"Right now!"

"Okay, fine," I say.

We start down the hallway, Carl, me, and Ratched. Some other orderlies or whatever they call themselves in a place like that and a resident or two join us, the bobblehead fellow included.

"What's your name?" she asks me. Her affect reminds me of someone who makes a living cradling a clipboard—which I suspect she does—but in the excitement of booting me out, she left it on her desk next to her Diet Coke.

I'm annoyed. "I gave it to you already."

More people come, making it a Pepsi commercial. I look for Carl but he's been excised from the group. Probably off somewhere getting his brain erased. No more answers to questions about the candy murder.

By the time we get to the door to the outside, more have joined the entourage. The intercom or someone's phone on speaker announces something about a code. The color blue? Red?

I try the door, but nothing.

"You can't get out without being let out," she says.

Seriously?

"I want out right now," I say.

She shakes her head and flatlines all expression, which I think is her normal look, but now I'm anxious.

I play to the crowd. "You are holding me prisoner in this facility! You are now holding me prisoner. Let me out. This is called kidnapping. It's a federal offense. I came here at the request of Mr. Badger. I did not know it was a psych facility. You can't hold me. Let me out of here. Let me out of here right now."

"You're confused," she says.

Right then I flash to every movie in which someone—reporter, ex-con—had been held in a prison or mental institution by mistake or because of some complicated revenge motive.

I resist the Reese Witherspoon, Dina Lohan, or Sam Worthington much-maligned retort: *"Don't you know who I am?"* Or *"I know Barbara Walters."* Or *"I'll tell Josh Mankiewicz at* Dateline.*"* Crap, Barbara's dead.

"You can't do this to me," I finally say.

"You've taken liberties that weren't necessarily okay. I'm not letting you out."

I'm starting to sweat. For real. Is this really happening?

"You better let me out," I say. "This is very unkind of you."

She purses her interlocked lips. "It was very sneaky."

I protest. "It wasn't sneaky. I asked Carl. How would I know? How would I know if he said fine?"

"We've called the sheriff."

Oh, this is just perfect. I'm getting arrested.

A woman in a mask joins the group. She's obviously a visitor. She wants out of there too.

Another employee arrives. Dressed better, so a manager, I imagine.

"This gentleman is having an issue," she says. "We're waiting on the sheriff's department."

"I want to leave," I say.

I take in the visitor's anxious eyes above her mask. Instead of seeing solidarity, I see alarm. She thinks I'm a resident or inmate or whatever they call them here.

I lean into it anyway. "Let us out! You're holding us prisoner."

Someone from the psych ward flash mob takes her away.

To freedom!

The manager revisits what happened and tells me the same thing Ratched did, but this woman seems more reasonable.

"I'd like to leave now," I say.

The door's lock finally clicks and I reach for the handle.

Ratched, who hates being upstaged, says the sheriff will arrive any minute.

I don't care. I won't be sticking around.

My heart is pumping pretty good by now.

I slip behind the wheel and take a deep breath, thankful that I'm not doped up in a shitty TV room drooling on a granny-square afghan watching *Bassmaster* reruns and trying to remember who I am.

I turn on the ignition and get the hell away from there.

What I don't know is my day is about to get ten times worse.

Make that a hundred.

CHAPTER THIRTY-SEVEN

The women at the front desk of the Millersburg Holiday Inn Express warn me that driving can be treacherous when it snows here, even as the plows and deicers have lined up in an endless parade and would give the powers that be in Washington State a lesson on how to deal with the white stuff. At home, every flake is a potential Snowpocalypse or Snowmageddon.

Here they call it Wednesday.

I drive under the speed limit and stay far back behind any cars as I wind my way to Des Dutch Essenhaus in Shreve to meet Levi Swartzentruber for brunch. This is where I'm not exactly going to put the screws to him, but I am going to ask him the hard questions that I've never had the guts to.

The snow-coated cornstalks look just like the evidence photos taken by the Nebraska State Patrol when they canvassed the crime scene where Danny Stutzman's body was found by a truck stop owner on Christmas Eve 1985.

Chuck Kleveland left his house in Chester that morning headed for the barbershop. Those plans weren't kept, of course. And no Christmas Eve would ever be the same for Chuck and the rest of the people of

Thayer County. That's because Chuck finds the body of a little boy wearing a Carter's blue blanket sleeper in a cornfield. His name wouldn't be known for nearly two years, but the world would be drawn into the mystery in ways that can happen only because of the clear and haunting juxtaposition of good and evil. A little boy taken in by a loving and grieving community, against the father who left his son there, a heartless Amishman named Eli Stutzman.

The snow falling along the roadway is silent. I think about Eli's story of the night he left his son's body. How he said that he'd put him where God could find him. He said he'd prayed for hours, trying to get an answer from God as to why this had happened. He said the light of a full moon illuminated Danny and the pale-blue sleeper as he covered him with snow.

Had Danny been alive? Had he called for help while his dad suffocated him? Did Danny die there near Chester, or had it been somewhere else?

So many things will never be known. That's really the bitter truth of true crime writing. We can never know for sure what truly happened. Not all of it. Sure, forensic science and witness statements can give us an excellent idea of what transpired, but that's only part of the *how*. Not the *why*. Not the reasoning behind the act. Forensics can't tell what the perpetrator was thinking as he or she took someone's life.

Had there been a struggle?

Had it been for money?

Another party pushing buttons to make it happen?

We don't get to know.

Not ever.

Even if Eli had been charged with the murder of his son, and a trial ensued, we'd never know for sure. That's because while they are billed as a search for the truth, trials are really a story with both sides narrating what they want the jury to believe. Crime writers mostly align with one side or another—usually with the prosecution. Some storytellers choose the middle space that selects facts that offer a more nuanced portrayal of a crime. A few of my colleagues speak with absolute conviction that they know what really happened in the cases they've written about. Podcasters too. I think that's totally fine. For them. And I confess, I've tried, especially on a TV show where a sound bite is more important than nuance. My truth is I don't have all the answers. And for those who think they do, why are there so many unsolved murders? You would think there would be a profiler's app and mysteries could be solved with a single click. The databases are there, right? Unless someone confesses or is caught on video, killers are not so easy to find.

With the exception of Glen Pritchett's murder, we don't know what happened to those who died along the trail of death that followed Eli Stutzman.

I think about all of this because as it turns out, I have a lot of time to think. Levi is a no-show. I try calling him. I ask Robbin to reach out to him. No luck. I buy a cup of coffee, and Des Dutch Essenhaus's owner, who has been very friendly, gives me a gargantuan cinnamon roll.

I put it on the passenger seat and it taunts me the whole slow, careful way back to Millersburg.

I never get to sample it.

Not a single bite.

It happens in slow motion. Everyone says that when they get into an accident. It's pretty much true. Especially in my case, because I swear to God, and my insurance company, I was crawling down the hill to the Holiday Inn Express in Millersburg. Seriously, barely moving. When I lose control on a nasty sheet of ice, I do what I was taught to do. I turn my wheels in the trajectory of the car as it slides.

It keeps going.

I realize I'm on the edge of an embankment that drops about a hundred feet to a parking lot below.

I try to turn, but it's no use.

And now I'm going faster.

A tree comes out of nowhere and all of a sudden, the airbags explode. Really. Explode. I sit there frozen, breathing in a toxic fume that I doubt the EPA would approve if anyone there had to breathe it. I just sit. It takes me a minute to accept this outcome and try to find a way out of the storm cloud–filled Jeep. The driver's side is crushed. I notice for the first time that the windshield is shattered too. And that tree? The front end of the Jeep has mounted it like a stallion.

I crawl out onto the snow through the passenger side.

As I do, my knee crushes that amazing, never-to-be-enjoyed cinnamon roll.

I call 911. The police come. I call Claudia. A tow truck comes. I call Robbin. I try to call the rental car company. I stand outside, my bald head dusted with snow, and replay what everyone says when I tell them what happened.

"It could have been so much worse."

I don't see how. I'm trying to solve a crime. I'm in the middle of Amish Country and I have no car. I don't know what I'm going to do. I'm going to miss my interviews.

Claudia texts me: Robbin is on the way.

I want to say no, but honestly, after making a dozen calls, I find out that there are no rental cars anywhere except the airports. I can't even get a cab to take me to the airport, though I'm told I can get a shuttle the following afternoon.

I text back: OK. Thank you.

A few minutes later, a Millersburg Police Department cruiser arrives, and a young, shorter version of no-nonsense Marge Gunderson of *Fargo* comes to the rescue.

She's bundled up in appropriate snowy-weather attire. Head to toe.

"Hit a patch of ice, did you?"

"You betcha," I almost say.

CHAPTER
THIRTY-EIGHT

The next morning, I find Robbin in the lobby of the Holiday Inn. She's got her laptop open and a stack of cards next to a coffee cup and her slightly crushed pack of Natural American Spirit cigarettes.

"Hey, boss," she says, "got here at two. Slicker than snot out there. Almost hit a deer coming from Columbus."

First of all, I used to cringe when Robbin called me "boss," but now I just go with it.

"You're a lifesaver."

"That's what I'm here for," she says, clacking away at her keyboard, drinking coffee, and smiling at the same time.

Are you for real? I think.

I get her caught up on who's on deck for the day and she's already heading for the door. I'm so glad she's there. Every muscle in my body aches.

"I brought some muscle relaxers," she says.

Mind reader, that woman.

First up is Stanley Smythe, a buddy of Jim Frost's from the early days. Stanley cut his teeth as a reporter at the Wooster *Daily Record*, where he covered the news with the kind of evenhanded, unbiased touch that has gone by the wayside. A compact man with dark-framed glasses and a crisp blue shirt, he'd been made by someone—I don't know who—to be the mostly confidential spokesperson for the gay community at the time of the barn fire.

Now retired, Stanley lives in a dusty-rose Victorian with cranberry-colored trim in Orrville, the home of jams-and-jellies-giant Smucker's. His place is partially shrouded by a huge magnolia. That's just fine with Stanley. Keeping up a century-old structure is more than a ton of work, he says.

"Seemed like a good idea at the time, right?" I tease when we talk.

He laughs. "Like a lot of things back then."

I'm unsure if that's a loaded response or just a friendly comment.

I ask how he's been.

"I've gotten so fat," he says, again with a laugh. "Huge. And I take care of a bunch of feral cats that, well, really shouldn't be feral. I feed them every night around seven. So, there you go. I'm fat and I have a bunch of cats!"

The very first time I came to Wayne County, descriptions of what was transpiring at the Stutzman farm before and after the fire were given mostly in the form of gossip and innuendo. Eli's English neighbors told me that they saw a bunch of guys come and go but had "no idea" what was really happening until after Eli and Danny left town. That's when Norma Moser got the shock of her life. A copy of *Stars* magazine, an analog precursor to Grindr, showed up in her mailbox by mistake.

Eli Stutzman had advertised in the meetup section with a photo now commonly called a "dick pic."

Stanley insists he'd never been a visitor at the Stutzman farm. He wasn't out at that time, so he did his meetups in the clubs in Cleveland and Akron. Never in town. Even so, he'd heard what was going on and had a good idea why it was happening.

"See, that was a fringe group," he says of Stutzman's barn party attendees. "I guess they got together in the barn and had—I don't know whether they drank or what—you know, anonymous sex or whatever.

And I never was in that scene. But I'm sure, you know, being out there in the hinterlands, you know, the farmers, the Amish, and the more closeted people probably found this to be acceptable. While I think the parties were sex-oriented, I don't think they were full-blown orgies."

Among those attendees were at least three men in law enforcement—two deputies and the sheriff.

Older. The world's changed. Fat. Has cats. Hard to say just for sure why Stanley is loosening up a little and shares things that I wish I'd known the first time I visited him in the late eighties.

He drops a bombshell.

Then, wait for it, another.

Stanley says he and Frost had an affair. Jim was a catch back then, he says. Handsome. Very smart. Dedicated to doing the best he could as the chief law enforcement officer for the county. He and Stanley were together briefly, and the parting of the ways was amicable. They remained friends over the years.

A short time after the Stutzman fire, Jim had shared with Stanley what actually had taken place there.

"Jim told me that what happened was Stutzman was feeling very trapped. He was gay, right? He was in a marriage that he didn't want to be in. He already had one child and Ida was pregnant."

I'm shocked. Really, I am. I don't let on, though. I don't think Stanley knows the importance of what he's saying.

"Jim Frost said this?"

"Right," he confirms. "Jim couldn't prove it. He wanted so desperately to prove it. But he could not or did not. And whether it's in the files, I don't know."

It isn't.

Stanley presses onward, sharing Jim Frost's take on Eli's motive.

"He did not want another child because he wanted out of the situation he was in. Eli hit her in the head with a rock. Knocked her out and then locked the barn and set it on fire."

"Jim Frost actually said this?"

"Yeah."

Robbin's waiting in the car. She's talked to Stanley a dozen times on the phone over the past few months. I had her drop me off because I hoped that one-on-one would yield better results. That's no dig against her. She's a total pro. Sometimes I almost burst out laughing when I play her preliminary interviews.

One she did with Tim Blosser was priceless. Because he loves dogs so much and has so many, she told him that she was sending him some dog food. She waited for him to call and thank her after delivery, but no call came.

"Mr. Blosser," she said, "did you get my package?"

"Package?"

"Yeah. I sent some dog food."

"No package."

"It arrived four days ago."

Blosser doesn't speak for a minute.

"Oh, that was dog food? I thought it might be a bomb, so I didn't open it."

"Not a bomb. Dog food."

"Thank you. I'll open it now."

Click.

Another time, when Blosser was weaving a tale about the unknown truth behind the Kennedy assassination, she tried to steer him back to the Stutzman story.

"That assassination stuff is fascinating, but let's focus on Eli and Ida. I want to learn everything I can from you, sir. You are so brilliant and have such a great mind. I want to be your student."

She was channeling Starling's encounter with Lecter.

I loved it.

CHAPTER THIRTY-NINE

The Harris County medical examiner's autopsy report on Jim Frost pings in my mailbox while Robbin drives us to our next interview.

I could grow to like the chauffeur thing I've got going. Except for the fact that I totaled a car, being driven around is kind of sweet.

This Harris County document dump contains five attachments. I wonder if any of the photos are of Frost's body. Autopsy images are right up there with crime scene photos, though far more invasive. Sure, the body is all cleaned up, head on a riser, supine, and serene. Well, dead. A generous Y incision from shoulders to sternum marks the entry point as organs are analyzed, cross-sectioned, and weighed.

A thoughtful examiner will place organs back close to where they had been plucked. A lazy or exceptionally busy one will treat the cavity like stuffing a Thanksgiving turkey.

In the case of 98-2278, conducted on August 19, 1998, the cause of death was listed as a perforating gunshot wound of the head. Manner of death: suicide.

And, thankfully, no photos.

The external exam noted that the body was that of an adult Caucasian male measuring seventy-two inches, weighing 190 pounds, and whose appearance could not be correlated with his stated age of fifty-four years due to moderate decomposition. Rigor was gone. Lividity could not be assessed.

Decomposition changes were moderate in the form of early mummification of the fingers, skin slippage, marbling, and bloating. Maggot infestation was recorded on various parts of the body and in different stages of maturation. The left eye had a cloudy cornea, brown iris, and a round, dilated pupil at 0.4 centimeters. The nasal bone was fractured. Additionally, the examiner noted a short mustache and goatee and straight brown hair, approximately two and a half inches in length. No identifying marks or scars.

Only a single piece of personal property was noted: a cross that hung about his neck with a leather string.

I make a mental note to find out if Frost was Catholic.

Next, the examiner focused on the gunshot wound.

The entrance was in the right temple with an exit on the left side of the head behind the left ear. The projectile passed through the skin musculature and related soft tissue in the right side of the head, transected the brain, and produced radiating fractures through the middle cranial fossa and the frontal bone.

There were three pathological findings at the conclusion of the report: one, a perforating gunshot wound of the head; two, moderate decomposition; and three, ethanol intoxication.

The gunshot injury was drawn in pencil in one of those line drawings that make every dead man look like a shrunken version of the Rock. The examiner added a few scribbles to indicate a goatee.

Another attachment is a handwritten report from the officer on the scene. Apartment manager Helen Graham said Frost was a loner and had no friends nor next of kin to her knowledge. No one had seen him since Friday, August 7.

The ambient temperature inside was seventy-two degrees.

> *Frost was an employee of the Marriott Hotel's Loss Prevention Department but had been fired the previous month for ethanol abuse. The reporting officer spoke with the employer and learned that the dead man's extended drinking binges forced his termination.*
>
> *No sign of foul play was found in the unkempt apartment. There were 75 to 100 empty beer cans throughout the residence. There were numerous books, magazines, and materials of a gay nature throughout the house and the manager Graham said the deceased was homosexual.*

Frost's mother was his emergency contact and she'd been notified, likely the worst call she'd ever received.

The irony of the thoroughness of Frost's autopsy is not lost on me. It was a stark contrast to the one Dr. Questel performed on Ida Stutzman in 1977. Frost and Ida were both from groups of people that had been given short shrift by law enforcement and by society in general. In the seventies, gay people were mocked, derided, and even ignored by law enforcement until cases such as Matthew Shepard's murder two months after Frost's suicide accelerated a change in attitudes that had been slow in coming.

Frost was gay, but he was given a thorough exam.

Ida was Amish, and she simply wasn't.

All of this makes my blood boil, because even now, I hear things that I know are not completely true. *The Amish want to handle things themselves. They are secretive. They don't like outsiders meddling.*

Those are the lies people say to themselves when they decide to look the other way.

As for Jim Frost, who once commanded a place on the front pages of several papers, no obituary was published to acknowledge the former Wayne County sheriff's death. Just a dozen words in the *Akron Beacon Journal* noted his passing, buried in the free listings, on August 19, 1998.

CHAPTER FORTY

Neither Robbin nor I can find a single person to talk to about Jim Frost's life after he left Ohio for Florida. A row of big fat zeros. Nothing other than what can be found by way of police records and court filings.

His life in Texas is even sketchier.

So, while his life in Ohio is revealed in bold brushstrokes, and in color, by detractors and admirers alike, his final years become more of a tragic and devastating connect-the-dots.

No one I interviewed over the years attended his memorial service in Orrville or even knew for sure if one had been held. Most would have gone out of respect for the man and the office he once held, not because they truly mourned him. Additionally, no one knew where his remains had been interred. Truth be told, not a single person was exactly sure where he'd died. Some thought he'd even been in Wooster when it happened.

By Stutzman redux, Frost's parents were dead, his first wife didn't return calls or answer a letter I overnighted to her asking for an interview, and finally his only son ghosted me after a short phone call with Robbin. I get it. I was opening up an old wound long after it should have faded to an imperceptible scar.

A public document request to the Houston Police Department brings back a single page of information—with a surprising notation that my request on the investigation into his death is denied, because the case is still open.

WTF?

I sic Robbin on the records folks, and she runs out her phone's battery leaving messages and taps out a half dozen or more emails. She reports her frustration almost daily.

"Those idiots are stonewalling," she says.

"Or they're just idiots."

A few weeks later, the records department gets back to us and says they'll release the documents.

And when they finally do, not only do I get the investigative reports, I also get the name of the Houston homicide investigator who'd been to the scene. One click and his phone number is right there too.

Larry Baimbridge exhales into the phone as he takes himself back to a particularly hot August in Houston some twenty-four years ago. In fact, the whole summer of 1998 was a stinker of the highest order, the kind where the muggy air rehydrates and resuscitates roadkill and keeps it from peeling away from the highway.

Every homicide cop knows the distinct odor of death, be it from roadkill or human being.

"I had so many decomposed bodies in a row that summer," Baimbridge says. "It was like, you know, you might get one every few months and they're never fun. And they always saturate your clothes, and you have to come home and change outside before you walk into the house."

Those who have never taken in a whiff of that peculiar stink always ask what decomp actually smells like. Larry concedes it's a tough one to pin down. Rotting meat? A little bit. Decomp practitioner Jeffrey

Dahmer blamed the stink fest emanating from his Milwaukee apartment on meat that had spoiled due to a malfunctioning freezer.

Nice try, but not quite.

"There's a certain pungency to it," Larry says. "I won't say it's a sweetness, but it's along those lines, nauseating. You know, decomposing human flesh is different than any other, maybe because of what we eat or the chemicals that we ingest."

I've never smelled a decomposing human body. When I was a fifth grader at Camp Sealth on Vashon Island, however, I found a rotting seal pup on the beach. I made the rookie mistake of getting too close. Just to see, of course. Not to poke it. I smelled it then, and as Larry said, it wafted a disgusting and cloying sweetness into my nose. It had staying power too. It was like the odor Velcroed itself to me for the remainder of camp.

I can imagine it right now.

As he continues, I'm convinced Larry is no wuss when it comes to doing his job. He says department-issued respirators frequently clogged, and since this was going to be his profession, his life, he opted to ditch his.

"So, I took it off, took a deep breath, and said, 'I'm not going to let it bother me.' And I didn't. After that, I could do it. No problem."

The call that brought Larry and a partner to 850 Briarwillow #253 in Greenspoint came from Helen Graham, the manager for the Briarwillow Crossing Apartments. She said a tenant that had been late on rent had not been seen for more than a week. That prompted her to enter the unit with a maintenance man, where they found the tenant dead.

That area, known by cops and those with necessary-for-coping dark humor as Gunspoint, was not the best part of the city. It was poorer by half in terms of the average income in other Houston areas. It was rife with crime, most infamously the unsolved 1991 kidnapping and murder of Harris County sheriff's deputy Roxyann Allee, thirty-four. The mother of two was abducted in the parking lot at Greenspoint Mall.

Her torched van was found a few hours later not far from the mall, her bullet-riddled body later in another location. Larry started working as a crime scene investigator in the area the following year. He knew the Allee case. Every Houston cop did.

If I know anything about law enforcement, they still do.

Referring to his handwritten notes, Larry walks me through the scene of Frost's death.

First, the eviction notice clipped by the door, a kind of surrender or warning flag. Next, Larry caught a trace of the insidious and familiar odor as it wormed its way through the weather stripping.

He made a note that there was no sign of forced entry. He twisted the knob on the unlocked door.

That smell.

After parting the curtain of stink in the entryway, Larry found Jim Frost, his gun still in his hand. Decomp well underway. A week was about right, he thought at the time.

"He was lying on a couch up against the wall," he says. "I know his head was to the north, feet to the south, across at the ankles. Which, you know, that doesn't sound like much, but when you're talking suicide or murder, it matters. Unless they're asleep, they're not going to have their legs crossed like that. It indicated that he had decided he was going to kill himself and lay down on the couch and popped himself in the head. Temple press by the right hand."

Larry reviews his notes.

"Red shirt, baggy pants with, I guess, with tennis shoes . . . gold watch on the left wrist, and I also know that he had beer cans all over."

He takes another beat. "Did I note that there was bloody puke in the sink?"

I look at the report. "You did."

"Okay. So that tells me that he probably had some serious alcoholism or something like a very bad ulcer. Just speculating. But usually if you see bloody feces, which I've seen a few times, where basically their intestines just kind of rupture from the heavy drinking and they just start either puking out or crapping out blood. I mean, it's really nasty. I don't know, maybe he realized his time is short. That's why he decided to kill himself."

Larry mentions a 35-millimeter roll of film and goes on to say that back in the day, film was expensive, especially Polaroids. Digital cameras were years away.

"Where are the pictures?"

He says the film was never developed.

"It was a suicide. No need to do anything more. Unless there's something really suspicious or, you know, the family inquires. This one was pretty clear cut. No sign of forced entry. He's got the gun in his hand. There's nothing whatsoever to indicate there was anything further. He was just a guy who lived alone and, you know, killed himself. So, we weren't spending more energy on it."

And the undeveloped film?

He says it went to the photo lab.

"I have no doubt there's some film of the scene somewhere. When I go in tomorrow, I'll contact the lab and see if they still have them."

Larry's email with the photos arrives. I have seen lots of grisly crime photos, and I won't lie and say that nothing bothers me. That I'm some super tough guy who can eat a bowl of spaghetti while flipping through pictures of someone's disemboweled body.

I swallow and hold my breath as I download the images. I have thought a lot about Jim Frost over the years. He's remained a bit of an enigma, a person I couldn't quite figure out. Naturally I sought him out when I wrote *Abandoned Prayers*. I'd left messages for him at a Cleveland hotel where I'd heard he was working security at the time. When I look back now, there was another reason why I didn't try a little harder. I had heard he was unstable and an alcoholic. I didn't want to push him over the edge.

I click on the file, and it opens.

The first photo shows the entrance to a ground-floor apartment wrapped in a brick façade and accented with Kelly-green trim. Very nineties. That one is followed by a close-up of the doorway, and a third features the doorframe with the eviction notice secured in place by a notebook binder clamp.

With the next photograph, I am inside the apartment. The door is open to reveal a trash-strewn carpeted entry with overflowing garbage bags turned on their sides as though the occupant had just given up on making any effort to conceal the chaos that was most certainly inside.

And the smell. The hot air of the sticky, stinky August that Larry described makes me hold my breath. It wasn't Smell-O-Vision or a virtual scratch and sniff, but my nose and brain reacting to what I was processing. As if the viewer needed a reprieve before the main event, the shutter blinked on the lock mechanisms of the front door to show that there had been no tampering.

Whatever had occurred inside Jim Frost's ground-floor apartment had been, almost certainly, a solo endeavor.

The seventh photo is a wide shot of a body clad in red and black on the couch with a mountain of silver Bud Light cans all around him. Probably hundreds of them. Part of me wants to count them, but I'm distracted by the banality of the scene. An artificial ficus tree, some yellow silk roses, and a blue-gray couch trimmed with oak. Claudia and I had an apartment like this when we were in college in 1980.

But this was 1998 and Jim Frost was in his fifties.

The next photo is an even wider angle of the same shot with a small computer desk, stereo system with a stack of CDs, and the body on the couch. It captures the top of the deceased's head and a gold watch on his left wrist, resting on his stomach. He wore a pair of jogging pants and white leather tennis shoes. Grocery World bags scattered about touted it as the home "For new everyday low prices."

It passes through my mind that if Jim Frost had been looking for any low prices, it would only be for beer, and only for Bud Light.

The next photo provides a visual narrative of his last days. He'd kind of wrapped—or maybe "trapped" is a better word—himself inside a tumbled and crumbled wall of beer cans. In a narrow passageway to and from the couch, it appeared he just tossed the cans aside, one after another.

A beer can fortress.

I think about his son. His parents. His ex-wife, even. This ending for Sheriff Frost is something no one could have imagined when he first came to the department. He was young. So sure of himself. Full of ideas. Ready to modernize a law enforcement agency that was woefully behind the times.

And it all ended here.

The next photo is a view from the living room to the tiny kitchen. Countertops buried in Bud Light cans and a sink full of dirty dishes are in marked contrast to the carpeting, where tracks from a vacuum showed he'd vacuumed recently. Had he planned on moving and just decided that there was nowhere to go? He had been fired from his job. Had he also been crushed by a broken romance? It's impossible to know, of course.

There is no note, after all.

Affixed to the front of the refrigerator I make out a schedule, a calendar of some kind. The writing is blurry. I zoom in. I darken the photo. I sharpen, but to no avail. There isn't enough detail to see what his routine had been that August.

The twelfth photo provides the real full-on view of Frost. His black pants are joggers or loungewear, emblazoned down one leg with *"Naughty By Nature O.P.P."* His ankles are crossed and his shoes are untied. The red shirt has a collar, and around his neck appears to be a necklace. His right hand is positioned on his chest, a .357-Magnum handgun still in it. A large stain of either urine or vomit discolors the carpeting next to the couch.

Welcome to Gunspoint.

The fifteenth photo on the film roll literally takes my breath away and forces me to look around to ensure no one is peering at my laptop screen.

Jim's face is a black-and-tan mask, slipping downward. His mouth leaks blood or vomit. His eyes bulge like a Black Moor goldfish. Gases? And though it is expertly focused, it is hard to discern the dead man's features. It is like the lens had been given the fading old Hollywood film star's remedy and smeared with Vaseline. The entry wound, visible on his right temple, is the scene of blowfly larvae's last stand. My eyes linger on the gun. He holds it in his hand with his thumb, not his finger, on the trigger. Kind of odd. His thumb? Who does that?

He has what appears to be a light beard or maybe a goatee. Or maybe it's just that he hadn't bothered to shave after he sequestered himself on the couch with a shopping cart—or more—of Bud Light.

Next is a close-up of paperwork sitting atop a bunch of beer cans. Though slightly crumpled, it is legible enough to read. He'd been given notice on August 4 to vacate the apartment within three days. He is $440 in arrears. He'd been living there since June 1.

I wonder where he'd been before that.

Another photograph shows that tiny kitchen. There, a SlimFast diet-shake mix and Totino's frozen-pizza boxes offer a reasonable suggestion about what Jim Frost's last meal might have been.

The microwave door is left ajar, the light still on.

There is something odd depicted in photo number twenty-five, taken in the hallway. On the right-hand side of the corridor, seven mirror tiles had fallen to the floor. Had Jim become angry? Pounded his fist against the mirrors? Or had the heat melted the adhesive?

Now the bedroom. A red shirt and khaki pants with the belt fully buckled are shown on the floor at the foot of the unmade bed. On one side of the bed is a desk, above it is a bulletin board, and on that is a color picture of a young man in a suit and tie. Who is that?

My eyes latch on to a shoebox on the bed.

What is that all about?

The photographer had zoomed in on just what I was wondering about in the next image. The box holds more than a half dozen pairs of what appear to be boys' underwear.

WTF?

One pair has a print with sneakers and pizza slices, and another is striped.

Next to the underwear is a box of .357-Magnum cartridges.

I pause over the contents in that box. The underwear and the bullets are nestled together. A shoebox. I think of how people store things in shoeboxes. Amos Gingerich put those letters about Eli in a shoebox. Claudia and I have a shoebox or two, probably more, of family photos. When my mother died, we found an old shoebox of hers with letters from my father and a bunch of her old silk scarves.

Keepsakes, all of them.

The underwear and the bullets were keepsakes.

The next in the photo series captures the side of the bed. Jim's shoes are on the floor and beer cans cover the top of the dresser; a bunch of videotapes and magazines sit atop a Reebok shoebox. Curious, I zoom in on the magazines to see what he was reading and watching on his VCR. Under the headline of "Man of the Year," actor Eric Roberts's blue eyes peer over sunglasses on the cover of *Playgirl* magazine.

The centerfold copy on a male model's shimmering torso touts his favorite place to make love: *"Under a full moon on a stretch of sand in Long Island Sound when the tide is up."*

Robbin texts me that she's scored a preliminary interview with one of Jim Frost's nephews. After getting nowhere with any member of his family, I tell her any relative is a great get.

He says that the interview will be on Zoom and he'll be recording it.

Go for it, I text back.

I remind her that whatever we've discovered is not ready for prime time. While we need to corroborate things about Frost, Eli, and others, we can't disclose what we've found.

Hey, what's the collection of underwear about?

True crime writers are gatherers first, I tell her. We look for the details that add to the framework of things that are irrefutable. After we collect and catalog information, we look for content and context from those who might know.

We want their true recollections, uncolored by what we've learned during our research.

Got it, she says.

Thankfully, no "boss" this time.

The next day, she texts an update about her Zoom with the nephew.

I started by telling him that I was doing a preliminary interview for you, and we were just trying to find out who his uncle was as a person.

Perfect, I send back.

Then it got weird. He asked if there was any "character assassination" that he should be worried about. I told him no. We simply wanted to find out what was happening in Frost's life leading up to his suicide.

I also explained that we were looking into the Stutzman case and wanted to ask him a few questions about that. He said he'd think about it and investigate your book and will get back to us by the next week.

Robbin is tough and undeterred. Like a terrier with a bone. She never lets go. She's followed up with the nephew several times.
Still waiting.

CHAPTER
FORTY-ONE

As I peel back the layers of Sheriff Frost's final years, I want to have sympathy for him. The underwear thing, however, is making that increasingly impossible. I realize it could be nothing more than a kind of fetish. Robbin sent me an ad from the *Advocate* where an Ohio man wanted to trade used underwear.

That's a far cry from pedophilia, of course.

I don't even want to go there. The idea of it makes me sick.

There is no denying it. James Frost was in a personal free fall between September 1988 and June 1989, when he was arrested at least three times in the Montrose neighborhood of Houston for driving while intoxicated. In every instance, he refused a Breathalyzer.

In the first arrest, the responding officer noted:

> *Frost was inside his vehicle, with the key in the ignition, and engine shut off, parked in the middle of the intersection of Claremont Lane and Chevy Chase Drive. The officer woke up Frost and stated that he smelled of alcohol and his eyes were bloodshot. Frost couldn't stand up and refused to take a breathalyzer.*

In the second:

Suspect was driving a blue 4-door vehicle when he was unable to maintain a single lane of traffic. His headlights were not on. Officer saw this and stopped the vehicle. Frost's pants were unzipped and unbuttoned, and he had urinated himself. He was highly intoxicated and unable to stand, walk or talk. Refused a breathalyzer.

The next was only a month later when Frost had gotten into a car accident.

The officer arrived and saw Frost leaning against the ambulance. As the officer observed Frost for a few moments, he had fallen several times. Witnesses reported seeing Frost swerve into a driveway/parking lot area. The officer stated that Frost was so intoxicated that he couldn't understand what he was saying. Frost was taken into custody.

CHAPTER
FORTY-TWO

Jake Weaver had proven himself a champion talker on the way to see Henry Hershberger.

I ask him if he'd take me out to see one of Eli's brothers. He told me last time we met that he knew where Andy and Chris Stutzman lived. Since it's late in the day, I suggest Andy's farm because he's only a few miles from our meetup spot at the Dalton Wendy's parking lot.

He fills me in on what he knows about Amish bed courtship, which is quite a lot. It's a fascinating discussion about rules and rule-breaking.

"What happens if a girl ends up pregnant?"

"The parents talk to the boy's family to see if marriage would work out or if it would be a further disaster. Sometimes the girl might have a baby that is raised as a sibling of the young mother's or there are plenty of instances when another man will accept the girl with the baby and raise him or her as his own."

"Seems pretty civil," I say.

"It usually is."

We park on the lane leading to Andy Stutzman's farm. Jake says to sit tight while he sees if he can break the ice, an appropriate metaphor given the frigid conditions of the weather. I sit in there freezing while eating the last of a bag of Cheetos for what seems like a very long time.

It's awkward. And risky. I've allowed myself to be an interloper with Jake as my guide because I know Eli's family can't be very fond of me. My first book brought them more unwanted attention than they deserved. While they had nothing to do with Eli's crimes, the whole world—and especially the Amish one—had more than a few things to say behind their backs about what he'd done.

Jake talks with an Amishman standing by the big white house on the driver's side of the car. He's too young to be Andy. The man is smiling and nodding.

I'm encouraged.

Next, Jake goes up some stairs to the front door. He's out of sight for maybe five minutes. When he returns, he gives me a look and crosses in front of the car. I'm thinking that he's going to get in, but he keeps walking. He knocks on the front door of a small red house on the passenger side. The door opens and he disappears inside.

And I wait.

And wait.

He's in there talking to someone, and I know that I'm missing out on whatever it is they are conversing about. That's the risky aspect of having a go-between.

Jake, it appears, may be too good a talker.

He comes out later and gets back into the car.

"Not going to talk."

"Crap," I say. "You were in with him a long time."

Just then a man in a wide-brimmed black hat emerges from the red house. I hold my gaze on him. It takes me right back to the courtroom in Austin and the murder trial. He looks just like his brother. Same eyes. Same build. Height. Facial features. He barely glances in our direction and goes on his way to the barn.

"That's Andy," Jake says.

No shit, I think.

"He's a ringer for his brother."

Jake agrees. "The first guy knew who Eli Stutzman was when I said Little Boy Blue. He was a relation, a cousin or something," Jake says. "He thought Andy might be interested in talking."

It turns out he wasn't.

Jake continues. "I had to introduce myself. They don't know me. I talked in German and that kind of warmed him up. It helps. You know, kind of keeping it local. The only people that speak that are Amish."

I know that, but Jake, it seems, is a marvel at filling in the gaps.

"You know, they would right away know that while you came from Amish, you're obviously not Amish anymore by the way you dress. Sometimes that's not all great, because they would think, *What happened to you? Why did you leave?*"

Note to self: *Having an ex-Amish guide might not be the best plan.*

"So sometimes they look at that as kind of a black mark a little bit on you or whatever, but it doesn't matter. I can talk my way out of that."

Good to know, I think.

"So, after the neighbor you go over to the red house here?" I say, indicating through the fogged-up window.

"Right. I knock on the door and his wife opened the door, so I had to tell her why I'm here. And I said, 'Well, do you think Andy would talk? Is he here? You think he would talk to me?' And I said, kind of like, 'This author is here from Washington State and is writing a book about Little Boy Blue.'"

Jake comes up for air. "I mean, I tried to make it sound about right. Yeah, that makes sense why we're here. She was pretty endearing. She laughed a little bit sometimes about some things."

I decide not to ask about the funny parts of the crime I'm writing about.

"It was dark in there yet and no lights on or anything," he goes on. "And then I said, 'Well, so, is Andy here? Do you think he would talk?'

And then she kind of looked around and said, 'Well, I think he's down at the shop.' I said, 'Do you think he would talk?' 'Oh, he might.' It almost seemed like Andy is a little bit of an eccentric person, a little bit, you know, like she doesn't know if he's going to talk. And so, then I said, 'Well, when we go down, I'll find out.'

"So, I just walked in and he's in a woodshop, nice and warm in there, and is working on some wood things. I said, 'Hello, hello,' you know, and he then said, 'Well, why are you here?' And you know, as I mentioned, like, 'This is a great guy that wrote that book, you know, some years ago about your brother. We're just here to try to get a little bit more information about Eli,' and like right away, he just shook his head. 'I'm not talking, and we have decided as a family not to talk.' I could tell that he wanted to be respectful to me, but he was also very adamant. And his expression was almost like, *'You won't get anything out of me.'*

"And I said, 'So, what should I tell the author?' And he said, 'Well, just tell him that I'm not interested.'"

Jake says he didn't give up.

"'Well, you have your opinions,' I said. 'I mean, you were his brother, and you obviously know how these things went. Obviously, you'd have good reasons to favor your brother. And it's not that you and your brother are favoring Eli in some way that you don't sort of want the truth. We all know kind of how it happened.'"

Andy didn't budge.

"'No, no, no. I have my opinion. I have my thoughts.'"

And that was that.

I don't know how hopeful I was for an interview with Andy. I don't know how honest anyone from Eli's family might have been to a stranger. Or particularly to me. They didn't cause Eli to do the things he did. Sure, his dad might have been completely terrible to him, but his lack of love or acceptance didn't turn his son Eli into a killer. Maybe it played a role. However, lots of people have lived through rotten child-hoods and they don't murder their wives, children, or friends.

Eli did.

I know it.

Andy probably does too. The stain of that truth is a shame that follows Eli's family wherever they go.

"None of the brothers would come into the hardware store for a long time and they never talked to anyone. Didn't want anyone to know who they were," Jake told me.

"That they were Eli's family."

"That they even knew him."

Later that night, I find myself alone in my room, going over shrink-ing numbers of index cards that guide me through the Stutzman story.

One is new. Robbin, in her typically enthusiastic fashion, says that Dan Stolfus is "a keeper." She'd found him after dialing every Stolfus in Wayne County, and when she got him on the phone, he'd promised he had a few choice things to say about Eli Stutzman.

"Not on the phone," she says. "Stuff he says he's never told a soul."

"My kind of interview," I say.

"I have a good feeling about this one, boss."

I'm not so sure. Sometimes it feels like I'm spinning my wheels. No one wants to break from the safety of their long-held silence.

No one seems to want to tell what they know.

Embarrassed? Ashamed? Involved?

One of those, I think.

Follow-ups are crucial. Stanley Smythe's disclosure about Frost telling him that he knew Eli murdered Ida but "couldn't prove it" has been consistent. I have no reason to doubt him. Even so, I reach out to someone close to him. Not a key player in the events that directly concern Eli Stutzman, but someone who knows Stanley very well.

"What he has to say is a bombshell, of sorts," I say. "Without getting into it, can you vouch for his honesty? Integrity? Can I trust him?"

The relative answers without hesitation. "He is very truthful."

"That's what I think too," I say. "He told me some things about Jim Frost."

"Whatever he told you was not a lie. He probably didn't tell you everything."

"Why not?"

"He was in love with Jim. At least he was at one time."

CHAPTER
FORTY-THREE

I'd heard of Daniel Stolfus decades ago as someone who lived with Eli Stutzman and Tim Brown in the early eighties. I knew little more about him than he was former Amish, but to be frank, his name matches hundreds of others, and I was unable to locate him back then. He was obliquely mentioned in *Abandoned Prayers*, however, as one of Eli's Amish boy renters who had taken Tim Brown's Wayne County sheriff's cruiser for a spin on the property.

Dan's house is a single-story ranch just dusted with light snow when I knock on the front door in late January. The storm door's latch is giving him fits as he struggles to open it, so he sends me in through the garage.

Dan was a seventeen-year-old Troyer Amish boy when he landed at Eli's door looking for a place to live after his mother told him that he couldn't stay at home if he owned a car, which at the time was a very big deal. Eventually he came to accept that he couldn't be Amish.

"I have nothing against the Amish," he says now at fifty-nine, while inviting me to take a seat at the dining table. He goes to the kitchen counter to pour some coffee. "It's just a lot of things are inconvenient. Seems like when you go to do things, well, you have to do everything with the horse."

Eli was working nights as an orderly at the hospital at the time he lived with Stolfus, and they had little contact since Dan worked days swinging a hammer at a pallet farm. Over the time he was there, Levi Swartzentruber, Sammy Miller, and most notably within two weeks of his arrival, sheriff's deputy Tim Brown took a room upstairs too.

Living there was mostly uneventful. Eli had some visitors now and then, English guys, mostly.

"When I look backwards, probably gay people. I didn't know anything about that. That it even existed. You know, I was raised in an Amish home, and I never knew there was such a thing as being gay."

Even when an Akron man kept coming for the weekends, ostensibly to clean house, Dan still didn't have a clue.

Eli wasn't around much so they didn't really talk, except for one memorable time.

Dan recalls an incident when Eli picked him up from work. Eli was out of sorts.

"He was upset about something and said something about someone being no good for him."

"Someone?"

"Yeah. Like someone was a bad influence on him. Not good for his soul."

Eli never said who that person was. Later, it came to Dan that it might be Levi Levi.

"I've got to know Levi, after all this happened. The only thing I remember of Levi is he could be really nice, but he was kind of like a snake too."

He tells me he's heard of Levi's confession but is reluctant to talk about what he heard.

"I don't like digging up somebody's past, you know? If he truly repented and converted to God, we're not to dig those things up. We're supposed to let that lie."

"I guess so," I say. "But doesn't it have to be a genuine repentance? I think his confession is half a truth and half a lie."

He gives me a look.

I fill in the gap I think he's searching for.

"He said he knew it was going to happen, but he couldn't stop it."

"Yeah."

"The second part is the lie, Dan."

His phone's ringtone sounds with "Amazing Grace." He talks to his wife, who had also been raised Amish, for a minute and then returns with a revelation that stuns me.

"Did I tell you on the phone that he was going to kill me?"

"Eli?"

"Yeah."

"No. Tell me now."

"You know, what happened, this is an act of God. Because there's no way that this is possible that you can be laying on your belly in bed and jump up in the air and land on your knees."

I'm not following, but I let him continue.

"I would say I went probably up in the air above two feet," he goes on, "knocked out a bit. I remember I kind of go like, you know, like I'm in the air. And when I came down, I looked over to the door. Eli was standing there with a shotgun pointed right at me. We both looked at each other in the eyes, and his gun went down. He ran down to the living room. And then I saw him go for his car, took off and left."

"I don't get it, Dan."

"The spirit of God lifted me," he says.

"A dream maybe?"

He shakes his head. "No. Real. I heard the noise of Eli opening the chamber and looked over at him."

Dan decides to demonstrate and goes into the living room with padded trim around the sharp edges of the fireplace. *Grandkids,* I think. He lies on the floor to reenact what it was that his body did that night.

"How can I jump up without using my hands? Jump up?"

"You can't," I say.

I get to the point.

"So, what happened before that?" I ask. "What makes you think Eli would want to try to hurt you, or even worse, kill you? That's the part I want to know."

Dan takes in a deep breath. "And you will hear," he says, now sitting back down at the table. "I had a hard time figuring it out, you know, because I was so naïve."

It happened a month before his eighteenth birthday.

Tim Brown and Eli Stutzman asked if Dan would like to join them at a cowboy show and auction in Cleveland. Dan liked the whole old west thing, cattle, horses, and the trappings of everything that came with it. Going up to Cleveland, the big city on Lake Erie, was cool too. The next day, a Saturday, a Mennonite man—a father of two from Sugarcreek—joined them for the drive to seedy Saint Clair Avenue in Cleveland.

With its steep pitched roof and wood-frame structure, their destination looked like Dorothy's tornado plunked it down in the middle of a row of flat-topped industrial buildings.

It didn't look like an auction place at all.

Its name didn't seem like one either: the Leather Stallion Saloon.

As Dan quickly learned, it was the city's oldest gay bar, and as it turned out, a favorite haunt of Stutzman and friends.

He was terrified.

"And I tell you what, I don't know if I ever prayed that hard in my life before or after," Dan says now. "I prayed there all night for God to protect me. I did not want to be involved in that stuff."

"What stuff?"

Dan gives his head a shake before he speaks.

"They auctioned the guys on stage. And they would hang their wang out. 'Hey, look, he's got a big wang' and stuff like that, right? And then they would auction them off for what? Sex! Yeah. If you bought somebody, they would take him home for the night."

Eli won the auction for the Mennonite man they'd brought along, and they returned to the farm. Dan says he prayed all the way home.

"That morning, Eli came up to me and asked, 'Dan, what do you think?' I said, 'Eli, that wouldn't be for me.' He was trying me."

"Of course, he was," I say. "He did that when he offered David Amstutz money for a blow job."

Dan pushes a plate of cookies toward me.

I take one and ask what happened next.

He says it was like a switch had been flipped. Eli was no longer buddy-buddy. He became cool to Dan. Icy even.

"Actually," he says, "right about then Eli said that I might have to move out."

"You were young, naïve, Amish naïve at that, but by then you knew what was going on at the farm?"

"Well, yeah, yeah, I knew. I knew."

When Dan's mother became ill, he went home and cooked supper for his family. He didn't want to be Amish, but he loved her. He and a brother got to talking about their mother's care. Dan and that brother decided that the older of the two, Dan, would move home to take care of their mother and the farm. Dan took his brother's job at a veal farm and moved into a trailer on the property.

Emotion creeps into Dan's eyes just then.

"I was thinking back," he says, "maybe if you look at this and all the people, take the whole picture, it looks like it took God's plan for Mom to get me out of there. It was a blessing."

Looking at things with the lens of experience has made Dan Stolfus rethink some of the things that happened at Eli's place.

"You know, Tim Brown was really nice to me. And, you know, I mean, just to the point where I was like, what does he really want? I was only seventeen. I just picture myself in my mind. He must have been close to thirty. One time he tackled me on the farm and was like wrestling me."

"Out of the blue?"

He nods. "Yeah, and it was too much. I told him to get off."

I ask if it was sexual.

"Exactly what I thought."

"At the time, or later?"

"At the point when it happened."

After that, Tim was no longer such a nice guy.

After the wrestling and the gay bar, things came into sharper focus.

"I remember they had a party in the barn. And, you know, Eli said, 'You cannot come to the barn, Dan. You got to stay in the house with Danny.' And so, I stayed in the house."

He stops, like he's holding something inside.

"What is it?"

He doesn't want to say.

"About Danny? Ida?"

Eli never even mentioned Ida the whole time Dan was living there. It was like she had never existed. Danny didn't say a word about his mother either.

"About Danny then?"

"Yeah, right," Dan says. "One thing I remember was one time I came down from my room and I heard him say, 'Oh, no, no, it hurts!' He was in the bedroom with Eli."

If Dan Stolfus said anything more after that disclosure, I didn't hear it.

After the interview I sit in my car in silence. Not Amish house quiet. As the defroster struggles to melt the crust of ice that formed during the interview, it gives me a moment to reconsider something that I wondered about for years.

Danny was crying and telling his father to stop doing something that was hurting him. Why were all these Amish boys ending up at the farm? What was the real reason so many of the men who lived or partied with Eli didn't want to talk?

CHAPTER
FORTY-FOUR

I'd been wanting to catch up with Levi Swartzentruber since my accident. He'd been embroiled in a drama with his daughter, but that wasn't the impetus of my call. It was the truth behind what his ex-wife, Connie, had been saying.

I mention Connie, and in that soft-spoken, lazy-voiced way, he tells me that he'd been in touch with his ex's son through Messenger, and he says that she is unwell.

"And we talked for a little bit and he's like," Levi says, "'She's got congestive heart failure' or something."

"I got the impression that she's very sick."

He's throwing her under the bus. Isn't love great? Anyway, I play along.

"Well, it may have messed up her brain, I'll tell you that."

"Yeah, I don't know," he says. "I told you about her coming after me."

"What happened?" I ask.

"She came at me and I'm like, *Man, I have no way out. Here she comes.* And I'm like, you know, *I got to stop her,* right? So, I stopped her. And, of course, there was a police report and everything on it. I just was like, I got to get the hell out of there."

"Was that like a domestic violence complaint? You didn't have to go to court, did you?"

"No, but I never pressed charges. Neither did she."

She's crazy and he's the devil. At least according to each other. I change the subject and bring up Dan Stolfus's name. I tell him about how he felt Tim Brown had tried to turn horseplay into sex play and how he didn't have a thing to do with Dan after he turned him down. How Eli made Dan stay in the house when he had parties in the barn. And finally, how he booted Dan out of the place.

"Dan felt they were kind of testing him, to see if he'd do the sexual stuff they wanted. Did they do that to you?"

Levi says they didn't, but after a moment of reflection, he recalls an incident with the man from Akron who'd come down to Dalton to be with Eli.

"They wanted me to come to his house, help them clean house. So I did. I had really nothing to do and he would pay me to help him. And I spent the night. I slept in my own bed. And I told him, I said, 'I'm just going to bed myself.' And he never really said anything then. But when he paid me, he said it could have meant a lot more. And I said, 'That's all right.'"

"Like he wanted sex?"

"Yeah. And I just lost it. And I was like, *I'm not going there again.*"

"Do you think that you were being tested? Like when he tried to give David Amstutz money for a blow job? Or when Tim Brown was wrestling with Dan Stolfus, it was to see how far he could go?"

Levi doesn't answer. I let the dead air linger.

"Do you have any feeling on that? Like, could I possibly be right? I mean, you left there, and if you left, is it because partly, *I don't want to be a part of this?*"

"That's where I got to. And Eli knew to get me out of there. And so he suggested that I go live with my uncle."

"Levi, I'm trying to find a parallel here with Dan Stolfus. Dan said after that incident with Tim and another with Eli, Eli told him it was time for him to move out: *"You're not doing what I want you to do."* Is that why you moved, why he told you to move? Because you wouldn't put out?"

He ignores the last sentence.

"I don't remember him really telling me I needed to move."

"Right. But a suggestion by the landlord is telling you to leave."

"Well, that's true. Because it didn't work out the way he wanted it to. He wanted me out."

"So basically, I'm right, aren't I? That this was his game with these young men?"

"Yeah, you're right. Like grooming."

I tell him that I'm headed into an area with poor cell service, and I will reach out later. He apologizes for the mix-up at brunch in Shreve.

"When you got in that accident," he says. "I'm like, *Oh, shit.*"

"Yeah! All your fault," I say with mock outrage. "Don't worry about it. I'm in one piece. And I would be happy to risk another accident to drive out and see you again. So don't worry. It's all right. You take care. I'll talk to you later, okay?"

CHAPTER
FORTY-FIVE

It's the right address, I think, getting out of the car. The address was on the old sheriff's report.

Robbin tells me that it looks like no one is home.

"Because there's no car?" I tease.

"Right?" she says in that strange way younger people do. Kind of an affirmative and a question at the same time.

We're there in search of the place where Eli Stutzman lived, and later, Ida joined him there after their wedding in 1975. It's also where a wife tried to keep her children and herself safe when her husband drank too much.

And, I've been told, where dying Levi Levi Hershberger finally told the truth.

"I knew it was going to happen, but I couldn't stop it."

While Robbin stays in the car, I walk through the crust of the freeze and thaw of snow past a mangled buggy waiting for someone to bring it back to life and into use. Even I can tell it is an older model. Yellow corncobs poke out like duck bills through slits between the wood of the barn walls.

No one answers my knock at the two-story white farmhouse, and I go over to another little building that could be a shop or a bunkhouse. Hard to tell. The windows are haphazardly covered with sheets and towels.

"Hello? Hello?"

No answer.

I return to the car and check the address.

It seems right. Damn GPS.

Coming all this way, for nothing. All this way and missing the element that I really need.

Someone to confirm what I've heard about Levi Levi.

We drive over to the next house, maybe a quarter mile away, just beyond a storage area for stockpiles of Scotts Miracle-Gro.

A young woman, who it turns out is Levi Levi's granddaughter, lets me inside to wait for her parents, Sevilla and Levi Hershberger. The couple is across the road using the telephone to talk with their son and others in Mexico for some kind of medical treatment. Her name is Lydiann. She's named for her grandmother, Melinda's sister.

I motion for Robbin to join me. The warm, dry air from the woodstove comes at us. Lydiann slides a couple of chairs in the kitchen to allow us to sit, but instead I ask if we can see what she's working on in the next room.

A quilt in progress is stretched over a frame. Neat white markings made of slivers of soap indicate the pattern of the needlework yet to come.

"Is someone in your family ill?" I ask. "An Amish friend of mine was down in Mexico to get treatment for cancer."

She shakes her head. "No, not that," she says. "My brother is there to get a stem cell treatment."

"Oh, like some kind of preventative measure?" I ask.

She gives me a nod.

She's a lovely young woman, in her early twenties, maybe a bit younger. I'm so used to seeing women of around her age with makeup that seeing one without reduces my ability to determine an age for her.

Amish homes are distinct in their loud silence. I notice it every time I'm inside one. The only noise is the ticking of a wall or mantel clock. No hum of a refrigerator. No background noise from a TV playing. Just complete quiet.

Above the woodstove is a drying rack mounted to the ceiling. Twenty pairs of dark socks hang downward like stalactites.

We make small talk. She's been to Florida, Minnesota, and Missouri where several of her older sisters live.

"One has five children. The oldest is five."

"Wow," I say. "That's a lot of little kids. Any twins?"

"No. One at a time."

Lydiann is in the middle of a dozen siblings herself. All were raised here in this house, which is cozy and, hopefully, much larger than it appears.

I tell her that her mom might be able to help me find out what happened to Ida Stutzman. I can see the flicker of recognition on her face.

"She knows something bad?" she asks.

"I don't know. Maybe."

She indicates she knows a little about the story from reading the book I wrote.

"I can't remember for sure who brought it up. I think maybe my sister did. Someone gave it to her."

"Did your mom tell you to throw the book away?"

"Mom said just to give it back to the person it came from because we shouldn't have it here."

"So, your grandpa Levi lived down the way from here?"

"Yeah."

"Do you remember him?"

She does, though only vaguely. He was mostly confined to a wheelchair for the nine years following his stroke. Speech was a challenge, a struggle.

"Well, some things you could understand," she says. "But a lot of things you couldn't."

I go fishing.

"Your grandmother had a hard time with Levi."

"Might be," she says.

"You know he had some problems, right?"

She nods, but it's clear she doesn't want to go there. I don't push very hard because she is sweet and maybe naïve, and I don't want to burst her bubble.

Her brother Henry comes in. He's fifteen and boy-band handsome with dark, wavy hair tumbling out from under his black hat. His face is pink from working outside on some task his dad asked him to do.

Lydiann tells him to go up to the phone and let their parents know they have a visitor.

Henry leaves right away.

I say something about how obedient he is, then ask for her sisterly assessment. "Is he nice?"

"Well, everybody's got their good," she answers.

Not everyone, I think. At least not the person I'm writing about.

When Levi and Sevilla Hershberger arrive, I introduce myself and Robbin and ask if we could visit about her father. I'd heard from others that it would be too painful for Sevilla to speak about him, but she's warm and invites us into the kitchen. It's easy to see where their children get their good looks; both parents are attractive. She has pretty eyes. He has a great smile. I am completely disarmed as we make small talk that ranges from the price of eggs to their phone call with their son and his stem cell treatment to the Pacific Northwest and so forth.

I hold back on the subject of the confession.

I ask Levi what's in the big bucket next to him.

He gives me a smile. "Oh, that's a good thing we have."

Sevilla makes a face.

He looks at her. "What? You're not sure it's any good?"

"Too hot," she says.

He opens the bucket. Inside is a mega snack mix of cereals, pretzels, and candy.

"Too hot?" he says.

Sevilla asks if I'd like to try it and I tell her I would. Levi pours a little pile on the table for himself and she fetches a little plate for me.

"So good," I tell her. "Not too spicy at all."

Levi gives his wife a look and she shifts a shoulder.

"I like it when she puts in the M&M's."

"I know," she says.

They know I'm there about Eli, or at least Little Boy Blue, but I launch into how I got there and how much I need their help. How important it is to find out the truth about what happened.

"One of the things I know now that I didn't know all those years ago was something that your father confided long after the fire."

They are listening to every word. Henry and Lydiann, both hovering behind us in the space between the kitchen and the living room, are taking it all in too.

I decide not to use the word "confessed," because it carries too much weight. It implies blame, and whether or not Levi Levi deserves that is something for someone else to decide anyway. I tell them about Dan Gingerich. I mention that I had seen her aunt Melinda and uncle Andy in West Salem.

"And one of the things that I found out now is that your father had mentioned something before he died."

If at all possible, somehow the room is even quieter than Amish quiet.

"He didn't kill Ida," I say. "It's not that, but he had knowledge that it had been a murder of her."

"Eli would have done that?" Levi asks, while Sevilla processes what I've said.

"Right. Eli did. Not Levi. Not your father."

I hate this part of the job. To sit across from decent people—who probably never did a bad thing in their lives—and ask them to pull up a memory of something that is so foreign to how they live is akin to pouring rat poison into their party mix.

Sevilla's face tightens.

"No," she says. "I never heard anything like that. I do not believe that. That is wrong."

"You don't believe that he ever said that?"

"No, I don't."

She looks upset, but not to the point of tears. Maybe just wishing I would go away.

"That was my dad," she says. "How could I say yeah, I believe that?"

"Well, he didn't do it. He didn't hurt Ida, but he knew it was a murder."

"Oh, but he didn't have anything to do with it."

"I'm only saying that he knew."

"No, no, I never heard that," she says.

And then Sevilla rocks my world.

"Dad and his hired hand were sleeping outside when they woke up and saw the flames, or the light, and they went over there."

This gives me a shot of adrenaline, but I don't show it. I ask for the name of the hired hand, but she tells me John Miller is dead.

"So they went over there? Saw the flames? Are you sure?"

"Yeah, they went there that night."

I seek clarification. "Flames, not sirens?"

"No, the light."

I think of the topography of the land north of Hackett Road toward Gerber Feed mill and the Stutzman Farm. There is a rise there, so I suppose it is possible that a glow could be seen. It seems a little fortuitous, or rather suspicious, that Levi Levi would just happen to be outside that night.

Sevilla further stuns me when she says she had seen Ida and Danny at the Stutzman farm the evening of the lightning strike.

I can scarcely believe my ears.

"The night of the fire?"

"Yes, visiting Ida."

She says that her father, mother, and John Miller, the family's hired hand, were all there.

"Did you go see where the lightning went?"

"The others went, I imagine. We stayed in the house with Ida and Danny. We loved Ida so much. Loved going to see Ida."

I'm truly dumbfounded. I think of those who happened to be there before the fire—and happened to come back during the blaze. Tim Blosser and Levi Levi? Seriously? Is it a magical coincidence?

"She was holding Danny and rocking and singing to him," she says.

"She was a good mother, a caring wife."

"Very caring, yes."

"But she married the wrong man."

"Yes," Levi answers.

"She waited for him for a long time, didn't she?"

"Yeah," Sevilla says. "I feel she fell for him."

Sevilla wants to share a memory, "an example" of who Ida was.

I watch her as she thinks a little, her eyes shifting upward. It's as though she's playing back a moment in time as she begins to narrate what she's seeing. It feels sacred. Special. Like a story she's never told anyone but me.

"She had a bonnet she wore when she got married; she probably made it new for herself. And after they were married, one day when I was there, she put it on my head and she said I could have it. She feels it's not big enough. Well, I wore it a long time, and then one time when her sister Lydia was through here, I asked her, 'Would you like to have her wedding bonnet?' She told me that Ida wanted me to have it, so I should keep it."

She gets up from the table and brings the bonnet from another room. It's beautifully made, an heirloom. I think of all the times Amos and Susie wrote to Eli asking about Ida, and later, Danny's Amish clothes. How sentimental and precious things like that were.

And how Eli said that everything was safely packed away.

Until it was all gone, of course. Until he killed Glen and left what he couldn't fit into his car.

We talk more about the night of the fire. How Ida was fully dressed and how all the lights were lit.

"All through the house they were on," she says of the lamps. "That's one thing I remember hearing all through my home life."

"So, what is that all about?" I ask.

Sevilla isn't sure, but her husband speaks up.

"She might have never been killed in the fire," he says.

"That's what I'm saying. That she was killed earlier in the evening."

"Why didn't the coroner find that?" Sevilla asks.

"That's a very good question," I tell her. "I'm going to figure that out."

"Did you make your book already?" she asks me.

"That's what I'm working on now."

Levi injects that Dr. Lehman wanted to find out what happened too.

"He was out visiting in the years later and it seemed like he was after the truth too."

"He was suspicious about Ida's death too?" I ask.

"Yeah. I think he was."

"And he came to see Levi Levi?"

Levi nods. "Yeah."

"Later, you heard Eli was doing things that he shouldn't do, that the Amish wouldn't condone. You know, like with other men?"

"Yeah," Levi answers. "Well, we were older, and I remember sometimes we heard stuff like that."

"Yeah," Sevilla says, "I guess you heard from here and there and I really didn't know what it was."

"Only after he left the Amish, or before?"

"After," she says.

Sevilla recalls seeing Eli around Christmastime after he left the community and moved out west. He came to visit the family, though he spent most of his time with her father.

"And Danny?"

Her husband answers this time. "He wasn't there. He was with his foster parents."

We all know what that really meant. Danny had been dumped in a cornfield in Nebraska.

"Looking back, what do you make of all of that?"

"It is not a great memory," Sevilla answers.

"Yeah," I say.

She shakes her head. "So, probably for a cover-up."

This couple could not have been nicer. Sevilla didn't seem like she was leading me away from any conclusion about her father. She loved him. I could think whatever I wanted. Whatever it was wouldn't change that. She probably didn't know the significance of her father being at the scene of the fire—and being there hours before the fire burned.

She'd never heard of the confession.

CHAPTER
FORTY-SIX

I'm not being a dog with a bone here, mostly because I haven't had anything on a bone since I started this trip. Robbin the rescuer and I have survived on drive-throughs and gas stations. Energy drinks have replaced coffee. Jerky is my burger; chips are my fries.

In any case, like that dog with a bone, I can't let go of the Badger story. I simply can't. Not only because of Frost's ridiculous announcement that it was solved, but because nobody seems to give a damn about the identity of a calculating killer.

Except me.

And Robbin.

"If my grandpa was offed by a psycho candy killer," she says, "I'd get to the bottom of it."

I would have said psycho CandyGrammer, but Robbin is in her thirties and has never heard of CandyGrams.

It is the early afternoon of January 24, 2023, when we drive to West Salem to ask Cliff Badger's family why they don't give a crap—though I wouldn't put it that way if we get a chance to talk. Snowfall the day before has softened the panoramic view of infinity-edged farmland, making it especially beautiful. The old white farmhouse, the scene of the crime more than a half century ago, sits at the end of a long gravel driveway.

I stay on the phone with the insurance adjuster discussing the claim process for the wrecked Jeep. Robbin heads to the front door, but no one answers. I watch as she peers through the windows, cupping her hands around her eyes to reduce the glare of the overcast skies.

Just as Robbin gives up, a woman approaches from an outbuilding with decided fierceness in her gait. I have seen this fast-stomping pace before. I try to get the adjuster off the phone. Robbin's body language is welcoming; the woman's is anything but. Their lips move, but I cannot hear what they are saying. Just then a man joins them.

I suspect he is Jerry, the grandson of Clifford Badger. Robbin shakes his hand.

Good, I think.

A minute or so goes by, and Robbin shakes the man's hand again, turns to the woman, waves, gets back into the car, and within seconds of slamming the door, I am now finally off the phone.

Before saying a word, she puts the car in reverse.

"That looked promising for a second or two."

"Right," she says. "Once I said my name, the wife acted irritated and said, 'I've already told you not to contact us. We don't know anything!' Then her husband, Jerry, walked up."

I ask what Jerry Badger is like.

"Not very personable," she says, "but he wasn't rude. I told him that we were looking at multiple other Wayne County cases that have no justice or anything being adjudicated this far from the seventies. And there's multiple other cases. And I told him his grandfather was one of them."

"What did he say?"

"Literally nothing."

"What were you thinking standing there?"

"I was nervous because they've told me not to contact them. However, I would feel that if someone was contacting me about a death in my family, and I felt it wasn't resolved and justice wasn't served, I would probably be a little more, you know, open to it at least."

"And then when you got into the car, you noticed he was doing something?"

"Right," Robbin says. "He went behind the car as he started walking down the hill back to, you know, the barn area and all of the animals, and took a picture of our license plate. I mean, so dumb because it's a rental."

Robbin takes my picture in front of the billboards as we head out of town. I keep hoping that something earth-shattering will come of my investment in outdoor advertising. So far, a few things have come my way. I need more.

At the Columbus airport for the flight home to Seattle, I tell the agent that I wrecked the car and called it in, but she says there's no record of it. She writes down my name and phone number on the back of a Target receipt.

"I have a bad feeling about all of this," I tell Robbin as we cram ourselves into the shuttle from Rentals to Departures.

"Badger? Stutzman?"

"No, Hertz."

We laugh. I'm tired. Robbin needs a smoke. I need a drink. By now my assistant is in this as deep as I am. We both want answers. I like having someone on my side.

PART THREE

Winter 2023

CHAPTER
FORTY-SEVEN

My billboards continue to yield tips, and I'm more than grateful that other advertisers' interest in promoting something in Amish Country has been soft—three of five are still up several weeks after the campaign expired. That, it turns out, is a very good thing.

An email to JusticeForIda.com was from one of the firefighters at the barn fire. He wants to stay anonymous and says, with convincing assurance, that back in July 1977, no one was suspicious of Eli.

I appreciate that. This is not one of those people who reassess a memory like so many do when learning the horrible truth about someone or something.

He says now, however, that after the Little Boy Blue story broke, most of those who were there hold deep regret over how things were handled.

> We should have investigated or done an autopsy, but at the time we didn't know who Eli was. No one did. You know, that was no one's fault. Over the years, amongst friends or other people that knew Eli or Questel or Frost, [they] said they wished they could go back and do something different.

Another man, John Steiner, also sends a tip about the night of the fire. He writes that he was the first person on the scene.

I call him the moment I get the chance.

John says he doesn't have much to offer, but he was indeed the first one at the scene—before the fire trucks arrived.

He had graduated from high school the year before and had worked for Harley Gerber the previous summer, so he was familiar with the area. It was around midnight on July 11, when working at another job, that he completed a run hauling a steel silo to a farm site and was returning home.

"And on my way back towards Kidron, I saw a glow in the eastern sky there. And the closer I got the bigger the glow got. And anyway, as I came into Kettering, the volunteer fire department were just starting to arrive. And so I thought, 'Oh, my goodness, nobody's there.' I realized what was going on, and it was Eli's barn, and I knew the fire trucks were coming. I parked out of the way and ran down there. There was another man down there. It was dark, except for the glow of the fire. It was just silhouettes, basically. And I'll never forget his words. He said, 'Call the ambulance. We've got a dead one here.'"

"I said, 'Well, Kidron's on the way.' He said, 'Do they have an ambulance?' 'I don't know.' He says, 'Well, go get one.'"

John ran back to his truck, took off, and just before Route 30, the first fire truck was coming across. He flagged it down, telling the driver to get an ambulance over there. He was just eighteen and pretty rattled by what he'd seen, so he went home.

That Saturday, John and his future wife walked around the remnants of the barn, and the tiled walls of the milk house were all that remained. Metal farm equipment and other odds and ends got so hot, they dripped and buckled into sagging forms, unrecognizable as to what they'd been.

He heard things about Eli afterward, and of course found out even more when he read my book.

"Did you ever have any thoughts on the cause of the fire?" I ask.

"I remember questioning a little the lightning thing because it isn't like there were any lightning strikes. I'm not going to say there wasn't any sheet lightning or anything or whatever you want to call it. But as far as lightning strikes, that had caught me off guard a little bit. It seemed to me that would have registered with me, you know, if it was lightning sufficient to have a strike that's going to support a fire."

The next day, I get another message from the Justice for Ida site. This time it is from a woman named Jamie Smoot.

> *My family knew Eli while he was Amish as well as after he left. It is rumored that on the day of the fire Ida caught Eli in bed with a law enforcement officer. It is rumored that he was involved with multiple officers, at least one is still active duty today. It is rumored that Frost helped Eli cover up the murder of Ida.*

When I call, Jamie answers right away and says without hesitation she will go on record. Now forty, Jamie found out about her family's connection to Eli Stutzman when she found *Abandoned Prayers* at a yard sale more than a dozen years ago. Her father had been Amish, and in fact, Eli had been his teacher at Cherry Ridge. Jamie's uncle is married to one of Eli's sisters.

"I was talking to some family members that knew him. On the day of the fire Ida caught Eli in bed with a police officer. He was involved with multiple officers."

"Right, I've heard that rumor. Tell me more?"

"Okay," Jamie says, "some family members were at a Christmas party, and they ran out of beer and Eli had instructed them to go to a house nearby to retrieve more alcohol. And upon entering they realized very quickly that this was the home of some cops. And then after going further into the home, they realized that these two cops were gay. And that really stuck out to them. Two gay police officers lived in this home and Eli was very close with them. He was involved with multiple officers on a sexual level."

I ask if she knows any more, but Jamie says her parents stayed away from Stutzman after that.

"My mother always got weird vibes from him at the parties that they would attend, and sometimes he would be there and sometimes not. But she said that he always made her very uncomfortable. She made her dad promise that he would never, like, leave her alone with him."

I ask if she knows the address of where the police officers lived.

"It was near the corner of Apple Creek Road and Old 30," she says.

Later I send some texts and emails to Jamie to get a better read on the location or address.

I'm still waiting.

A few days later another email tip arrives:

> *I am sure that Levi killed her. I think the sheriff office didn't investigate thoroughly. Those creepy Amish know and won't tell. Levi hit her in the head rendering her unconscious and started the fire. I really believe that is probably what happened. Good luck on your investigation.*

All right. This is a tipster I really want to talk to. I try multiple times emailing her. No dice. I never hear back.

I'm wondering if I really got my $5,000 worth from those billboards.

An anonymous letter writer from Cleveland does little to dispel that notion.

I suggest that you trace back the genealogy to Europe. The Amish came over to America to escape persecution. Check out the story of Behalt! This energy is still being played out today as you are well aware. Many just want to help but cannot due to restrictions imposed. Keep going. There may be a reason the Amish are so isolated. Can you free them?

I check out Behalt, and it turns out it is a mural of Amish history at the cultural center in Berlin. As for the Amish, I'm unsure if I can actually free them.

Around the same time, ever-ready Robbin leaves a voice mail and I press play. I roll my eyes at her cheerful "Hey, boss!" salutation and listen as she bulldozes through content gleaned from a preliminary interview with Travis Hutchinson, Wayne County sheriff for more than a decade.

"Just got off the phone with the sheriff. He deeply respected Frost and when he was a young deputy, he did odd jobs for him like washing his car . . ."

That white Corvette, I think.

"Frost gave him an opportunity when no one else would. Oh, Frost threw him a surprise birthday party at his house and invited all the deputies. I asked how he felt about Frost's death, and he stated that it was sad as he really liked him. He'd be more than willing to sit down with you and discuss Frost and Ida's case the next time you are in Ohio."

CHAPTER
FORTY-EIGHT

Eli never confessed to anything or anyone. Just made up lies or excuses. When he talked about Danny and the night he covered him in snow, it was an act of love and faith. He was leaving his son where "God could find him." He said he was afraid. Confused. With Ida, it was a bad heart. With Glen, he'd said he was headed on a bus back to Montana.

Being a naïve Amishman was a great cover.

I know I owe Dan Gingerich some kind of an update call. He's not expecting one, I'm sure. He gave me access to the letters. It was like blowing on a dandelion, I think. Sending me on my way with a wish that I'd find out everything he and I both needed to know.

I'm not there yet. I know it.

I return to the letters and pick through those sent after Eli had enough of Ohio and moved west. The distance from Ida's family emboldens him; each word is a brick in the foundation of lies he created after Ida died:

> Yes, it is true that I sold the farm. The deal finally went
> through two weeks ago. I had some trouble with the deed
> earlier. I have not bought another farm yet as I intend

to. I'm looking for a farm in another area where the land
is not as high.

No, I do not feel I was misused for the reason I left
the church, much more God's will and I'm sorry if you
feel that way.

A month later, he writes about Danny's upcoming birthday and
how much the boy is enjoying school in Colorado.

On a piece of legal-ruled paper, Danny writes:

I am fine I like Colorado I like school I have a girlfriend
Samantha I like to go skiing better than I like sledding.

A year after that, Eli writes the Gingeriches, this time from Texas,
where he and Danny had moved.

We rented out the ranch in Colorado and rented a house
here with two acres. Danny likes school better here than
in Colorado.

He encloses a page from a coloring book with a spotted dog that
Danny put his name on.

A year after that, on August 26, 1984, Eli says that Danny is starting school the next day. He says that he had been hired by the university
and will start working there in a few weeks.

In a letter to Amos and Lizzie, dated September 8, 1985, Eli says
he's back in the Four Corners area.

I arrived here safe and sound a week ago Friday after a
2-month vacation to Utah, Wyoming, Kansas, Illinois,
Indiana, Ohio and Pennsylvania. We moved back here
on June 15th but can't get back in the ranch in Colorado

until January because of the rental contract on the ranch. Danny spent July and August in a summer children's camp with some friends of ours in Wyoming. He chose to go to this camp instead of traveling. Danny said he enjoys school here more than in Texas. School started September 3rd. He is getting tall [and] hard to keep in clothes. He had his 9th birthday yesterday.

This is a letter dated November 2, 1985, purportedly written by Danny:

How are you? Dad and I are fine. The weather here is not very cold. I like school. I play soccer in school. My team won second place. I got my report card this week. I got good grades. I'm in 3rd grade.

I determined during my investigation back in 1989 that many of these letters were fakes. What kind of grotesque monster, father, human being forges a son's letter to his grandparents? What kind of a father sends his son to live with people he doesn't really know? I'd never talked with Cary or Relta Cox. I didn't want to bother them. I'd learned from Thayer County sheriff Gary Young, who ran the Little Boy Blue investigation from his office in Hebron, Nebraska, that Cary Cox and Eli Stutzman had been lovers.

"They met at a chicken show in Albuquerque," Gary told me.

Twenty years ago or so, I'd exchanged emails with one of the Coxes' daughters. She indicated she'd had something she wanted to tell me, but after multiple attempts and some back-and-forth emails, she never did.

With her mother now deceased and her father living in Kansas, I reached out again.

She seemed like she wanted to help, but once more turned me down. She didn't want to have her father turn against her. I'm thinking now that when she first contacted me a couple of decades ago, she'd likely been a teenager. She wanted to say something, and at that time in her life, she didn't care what the ramifications of disclosure would be.

Now she does.

Conventional wisdom within law enforcement had it that Danny had witnessed Glen's murder and had been shuttled off to Wyoming until Eli could figure a way out of his escalating troubles. Maybe he thought Danny would do what he was told. Keep his mouth shut. After all, Danny had been separated from the only person in his life—his father. Eli might have miscalculated that. After picking up Danny from the Coxes, he needed to do what he felt he had to do.

Like he'd done to Ida.

Shut him up permanently.

That night I talk to Claudia about it.

"Some people think that Eli killed Danny because he was going to tell someone about what happened to Glen."

She looks up from her phone.

"Okay," she says.

"And Ida . . . what if he killed her because she was going to tell something to the bishop about Eli?"

"You don't kill your wife over a camera."

"Probably not," I say.

"She caught him doing something and there was no way she'd put up with it."

I feel like a conspiracy theorist. Claudia goes back to her phone. What if it was worse? What if Ida was killed by her husband not because she caught him with a camera—or caught him with another man, even?

Something worse.

Howard Runck comes to mind just then.

CHAPTER
FORTY-NINE

If I'd ever had a *Perry Mason* moment, it was only in the process of researching *Abandoned Prayers*. I was on the hunt for anyone who knew Eli after he took Danny and left Ohio in 1982. I knew he was advertising in the *Advocate* for companionship, and there was only one library in the country that had the gay magazine on microfilm—Washington State University, on the other side of the Cascades from my home near Seattle.

I hired a student named Pede to go through the advertisements to see what he could find that would tie Eli to his next destination after Ohio: the Four Corners area of the US, particularly Colorado.

The conversation with Dianna and Chris Swartzentruber had brought all of that back.

"Wonder where he got all of that money he had," Chris had said over the table in the Kidron restaurant.

"Did he have insurance?" Dianna had asked, sparking a memory of my meeting with Howard Runck in Durango, Colorado. I remember how my heart pounded when I opened my hotel room door to the man who told me on the phone that he was Eli's business partner.

"Nothing more," he'd told me when I called.

In the book, I called him Terry Palmer.

He was in his sixties, a shy fellow who wore a cowboy hat and boots and Wrangler jeans. I invited him inside my room. He worked for Head Start and didn't want to be mixed up with any of the sordidness that had followed his business partner after he left Colorado.

He said he didn't know much about Eli, only that he was concerned about Danny.

We talked for a while and got nowhere.

Finally, I gave him my best shot.

"I don't need to use your name."

"I wish I knew something."

"Don't you?"

I remember feeling awful as I pulled out the copy of an advertisement my researcher at WSU had found.

"This was in the *Advocate*."

His eyes fastened on the microfilm printout.

"Please help me, Howard."

His gaze stayed downward. "I wish I could."

"I won't use your name."

"Sorry, but I don't know anything about that. It's not mine."

My heart was racing, as I imagined his was too. "Did you know that for one dollar you can find out who is the owner of a box number at any post office?"

He shook his head.

"Your name came back. Your box number is one that Eli used too."

His face turned pale, and I reiterated my promise.

"I'm not here to hurt you. I'm here to find out what happened to Danny and Ida. This is all your choice, Howard. You don't have to help. I won't write about you or anything."

A long beat of silence filled the hotel room.

"All right," he finally said. "I'll tell you everything."

In the summer of 1982, Eli arrived in the Four Corners flush with cash from the sale of the farm. He and Howard bought a place, with Eli plunking down $65,000 for the down payment. Runck agreed to make the monthly payments until their equity in the ranch matched.

The down payment had come from some of Stutzman's cash reserves. Howard didn't know how much money Eli had, but it was an impressive sum—from his horse business, the sale of the Dalton farm, and other sources.

Like insurance from his wife's death, maybe?

I didn't ask that specific question, though I should have.

Howard told me about his life, his fear of Eli, and the fear of being found out. The term "outing" hadn't entered the lexicon until a *Time* magazine article a year later. While no one used the word, everyone understood the ethics involved in invading someone's privacy when it came to sexual matters. Howard, like the other men Eli knew, had no reason to worry. I understood being outed could cost a man his job. His family. His life.

Anonymity was a promise I'd never break.

The next day, I drove out to the horse ranch near Ignacio where Howard, Eli, and Danny had lived. It felt eerie and abandoned. The wind swirled all around and the bright light of the sun blasted my eyes. I stood still for a long time, thinking about Eli and Danny and how this had been their first stop away from the Amish. It was a plunge into something very dark. Howard had told me Eli scared him. Threatened him. Harassed him when their business and personal relationship soured.

He was terrified of Eli.

I poked through the contents of an outbuilding and found a kid's swimming pool, a toy shovel. I let myself think the shovel belonged to Danny, only five, and I picked it up. Held it. Put it in my back pocket.

It might not have belonged to Danny Stutzman, but I still have it.

I'm not a forensic scientist or a crime scene investigator. I admit that I've looked through garbage and once even sifted through a burn barrel on the property of cyanide product-tampering killer Stella Nickell. I actually found a couple of half-melted Excedrin bottles the FBI had missed.

Underneath the plastic pool were remnants of the *Budget*, the Amish newspaper. Eli may have left the Swartzentruber church, but not entirely. He still had a need to know what the scribes were writing about after Ida died in the barn fire.

I thought of all of this as Dianna and Chris and I talked over a burger and those BLTs. Where did Eli get all of that cash?

Insurance, of course.

I had dismissed that years ago because, well, Eli was Amish. Amish don't buy insurance.

Stupid me.

Amish don't have driver's licenses either.

Eli did.

"If he came back to the church, really knowing and committing," Chris Swartzentruber said, "then he'd have destroyed his license."

✕

I hadn't talked to Howard Runck since the awkward interview in the hotel room in 1989. He was a good man who I knew had been like a father to Danny. He took the boy to school. He fed him. He made sure he was tucked into bed every night with a story. Howard even tried to help Danny with a worsening stutter.

Eli, it seemed, couldn't be bothered with any of that. He was too busy on the prowl for tricks.

And whenever Eli brought new friends over to party, Danny was often in plain sight.

I knew that scenario haunted Howard. His situation was untenable. His mail-order Amish boyfriend was a monster, and if Howard went to the authorities, he'd lose his job and his standing in the community.

If anyone knew for sure about insurance as the source of Eli's money, it would be Howard.

So I Google him.

In two seconds, I learn that he can't help me. Howard died in 2013. I'm disappointed, of course, but in a way, his obituary makes me happy too.

"Howard was the first male nurse commissioned as a lieutenant in the United States Air Force in the 1950s. With nursing quarters being all female up until then, he spent his first nights sleeping on a couch in the lobby while housing arrangements were adjusted."

Howard, the write-up continued, had spent the final two decades of his career as the health and safety coordinator for the Tri-County Head Start program in southwest Colorado.

And then came a welcome surprise.

Howard's life was no longer in the shadows.

"When his partner's autistic grandson came to live with them when he was 2, Mr. Runck dived into helping care for him, taking care of medical and school issues and taking on the role of mother," his partner said.

That partner of thirty years was a man named Steve.

I wish Howard and I had stayed in touch. The last time I'd heard from him, after the book came out, was in the form of a manila envelope with some crayon and pencil drawings made by then-five-year-old Danny on notebook and green-and-white computer papers. They were typical kid renderings of stick figures with one disturbing exception.

All were male with large phalluses.

They were like those drawings made for the benefit of a police psychologist investigating a sex abuse crime.

What was going on inside the mind of that little boy?

CHAPTER FIFTY

It's late. Claudia had surgery for a detached retina and is face down in a donut contraption in the guest bedroom. The dogs are with her, of course. I'm only an option for those two when she's out of the house. I can't sleep anyway, which has been an ongoing problem for most of my adult life. Can't turn off the brain. It's a relentless computer, albeit an Atari at this point, that whirls away at whatever story I'm working on.

The photo of the boys' underwear at Frost's suicide scene is in the queue at the moment.

If I had one of those TV detective walls going now, I'd be putting up strings of yarn from Texas to Ohio to Colorado, trying to make connections between the underwear, Danny, and Ida.

There are two primary theories about why it was that Danny ended up in that cornfield. The first is that he'd witnessed his father murder Glen. That's the "he knew too much" theory. Or he'd aged out of being compliant with his father's sexual abuse. That one is the "Danny was old enough to tell his dad to fuck off and stop" theory.

The forensic credence for the latter had been findings in the Scottsbluff, Nebraska, pathologist's autopsy report, which indicated Danny's anus had been dilated. It was inconclusive, however. It could have been the result of sexual abuse or the result of expansion and contraction of the body.

People I interviewed told me about things that were more than inappropriate when it came to Eli's behavior with his son. A Four Corners rancher recounted how he'd seen Eli "jacking off while Danny was sitting on the bed with him." An army officer from Texas "got the hell out of there" when Danny tried to put his hands on his crotch. Howard Runck sent me those drawings that showed a large phallus between each man's legs.

No one was more specific than Alta Northrop, who sat down with me in a café in Durango and told me what I knew at the time were serious allegations and unequivocal tales of sexual abuse.

As I write this, I can't help but think of a case that has been in the news. Two young men on the East Coast had been charged with pimping out their adopted children for sex with other men. I mention this only because it is such a rarity. That Eli was gay and might have abused his son was as unheard of back then as the current case. Being gay doesn't create a propensity for child abuse. In fact, children in same-sex partnered homes are happy, safe, and well loved.

Just like in any home.

And just like in any group of people, there are bad apples in every barrel.

Alta Northrop's disclosure all those years ago was stunning and revolting at the same time. It was so disturbing that I gave her an alias in the book—not because she asked for it—because I thought it took real courage to come out.

She could be brought up on child endangerment charges, I thought at the time.

Glasses, I think, as my mind whirls back three decades. Alta wore dark glasses with big oval frames in the café. The other glasses that come to mind are the red-framed lenses of talk show host Sally Jessy Raphael. The bespectacled women collided on Sally's show in 1991.

Back then, getting on a daytime TV talk show was huge. Sally had great ratings. It was not unusual for her to have eight or even ten million people tune in on any given day, a figure bested only by Oprah. Warner Books booked me on the show along with Dianna Swartzentruber, Abe Stutzman, Ted Garber, Jeff Cothran, and Alta Northrop, who, to my utter shock, decided to use her real name.

I start to play the recording and cringe as I come into view. I was only thirty-four, but my balding head is crowned with a wisp of a comb-over. Above my lip is what my daughters later would term my "porn star" mustache.

Some things are truly unforgivable.

Dianna is up first. She shares her suspicions about Eli and his abuse of Danny, how she'd seen a porn magazine in the boy's bedroom at the farm.

Then Abe talks about his cousin and his suspicions about him. He brings out his Amish hat and explains the significance of the brim size as it relates to a man's standing in the church or in life.

Alta brings the greatest reaction from the audience.

> Sally: Eli took his young son to Durango, Colorado, where he began to get involved in gay sex and his interest in drugs deepened. Our next guest says she saw Eli and Danny at many gay parties. This is Alta Northrop. Alta, I guess the first question is, what were you doing at all these gay parties?

> Alta: Well, they weren't strictly gay parties. There were all sorts of people at the parties, but there was a large group of gay men who were our friends. Some still are.

> Sally: Uh-huh. So you were in the gay male community in this area. All right. How did Eli act toward other men in front of his son that you found very, very disturbing?

> Alta: Well, all of the men in that particular group of gay men were very overt sexually at parties. They would do

things like grope each other's crotches and kiss and smack each other on the rear end, that sort of thing.

Sally: That wasn't the kind of party where you're having some drinks and discussing the world situation. No, there was overt sex at these parties.

Alta: Yes, there was one New Year's Eve party where people were openly having intercourse on the floors and in the spa and sort of all over the house.

Sally: Those kinds of parties.

Alta: Yes.

Sally: And it's not common to bring children to those kinds of parties?

Alta: We didn't. I'm married and have five children. We didn't bring ours to those parties.

Sally: But Eli always brought his son.

Alta: Yes.

Sally: And this would go on in front of the child?

Alta: Yes. What I guess he would say would emulate his father. He would do things like walk up to a man and grope his crotch or something. And on one occasion I said to Eli, "Do you really think you should be letting a little boy do that kind of thing?" And he said, "You're being really judgmental. I want Danny to grow up to be gay, so he'll never have to deal with women."

Then in a head-spinning non sequitur, Sally says, "Eli was into rough sex."

Alta: Well, I don't for a fact know that, but I suspect so many people in that group wore black leather and studs, and a couple of the men had their nipples pierced and sent cards with S&M kind of pictures on them at Christmas, things like that.

Sally: You told our producer—this is the most horrendous—that you thought perhaps Eli might have sold Danny for sex.

Alta: Now, that was just a gut feeling, nothing he'd ever said. But when the police in Durango first contacted us, I suppose after Danny's death, to ask if we had stayed in touch with Eli and knew where he was, they told us about Danny being found dead and all. And my husband and I both, our initial question to each other was "Oh my God, do you suppose he sold that little boy to someone for sexual purposes?" That that maybe was the cause of death.

Dianna: If you felt that he did these things to his son and you witnessed him at these orgies, how could you have not reported it? That's what I want to know.

Alta: Believe it. This won't make me any friends among the Durango Social Services Department. But we had already had some experiences with them where we had tried to report other people and they had just kind of blown us off and more or less accused me of being a busybody. So, we felt that nothing would be done about it if we had reported it.

I remember that moment. I felt sorry for Alta. Stupid, honest Alta. She used her real name, and the audience—led by pitchfork-holding Dianna—are out to get her. I try to throw her a lifeline.

Me: And many, many people saw these things. She was not the only one, but she is the only one that confronted Eli and said, "Don't do this to your son."

Audience member: She's the only one who does. Only one? How can a room full of people, even if you're enjoying yourself? Okay. I mean, that's your business. But a child should not be allowed in. Isn't anyone acting responsibly?

Dianna: That's exactly right.

Alta is sinking under water, and it turns out my lifeline is made of lead. She tries to redeem herself.

Alta: Now, my husband would usually try, like at the New Year's Eve party, Danny had gotten his first electric train for Christmas, and Eli had no idea how to put it together. So my husband used that as a reason to get Danny out of the party for several hours. They went downstairs to put the train together and played with it.

The audience and Sally blow off the attempt at redemption, and Alta sits there like she's been put before a firing squad made up of the blind. The bullets are flying, but there is no direct hit to put her out of her misery.

)(

After the taping, we hung out in the green room and drank coffee and ate room-temperature honeydew melon and cantaloupe slices left over from the morning. Azle's police chief, who'd arrested Eli, and Dianna Swartzentruber had no sympathy for Alta. In fact, I'm all but certain Dianna would have bitch-slapped Alta if she'd opened her mouth one more time. The feeling in the airless room was tense to say the least. As best she could, Alta had atoned for her poor judgment when she spoke about Danny at the parties.

Eli had sex on the brain. Hookups ruled his every move. In all likelihood there were probably dozens, if not hundreds, who'd seen something similar but just clammed up.

To save themselves, of course.

Alta not only admitted what she witnessed; she talked about going to sex parties on national TV. And she used her real name.

She was the first to leave for her flight. I remember walking her out past the *Sally* wall of fame and promos. She was shell-shocked.

"I guess I deserved that," she said.

"I think it took guts," I said. "I hope there aren't any repercussions in Colorado."

"Do you know when the show will air?" she asked.

"They'll call us," I said.

I remember standing there asking her the one question that I had been afraid to ask when I was researching. It seemed so dark and even beyond my ability to assess what I'd do if the answer was in the affirmative. The book was out in the world. There was nothing I could do with the information anyway.

In the book, I'd referred to Danny being used as a "sexual party favor," a line my editor liked for its grotesque imagery.

"Alta, did Eli prostitute his son?"

She looked at me through her dark glasses.

"You mean did guys pay him?"

"Yeah."

Alta waffled a little. "Maybe for drugs. Maybe for money. Probably so. Whatever was going on had been going on a long time. Danny was used to that stuff going on around him."

That was the last time I saw her.

I poke around online a bit only to find out that my chance to ask that question, to really push her into telling me what she had left out, is gone.

Alta died in 2008.

CHAPTER
FIFTY-ONE

I don't know what I really expected to find when the prison visitation logs finally arrive from Texas. Eli had been the subject of great curiosity after his arrest and conviction. He'd been featured in a spread in *People* magazine, Dan Rather covered his case, and there were stories all over the wire services. And, of course, my book. Honestly, I thought there would be more visitors as I start to scroll down the list.

Lewis McDorman, a Mennonite preacher from Austin who I remember attended nearly every day of the murder trial, was the first to see Eli. He also was the most frequent name listed as a visitor.

I make note of people I don't know, but there are only a few of those.

Jeff Cothran was a consistent visitor. I interviewed Jeff and we appeared on the *Sally Jessy Raphael* show together. He'd also been the one to connect Eli with the lawyers Connie Moore and Debbie Hunt, who defended Eli at the Austin murder trial. When I started revisiting Eli and Ida's story, I tried to reach out to Connie and Debbie, but both had died of ovarian cancer. A married couple, Connie and Debbie were lauded by the Fort Worth LGBTQ community for work they'd done on its behalf.

That's the hard part about revisiting an old story. It confirms that life is tenuous and brief. A writer comes in and captures a moment in time, and that time plays out forever on the pages. In that sense, a book is no better than a photograph. It captures a moment, and the people portrayed inside create another narrative. All their own.

I scroll through the names until landing on what shapes up like old home week, Wayne County style.

On June 15, 1991, Dr. Elton Lehman and his wife, Phyllis, visited. Interesting. I wonder how that went. Dr. Lehman was very suspicious of Eli's story about Ida's condition the night she died.

"She did not have a bad heart," he told me.

Two days after the Lehmans, Chris and Andy Stutzman saw their brother. That surprises me some. Eli was not only a notorious killer, but also under the bann. I knew none of his family came to his funeral, nor did they want his body back in Ohio, but they came to see him.

They weren't the only ones either.

In June 1992, Eli's brothers John and Dan Stutzman came for a pair of visits. Again, a little surprising but not shocking.

The next one, however, was.

On July 24, 1993, Eli H. Stutzman saw his son. His closest brother Andy was there too. One-Hand Eli, as he was known, was a preacher. He was as strict as any. From the way Eli talked about him to his friends, he could do nothing right in his father's eyes. When Eli was put under the bann, he told friends that he could sneak a visit with his mother, but seeing his father was out of the question.

Dr. Morton Bissell made his first appearance in the prison visiting room in November 1995. A second visit was made in January 1997, a third that fall.

Over two days in January 1998, Mose Keim—who took care of Eli when he had a nervous breakdown—and Eli's cousin Emery paid a visit.

Gerald and Janelle Gould were the last visitors, coming in 2001.

Eli was released the following March, in 2002.

The next day a call to Lewis McDorman is marked by gaps of silence as the elderly minister tries to retrieve memories of his time with Eli. His hearing has declined, making it necessary to ask each question twice. His answers, well, they make me smile now as I review the transcript.

> Me: What were your visits like when you would go to the prison?
>
> Lewis: Oh, they were good.
>
> Me: All right. What would you talk about?
>
> Lewis: Talk about anything he wanted to discuss.
>
> Me: And what typically did he like to talk about?
>
> Lewis: I don't know that he had any particular thing that he wanted to talk about.

Lewis is not being evasive. Not at all. I've experienced numerous interviews during which I wished I had pliers to pull out whatever information I was after. Not this guy. It seemed that the prisoner and preacher shared a cruel and unusual punishment of their own making—excruciatingly boring conversations.

The subject of Ida and the fire comes up.

Lewis echoes what others had heard from Eli.

"She might have had heart problems," he says. "I think she was helping get the animals out of the barn or something and that's how she got killed."

When the conversation veers to Danny's death, Lewis says that Eli told him how it happened.

"He was going back home for Christmas and the boy was in the back," he says. "There was a leak with the muffler or something. The fumes came through the floorboard and killed the boy."

Lewis doesn't hesitate when asked about Stutzman's character.

"I thought he was relatively forthcoming," he says. "I didn't feel that he was ever trying to hide anything."

The call over, I look through my stash of Eli's correspondence from that time.

In a lengthy letter, Eli writes about taking classes and working in the laundry. He says he receives a lot of correspondence from the Amish and is doing his best to keep up with all of it. He closes with this:

"As this holiday season draws near, let's again celebrate the birth of our savior, with joy, hope peace faith and most of all love."

What a bullshitter.

I wrote to Eli at least twice while he was incarcerated.

I received a single reply.

"I will not tell you my story if you don't pay me 100,000 dollars for the rights."

I had mixed feelings when I learned from one of his old flames that Eli had been paroled.

"That fucking Amish psycho Eli's been released."

"He'd had forty years," I said.

"Yeah, this is what we get now, justice. Thought someone would have taken him out. What that piece of shit did to that boy of his."

"Yeah," I said. "And to his wife."

I called the Texas Department of Criminal Justice right away, and they could only confirm that he'd been paroled to a halfway house in Fort Worth and that he'd be supervised for several years.

The mixed feelings? Claudia had always been wary about this whole true crime endeavor of mine. She told me the people I write about might eventually get out and want revenge. So that was one thing. The other was this former Amishman, who I was sure was a serial murderer, was free to kill again.

CHAPTER
FIFTY-TWO

I hadn't had any reason to request Eli's autopsy report when I learned of his death, at age fifty-six, in 2007. After all, he died of suicide and had left no note. I hadn't asked because there was nothing more to do on the case, though it still haunted me.

But now, the Tarrant County medical examiner's autopsy report and tox screen fall into the category of due diligence.

Even though I'd seen Eli in court during the Texas murder trial in the summer of 1989, as I'm looking over the report, I'm surprised by how small he was. At only five feet four and 110 pounds, he was the size of an eleven-year-old. Seems strange to me now because over the last thirty years, I'd built him up to be such a monster—menacing, ruthless, and without fear. He had those attributes no doubt, but each was veiled by his stature and his soft-spoken nature by a mile.

I open the PDF file labeled *"tox screen."* Analysts turned up cannabis and cocaine, which I knew was crack cocaine, though it wasn't specified as such.

Then, the autopsy report. First, it noted the circumstances of his death. Eli was wearing only blue underwear with gray trim when he was found on a couch in his bedroom with an injury to his left arm, a shallow *"incised wound of left antecubital fossa with penetration of the cephalic vein."* He had a full gray mustache and an unshaven face.

Next, the cause of death: sharp force injury of the left arm.

Manner of death: suicide.

Everything about Eli's body presented without any significant abnormalities. He wore a full set of dentures and had a four-inch scar on his forehead and a one-inch scar on his left arm.

Only one thing of interest was noted on the internal exam.

"Calvarium has evidence of a remote, healed craniotomy involving the left parietal and left frontal bones measuring approximately 8 centimeters in greatest dimension with anchoring metallic hardware in place."

I'm no doctor, but I do know a few. I also can Google.

As it turns out, the operation that Eli had undergone at some point in his mysterious, nomadic life involved a surgeon removing a bone flap and going into the brain to remove a tumor, blood clot, or maybe a bullet.

What was that all about? Was it because of violence done to him, or was it an indication of a medical reason behind his behavior?

The medical examiner finished by collecting fingernail clippings, palm prints, fingerprints, blood, oral swabs, anal swabs, and finally, trace evidence from Eli's hands.

CHAPTER
FIFTY-THREE

It has been a long time since Charles Turner and I spoke. How long? I can't be sure. When Charles answers the phone, however, it brings the welcome feeling that comes from talking to a friend you've missed more than you realized.

Charles Turner was Eli's last lover.

The Courtyard on Calmont apartments is a small two-story complex with a frame-crushing black mansard roofline. Most units are one bedroom with galley kitchens that promise solo cooking and efficient cleanup. The complex is located on the west side of Fort Worth on a bleak but busy stretch of road glued together with ribbons of tar. Eli lived in number 118 since paroling there in 2003.

Charles Turner lived in a one-bedroom apartment just across from Calmont.

While there was a kind of attraction for this Black and White, gay Mutt and Jeff, it wasn't a great love story.

"I wish that I could make it more of, like, a relationship," Charles said years later. "With like baroque music and, you know, flowers, butterflies, and open fields and waves or something? Oh, you know, it just wasn't like that."

"But it was real and mattered to both of you."

"It did," he said.

Though we have never met in person, Charles and I formed a bond after Eli's suicide. Charles is brilliant. Funny. Kind. He's everything you'd want as an ally. He's devoted to his schoolteacher mother, now ninety. The love of his life wasn't Eli, but Jeremy, a young man who'd died of complications from HIV/AIDS. That loss clings to him now, and likely forever.

"You sound the same," I say. "How are you?"

"Oh, actually, quite well," he says. "I went to the doctor today, so everything came out well. I mean, blood pressure, everything's okay."

"That's good."

He goes on to tell me that he'll be moving from Fort Worth to take care of his mom in his hometown, Tyler, Texas. Mrs. Turner is suffering from dementia.

I share my family's struggles with my father, now gone from Alzheimer's, and how it brought us to our knees.

"There's no road map for this kind of thing," I tell him.

He understands. "You have no choice but to make it up as you go along. Yep. I know it's only going to get much worse, and I'm not even prepared for it."

We talk about Washington and how much he wishes he could come visit. How he'd love to see the San Juan Islands. He's made friends online with people who live there. I remind him about the vintage postcards he'd sent to me.

"And the fossils?" he asks. He sent me an extensive collection of Fort Worth limestone. Each was in a separate bag, all meticulously labeled *Nautilus texanus*, *Hemiaster elegans*, *Pecten bellula*, and more.

"Henry loves them," I say, referring to my oldest grandson, now ten. "Pete is probably old enough to appreciate them now too."

He muses about the passage of time. Not with the fossils, but my grandsons. He asks about Doug, my student intern from way back.

Doug camped out on Charles's sofa when passing through Texas to build homes for hurricane relief in Louisiana, post-Katrina.

And then I turn to the subject at hand—Ida's death.

"If there was a cover-up," I tell him, "it was a conspiracy of silence. Not solely on Eli's part. On the part of others too. I want your help."

"Okay," he says. "Tell me more."

"So, Charles, here's the thing. I want you to look back to 1976 and '77 when all this stuff is going on. It was a different world for gay people then, right? Same's true for 1989 and '90 when I was writing the book. I wasn't doing 'Don't ask don't tell,' but I never pried into anyone's sexuality. It was private. If they brought it up, then we talked about it and how it was a big part of the story. And then, of course, there's the Amish. They were private and many believed that they didn't want to be a part of our world. So, I'm looking at these two factions that come together in Ida's story. Their combined silence kept the truth from coming out and ultimately let Eli roam the west to kill other people."

I lay out more details—the incident in Marshallville, how Ida took him back, the Wayne County sheriff connection, the men who came out to the farm to see Eli, all the red flags.

"So, let's talk about the way things were back then. Your story. Eli's story."

Charles tells me about growing up gay and Black in the seventies and how loneliness and shame played on his psyche every moment of each day.

"Being gay in Texas was simultaneously a crime and a psychological aberration. What was it that the American Psychiatric Association had just declassified, being gay or homosexuality as a mental illness in like 1973? And so, we were all there, you know, no positive role models in the media. Just silly. Swishy. And by the late seventies, things changed a little. Eli got some of those magazines so he would have gotten some inkling of what was going on in like New York, San Francisco, Miami, all the really large gay meccas. He'd see what was going on, what was going on in your town, you know?"

"His world before then was small."

"I think so."

"When I was growing up, having a Black president or a Black female vice president wasn't even in my world. Eli couldn't know or even imagine what his life could be. Being Amish made it even harder to figure out things."

"And he wanted all of that," I say. "Before Ida."

"Yeah, I could see him getting information on that kind of thing and maybe trying to replicate it. And then I think it just came to a point where that life wasn't going to fly anymore."

A few people in Eli Stutzman's circle in Fort Worth might have known that he was the father of Little Boy Blue, but Charles wasn't one of them. When we first spoke all those years ago, he was reeling over the idea that his lover, a gentle, quiet man, was not who he'd said he was. Eli told Charles and others that he'd been raised in an Amish home and said that the Amish people were kind and hardworking but repressed and overbearing and unaccepting in their ways.

Eli kept some Amish clothing and wore it to costume parties.

Photos Charles shared with me from back then show a smiling, happy Eli Stutzman. He was gray then, sans beard, only a mustache. He wore wire-framed glasses of the style that Amish people often choose.

Charles was intrigued by the inexplicably incongruent trajectory of Eli's life—it was like this man had been transported from one extreme to another. First, the rolling pastoral world of Amish Ohio to the hard-edged, caged spaces of the Ramsey and Beaumont Units of the prison near Huntsville, Texas. Charles was also charmed by Eli's accent and playfully teased him when he mispronounced a word like "nicotine."

When we talk fifteen years after Eli's death, Charles still holds a fascination with the small-framed Amishman and his people.

"I had never met an Amish person before, ever. And so, I started asking him about his religion. And, you know, what do we all really know? We rarely get to meet someone who actually was part of that religion. So, I talked to him about it quite a bit and he was actually quite stunned that I even knew anything about them."

Eli kept a sewing machine in his apartment and made leather goods he sold mostly at LBGTQ gatherings like the Texas Gay Rodeo.

"He made me a pair of moccasins, which I still have," Charles says.

The way Eli spun it all made the Amish world seem organized and quaint, and Charles couldn't understand why anyone would leave it behind. From the outside looking in, it had the romantic appearance, the sentimental ambience, of a time gone by. It was a snow globe.

Eli, however, was candid about the downside. It was a repressive society. There was no chance for education beyond eighth grade. Women were relegated to household duties and having babies while men gave their full attention to running the farm.

Everyone had a place and expectations were rigid.

"Homosexuality in the Amish," Charles says, stopping to make sure he frames it fairly. "Well, there was no such thing. It wasn't known. And it wasn't approved, obviously, or accepted."

"Well, it was known to Eli," I say.

Charles doesn't disagree. "Yes, he knew that he was different, and he rebelled against it. He couldn't stand it anymore. He had to give up everything he had. Had to leave what he knew to be his first and only child, Danny."

"He actually didn't leave Danny until he left him in that ditch in Nebraska," I say.

"Gregg," Charles says, "that's the strange part. Eli spoke about Danny as if he was alive. Grown. And he was in communication with him."

I have no idea how to process that, but it makes me wonder if Eli could have conned himself into believing his own lies.

If anything, Charles is a trusting soul. Maybe less so today, post–Eli Stutzman. Who could blame him? He took every word that Eli said as the truth. Eli was that sweet, honest Amishman, who had unblinking sky-blue eyes that never communicated a single bit of pretense.

"But you caught him in a lie, didn't you?" I ask, remembering a story he once told me.

Charles goes quiet. "Yeah," he says. "I don't know the guy's name anymore—probably a homeless hustler—he had over there, and he said the guy was another gay expatriate from the Amish Country. And he was trying to help him. Get used to life outside, right? But he never wanted me to meet him. Okay, well, you know, maybe the guy's shy. He said he didn't speak English. His German was better than his English."

Later when they finally met, Charles said something in German to the visitor, but the guy didn't seem to understand a single word.

He wasn't from Amish Country at all.

"And that was a lie right there," Charles tells me. "But it just didn't register because maybe I didn't want it to. You know what I mean?"

I think I do.

Other moments haunt him.

One time, Charles was looking at a genealogy book and noticed that Eli Stutzman had a wife and son, both of whom had died.

Eli snatched it out of his hands and insisted that it was another Eli Stutzman.

"It's a common name," Eli said, shutting down the conversation.

Another time, Eli told Charles that he'd been able to visit Danny in Ohio.

Eli's apartment, while always immaculate, was sparsely furnished. No family photos, of course. He had a seashell collection, a wooden clipper ship he'd made in prison from squirreled-away wood scraps and linens, a computer, and a TV.

He also had a lap-size mutt named Sport.

"And I have never in my entire life, even now, seen a better-behaved dog," Charles says. "You know, the first dog I had ever seen that did everything on command, the usual stuff, just sort of roll over, beg, and all that stuff, but a ton of other things and just very, very, very well behaved. Oh, he was just incredible. So, Eli was really incredible with animals."

"What happened to the dog?" I ask during a call.

Charles suddenly becomes wistful.

"He was going to give Sport to me," he says. "But I couldn't afford to keep him after everything happened."

After the call with Charles, I turn my attention to the last words on Eli's life.

While I have no intention of grassy-knolling Eli's death, there are some things that don't quite add up in the investigation conducted by Houston police. As I look at the police report, a few things jump out with face-smacking force.

When his parole officer visited Eli only two days before his death, why didn't she make note of his missing belongings? His TV? Computer? One would think it would be a warning sign that Eli was planning on leaving Fort Worth.

Or maybe even worse.

In addition, his phone was "not working" the day he was found. However, Charles left a message on the machine the day after his body was discovered; that's how the police found him.

If the entire apartment was neat and orderly, why was the bedroom scattered with clothes? Had Eli had a tryst with someone who became violent?

The report mentions blood on Eli's feet but no bloody footprints in the apartment. How does that happen? Had someone cleaned it up? Along those same lines, some people who were in the apartment say they saw a knife in the bathroom.

From the investigator's write-up:

"Officers searched the apartment for any cutting device that may have been used however no knives or cutting instruments were located in the bathroom or near the DEC."

So where did it go?

Charles noticed things were heading in a downward trajectory. Eli said that someone got into his bank account and took all his money. The idea that someone would take advantage of him was a complete puzzler.

"Everyone liked him," Charles says. "No one who knew him at all would steal from him."

Around the same time as the bank theft, things started disappearing from Eli's apartment.

"Unbeknownst to me, his apartment, a rather scandalous apartment at that, had become a revolving door like in a bad comedy. People said that every junkie in the area was going in and out of his apartment at night. So, they go over there and now he would sell or trade for drugs. You know, I'll say I probably knew all these people. You know, I'm not perfect. But I certainly would not have let them hang around me."

He asked Eli about his vanishing belongings, and he said that he'd put his valuables in storage for safekeeping while he was away.

"Where was he going?"

"He wanted to go visit his dad in Ohio."

"Oh boy," I say.

"Yeah," he answers. "At the time, I told him it was fine because 'you do live in a kind of dicey place.'"

"Seriously," I say, just because I can't think of anything else.

Charles goes on, telling me that Eli gave him the ship he made in prison, some periodicals he'd been given by his relatives, and the Amish genealogy book.

Charles told him that he'd keep the items until Eli returned to Fort Worth.

He still has them.

In the first hours following the ambulance's departure from the Courtyard on Calmont apartments, talk that Eli had been murdered filled the ears of the residents of the complex. Many were completely convinced that a frequent visitor, a known heroin addict, had been the killer—probably over an unpaid debt. Maybe a robbery gone wrong.

Charles didn't know what to think. The apartment manager, her daughter, and another neighbor just didn't think that the man in number 118 was the type to kill himself. So quiet. A gentle, not-able-to-hurt-a-fly type of guy.

My mind flashes to the final scene in *Psycho* where Anthony Perkins lets a housefly crawl over his face in a bid to show detectives that he couldn't be a killer.

The name that came up most frequently as the killer was Hammer, a man Eli knew from prison.

A man who gave Charles the creeps.

"People didn't trust him, and he really was worthless, a POS. But anyway, he was the only person from his past that I've ever met because they were in prison together."

CHAPTER
FIFTY-FOUR

Charles now calls the week following Eli's death a "tsunami of revelations." First and foremost, he didn't know anything about Glen Pritchett's murder, the reason Eli had been incarcerated.

"No mention of a murder. And I didn't think to look it up. I just took him at his word."

"Eli kept so many things private, locked up," I say.

"Yeah. So that week, I heard everything. And that's what really baffled me that entire week that the story started. I had zero, less than zero, idea what had happened."

Charles never knew any specifics until a reporter from the *Fort Worth Star-Telegram* phoned him.

The disclosures shook him up.

"Imagine, like a river with ice floes and ice chunks, right? Just leaping from one ice chunk to the other, you know, all lies. And I just went from one to the other because I was so," he says, hesitating before adding, "I was willing to put my faith in people. I was very, very lonely at the time. Everything he said was a lie."

A *Star-Telegram* front-page story ran on February 25, 2007, with the headline "Long trail of mystery and bodies ends in Fort Worth."

While the afternoon sun waged a losing battle with a misty rain, Hammer, Eli's friend from prison, pounded on Charles Turner's apartment door. It was Wednesday, January 31, 2007.

"Someone killed Eli," Hammer said.

Charles couldn't quite grasp what the man was saying.

"That can't be," he said, because he thought Eli wasn't home. "He went to visit his dad."

Eli didn't have any next of kin listed anywhere. Charles made calls to some numbers in an Amish magazine that Stutzman had given him and left messages for someone who knew Eli's family to call him.

When a man finally did, the first thing he asked was "Are we talking about Little Boy Blue's father?"

Charles had no idea about the reference.

He followed Hammer to the end of the driveway and saw the ambulance drive off. The lights to Eli's apartment were off.

It had to be true.

Who, he wondered, would hurt the nicest man in the world?

He left a recording on Eli's machine.

"I heard what happened, Eli. I don't know what to say. I guess you are at peace now. Whatever torture you were hiding is gone."

The next day a police officer knocked on his door, asking to see the items Eli had given Charles. Gossip shot from one apartment complex to the next. Lots of talk about blood found all over the apartment, in the sink, a bloody light switch. The officer told Charles that it appeared to be a suicide, but the medical examiner would make the determination.

CHAPTER
FIFTY-FIVE

Dan Gingerich packed a set of Amish clothes for Eli's burial and took the long bus ride from Minnesota to Texas for the funeral. Dr. Lehman had called Ida's brother and asked him to come to make sure it was Eli. When word circulated Eli had died, many dismissed it as another con. Eli was clever. Conniving. A practiced liar and fabricator.

"I never regretted going," Dan says. "Some people thought I shouldn't go. And even Eli's family, some of them thought I should know why they were so shaken by that."

Abe Stutzman drove his pickup from Illinois to attend his cousin's funeral. Dr. Lehman and a couple of others drove down from Wayne County.

Charles Turner, of course, was there too.

Everyone had a different reason for coming. Some to say goodbye. Some to make sure. One even came so he could brag about his attendance.

First there was a viewing at a funeral home, followed by a brief graveside service.

"It gave me the shivers," Dan tells me about going to Cedar Hill Memorial Park to bury Eli. "I felt really sorry for him because he told me way back in the late seventies that he knows he won't go to heaven. So I felt sorry for him, but I couldn't do anything about it."

Dan recalls Charles Turner speaking.

"He said, 'All we're doing is closing the chapter. I don't know anything about this guy. I can't condemn him. I can't praise him. I don't know. I'm just here to close the chapter.'"

CHAPTER FIFTY-SIX

I tried to catch up with the Miller brothers back in 1990 but never managed to reach any of them. The self-inflicted stabbing incident at the Marshallville dairy was and is essential, I think, to understanding the lengths Eli would go to in order to wriggle out of trouble. I tried again, going so far as to knock on doors, send emails, and make a number of dead-end calls.

I got nowhere.

That is, until an email tip from the billboards arrives. I lift my jaw off the keyboard. It's from Earl Miller, one of the brothers caught up in the misguided and ill-fated Wayne County sheriff's marijuana sting.

> *Eli Stutzman was an interesting character as was the Wayne County Sheriff Frost at that time. There is a lot to this death of Ida Stutzman that time on the farm on Moser Rd up from Harley Gerber's Feed mill. I don't know if you knew that Sheriff Frost and at least one of the deputies, Taylor, were gay and made visits to Eli's farm in Dalton. My brother was close friends with Dr. Elton Lehman who was the coroner of Ida's death and was a little sloppy and let her not have an autopsy,*

which would have gotten Eli caught for murder. There was a lot that Eli did that other people know about that has never been told.

He ends the tip noting that he's in Florida for the winter, so given the hour I wait to call until the next day. Something stands out in his note, and I assume it's a mistake. He must mean Tim Brown, not Jim Taylor, as the deputy who knew Eli personally. It's been a lot of years and we're all getting older. *An error,* I think.

And it isn't so much a conversation that follows as a monologue. Earl has a lot to say and well, I'm all ears. He's got so much energy behind his words, he's like a geyser that's been dormant up to now. "Anyhow," it seems, is his favorite word. It gets a workout in his diatribe on the events of late 1974. He says the connection between Eli and the Millers was a "Swartsie" Amish boy, confusingly named Henry Miller. Henry worked for Earl and his brothers, as did other Amish boys before and since. Henry set up a buy for his friend Eli Stutzman.

"Earl," I ask, "this is not like you had some big grow operation, right?"

"Like hell no," he says. "We had like a couple pot plants behind the barn in the pasture. We never sold anything. Henry was like our first customer. Said he wanted it for this friend of his, Eli. I forget why, said he needed it for headaches or something. Anyhow, we went down in the basement where we had a little box of pot and I gave it to Henry. And the next day we saw the goddamn Wayne County sheriff cars coming up our road like maniacs. We had no clue what was happening or anything. It was Sheriff Frost and Deputy Taylor."

"Jim Taylor, are you sure?"

"Yeah. A big, big boy, that Taylor. He picked up dead cattle on the side. And anyhow, Eli was working up at Stoll Farms in Marshallville. And anyhow, Taylor would go that way to pick up dead cattle. So he knew Eli. And that's how the connection came through there."

I ask for more about Taylor.

"Taylor was a sight to be seen in that stinky truck cab of his, and he always had a big German shepherd dog with him. I think Taylor had the dog to protect himself in case someone wanted to get even with that old queer, because he obviously was corrupt."

Tell me how you really feel, I think.

Anyway, it's a good thing that Earl is a talker because I'm actually stunned. Jim Taylor's name was in Liz Chupp's diary; writing in it was a daily practice she kept since girlhood. Taylor was Eli's best friend at Stoll Farms, according to Liz. They used to go "coon hunting" at night, but they never caught anything.

I didn't make the connection between Eli and Jim Taylor, though I should have.

"So anyhow," Earl continues, "we knew who squealed on us, because we had never sold any pot to anybody else but him. So, my one brother who was not involved with it at all went up to Stoll's and wanted to confront Eli about it. The next night the sheriff came down to our farm at like seven thirty. Hadn't eaten supper and stuff."

It's hard to keep up with this guy. He's seventy and he's on a roll, telling a story that he's been waiting to tell for fifty years.

"Anyhow, Christ, I think we had a dog. Maybe. And some god-damn ruckus or whatever by the barn, you know, and something's up. We had had a little shed up above there where we kept the cars, and they were screwing around out there. And finally, they came to the house."

"They were there because of Eli's story about the men who jumped and stabbed him," I say.

"Right," he says. "Oh, they said they were hoping they would find a car there with a hot motor. And anyhow, we weren't real happy. Frost was a liar and a crook."

"And then Eli recants, right quick," I say.

"Yeah," Earl says. "And they had to put something in the paper. It was hush-hush."

I talk about that sudden about-face, the switch from a supposedly big pot bust to no charges. The big question for me has always been why Eli would have been a drug informant; on the face of it the whole idea is ludicrous. I kept thinking, *Why would Eli Stutzman be an undercover informant for the authorities?*

The answer was Jim Taylor, someone I'd never even considered a relevant part of the story. All I knew was that he ran for sheriff against Frost, lost, and was booted off the force. He died in 2013.

"Jim Taylor was Eli's buddy," I say, really making sure.

"Oh, that son of a bitch," Earl says. "He was an old bastard. But anyhow, those two boys were both gay."

"Taylor and Eli?"

"Yeah. And Frost too, but we didn't know it at the time. They had at least a couple in the sheriff's department."

Actually, four, I think, adding Ken Kerr and Tim Brown.

How everyone in the county thought the Miller brothers were major pot growers still pisses him off.

"Over the years or whatever, this and that, we just kind of let it die or the whole thing is everybody thought, oh my God, we were big drug dealers. Crazy. We, you know, that was the only thing we sold. I think that was twenty-five or twenty-seven dollars we got out of that. But yeah, like I said, some people always try to rub it in, you know, and so, hey, it was twenty-seven dollars. Everyone makes mistakes."

And regarding Jim Frost, Earl can't say enough about him.

"He came in there that night without a warrant, checking them motors. He's lucky that we didn't clean his clock. Yeah, he was a bastard. He was crooked. People thought he was God. They never knew the real side of him."

The call winds down and I tell him that I'll send the sheriff's incident report, which I do right away.

The next morning, I get this email from Earl:

I had never seen or knew of these reports. If I had known what I read in these reports, I would have sued every one of those assholes and queers on that force. They were pure dirty, outright scumbag liars. I can't believe the undertaker did not remove her head covering. Eli really controlled things.

A few minutes later, a second email pings:

It was kind of funny reading this bunch of lies Eli had to cook up. We knew Eli screwed us because it was not hard to figure out who squealed. We had never sold any pot except to Eli and I think Henry was his connection or it would never have happened.

So now I know whom I have to coax out of the woodwork: Henry Miller.

CHAPTER FIFTY-SEVEN

I sift through more letters from Amos Gingerich's Wolverine boot box. This group had been sent after Little Boy Blue was identified as Danny. I can imagine that the intent of the correspondence was to provide comfort, but still, each had to hurt. So many were imbued with regret too.

An Amish relative wondered if Ida knew about all the things that happened in the ten years since her death.

> *We all imagine she'd be a heartbroken woman the way we hear he might still be trying to lie his way through all of this.*

One of Eli's sisters wrote to Susie Gingerich just after the news came out that Danny was Little Boy Blue. The letter shows the depths of Eli's deception, even to his own mother.

> *Little Danny is far better off than his dad but what did he do to bring his death?*

She writes about Eli's visit in January 1986:

I remember mother asked why he doesn't have Danny along? He said it was hard to not be bringing Danny along but Danny went to school. Then he showed mother some school papers Danny had done but she said he took them along when he left. Now I think maybe I know why this could be some fingerprints on the papers.

I was up home yesterday afternoon. Mother doesn't seem so good which I expected with all this talking about Eli and little Danny. Seems . . . people from far and near are talking about it all . . . and you know so often some talk is not true. It is hard on mother with all this sadness.

CHAPTER
FIFTY-EIGHT

A call to Earl Miller's brother Les Miller confirms that Dr. Lehman knew the investigation into Ida's death had been bungled. Les and the doctor were in a church group together.

"Anyhow, we had a men's group, and we discussed this thing one time, and he says, 'Yeah, it's just too bad that it wasn't checked out. They just assume the Amish don't lie. And they said she had a heart condition.'"

That's not quite right, of course. Dr. Lehman made no mention that he'd been her doctor and that she'd never had a bad heart. If he had known it was a lie, then why did he go along with it? Further, a "bad heart" is hardly a definitive medical diagnosis.

It was Frost who ramrodded the theory to Dr. Questel.

"Did Dr. Lehman know that Frost was gay?"

"He was a man and he wasn't stupid," Les says.

He goes on to share something else I'd heard before from the Amish.

"Somebody said she had bit her tongue. I don't know if that's true or not. If she did, possibly he was trying to suffocate her. I don't know who said that either," he says, stopping for a beat, before adding he's certain it was Dr. Lehman who told him that.

"Yeah, I do know. I mean, I thought I knew Elton very well. I could practically finish his sentences."

I'd heard versions of the story of Ida's tongue for years, but there had been no mention of it on Dr. Questel's autopsy report.

Before the call is over, Les provides some thoughts on some of the key players in the Stutzman story.

> **Tim Blosser**: "Tim was in my class. He can be real nice. He's just gonna be real nice, then he is shrewd as can be. Oh, money was all that man knew. That's all he knew. His number one object is himself."

All right, fine, I think. If that's so, what was in it for Blosser on preparing a will that was never finished? Why did he keep coming back to Stutzman's farm? Maybe he represented Eli with the insurance companies?

> **Tim Brown**: "He was a gay guy, a real nice kid. I saw him up at the fair and not too many years ago I saw him down at the Walmart with his mother."

A little Facebook stalking lets me know Tim is now married to his second husband. Pictures posted by his husband give an impression of a happy family, trips, holidays. Tim probably *is* a nice guy. And I'm sure the reason he ghosted me is that what happened with Eli and Ida and Danny is probably the worst thing in his life. Tim denies having an intimate relationship with Eli or any involvement in the cover-up relating to Ida's death.

> **Levi Levi Hershberger**: "Well, he knew his horses like nobody else did, and he liked his alcohol like no other Irishman did."

Nothing new there, though the chronic drunk seems to define almost everyone's memories of the man who was by Eli's side at the fire, and at the barn raising.

Did he drink to forget like Jim Frost did?

What I find next could be nothing or it could be something monstrously big.

That's the thing about the internet. So much content is out there, and it is easy to draw connections that may or may not be something. That's what conspiracy theorists do all day long. They find and they connect, no matter how tenuous.

Any name is a possible source when found on a document and is worth the chase. Most of those are dead ends. People move. People die. Clerical errors are rampant too.

When reviewing documents related to Jim Frost and any of his residences and associated financial transactions, I capture names and pass them on to Robbin to include as potential source hopper.

Tonight is different. I decide to run a name myself.

In 1995, a man named George Zirwas bought James Frost's condo at 611 NE Fourteenth Avenue in Fort Lauderdale. I run the name and, just like that, I get something that is either golden or a deep, dark rabbit hole.

George Zirwas was a Catholic priest.

Yes, sadly, *that* kind of priest.

His first mention in connection with any crime was an article in the *Pittsburgh Post-Gazette* in 1989 in relation to another priest being charged with the molestation of boys at a resort near Seven Springs. The incident occurred in 1984. Zirwas was in the same resort in the presence of two other boys but was not charged.

After a dozen mentions as an officiant at a wedding or funeral, or as the writer of a series of letters to the editor in Pittsburgh, Zirwas's name resurfaces in the newspaper archives of 2000, weighing in on the Elián González case. He's an advocate for family values, he writes in the *Miami Herald*, and no boy should be separated from his father.

The next time is a headline from the *Miami Herald* on June 1, 2001: "American Priest Strangled in Havana."

The Diocese of Pittsburgh said Zirwas went on a personal leave of absence at the end of 1995. *"That isn't common, but it happens . . . It was extended periodically by mail every six months."*

Sadly, and predictably, anyone could see where this is going. The fact that it took another decade and a half for the truth to come out is truly the only surprising part of Zirwas's sordid story.

It turns out that up until 1995, as many as five separate allegations by boys and their mothers were made to the diocese, which shuffled him to as many as seven parishes as a fix for a very serious problem. A former altar boy said Reverend Zirwas raped him two to four times a week between 1982 and 1987.

Zirwas was also identified as part of a ring of four predatory priests who created and circulated porn of their victims. Some of the poses were imitations of Christ on the cross.

It gets sicker.

As it frequently does.

Zirwas and the deranged crew gifted their "special boys" with gold crosses so other predatory priests could identify them as easy targets for additional abuse.

As I sit here and stare at my laptop, I wonder if this is just a grotesque rabbit hole that I've taken a deep dive into. Is this how Pizzagate began? QAnon? Oliver Stone movies? Is it fair to draw conclusions and connections to things that people told me about Danny and Eli?

I answer my own question by making a list.

1. Dan Stolfus hears Danny begging his father to stop doing something that was hurting the boy.

2. One of Eli's dates bolted out of the Colorado ranch house because he was terrified when Danny groped him.

3. Alta Northrop went on national TV to say she suspected that Danny was being passed around by men at a sex party.

4. A Colorado rancher told me back in 1989 that he saw Eli "jacking off" while Danny sat next to him on the bed. What dad does that?

5. The Nebraska pathologist who examined Danny's body said his anus had been dilated but couldn't determine whether he'd been abused sexually. It might have been the freeze and thaw of the winter weather.

6. Howard Runck saved Danny's drawings because he was alarmed about the sexual nature of the pictures. What else was he terrified about?

7. And Jim Frost? His lover Ken Kerr was barely out of high school, and Frost had a good ten years on him. Obviously that in no way makes him a pedophile.

8. Yet Frost sold his place in Florida to Father Zirwas, a pedophile priest; isn't that something?

9. And what of the boys' underwear found at Frost's suicide?

10. And, as far as I know, Frost wasn't Catholic. Why was he wearing a gold cross like others in Zirwas's pedophile ring?

CHAPTER
FIFTY-NINE

Amos Gingerich told me that the failed blood tests had always troubled him. Amos was not a worldly man, but he knew the outside world better than many Swartzentrubers. He understood that the premarital blood test was about venereal disease and doubted any herbal tea could cure it. No one knew what doctor Eli had gone to see.

It was someone outside of the community.

Among those who contacted Charles Turner after learning of Eli's death was Dr. Morton Bissell, the chiropractor from Brewster, Ohio. Bissell treated Eli for "nerve pressure" following one of his breakdowns when he left the Amish. It was also Dr. Bissell who helped Eli with his "bad blood" so he could obtain an Ohio marriage license.

The mystery of Eli and Dr. Bissell's close connection is answered in correspondence between Charles Turner and the chiropractor. Charles had never heard Eli talk about Dr. Bissell or their relationship.

"Eli rarely talked about his past and whatever he said, I now, pretty much, consider a lie," Charles tells me when I get back on the Eli trail with a phone call to his Texas apartment.

I ask Charles to send the correspondence he received from Dr. Bissell after the suicide, which he does right away.

What had been going on between Eli and Dr. Bissell all those years is revealed between the lines.

The first time the chiropractor writes to Charles is on March 2, 2007, after the two made contact in the comments section of a newspaper article about Eli's death. Bissell says he'd written weekly to Eli during his incarceration, talked with him on the phone often, and visited him at least once a year.

Bissell writes how it's very hard for him *"to believe . . . all the things they are digging up on Eli. It sure isn't the Eli I knew."*

At the end of the letter, he notes how he'd like to meet Charles, though he expects that Charles is much younger than he is. He adds he'll be eighty-one in June and encloses a photograph of an exceedingly heavy white-haired old man in glasses, seated behind a table layered with pieces of a jigsaw puzzle. Also in the photo is his cat, which he identifies as Mr. Tricks.

Two weeks later, on March 17, another missive arrives from Brewster. Again, the doctor reflects on the quality of reporting in the Fort Worth newspaper, pronouncing it "garbage." He laments his own loneliness. He has a "cozy" little apartment, but no one to share it with. *"My cat is great, but there are areas he can't satisfy. I have to stop wishing and move along."*

Charles knows where this pen pal relationship is headed—and, by his estimation, not in the right direction. He backs off and declines to respond.

Dr. Bissell, however, remains undeterred. On May 8, he writes that he hasn't been able to reach Charles. He keeps getting a message that the phone number is no longer working so he decides it would be best to write. *"I often wonder what has transpired with regard to my good friend Eli. I have always heard no news is good news and I hope I am right."*

He asks if Eli's body is still at the medical examiner's office and says that he has not heard from anyone who knew Eli. Possibly, he could talk to the Stutzman brothers, but he's not sure how they would react.

Charles sends a short note in return, updating Dr. Bissell about the funeral and the fact that Eli's immediate family had declined to participate. He avoids giving out his current phone number.

On July 28, Dr. Bissell selects stationery featuring an Amish horse and buggy for a letter that starts with a ramble about a fishing trip and the number of bluegills (forty-one) caught by an Amish group he'd driven to a lake.

He says Eli's Amish relatives are tight-lipped about their wayward and troubled family member.

> *They have ways of being very secretive. Mum is the word with them. I would enjoy taking you to visit their houses and introducing you to them. They might let you talk but I can assure you that they will not converse with you about Eli. When he left the Amish church, they had a funeral for him and as far as they are concerned, he was dead. I understand why relatives like cousins went down to receive the body and see it buried. They were from another church and were not under the church bann.*

While the letter is about Eli, it's also about something else. Something, Charles knows, is coming.

"I often imagine I'm having sex with someone else when I masturbate," Dr. Bissell wrote. *"Now I will imagine it as you. You can imagine it is me if you care to. It would be nice to share by letter or phone exactly what we experienced."*

More letters pass between them throughout the fall. Much to Charles's relief, Dr. Bissell says he's given up on a previously planned trip to Texas. Unexpected expenses had cut deeply into his finances.

On January 9, 2008, Dr. Bissell writes in response to the article suggesting that there wasn't enough evidence to tie Eli to the Colorado murders of Dennis Sleater and David Tyler.

They are not done with trying to blame him yet. And even if they find he was involved, I am not able to see what good that is going to do. Both men are dead. It seems like a waste of time and money. Maybe someone needs a job.

After that little screed, he goes further in expressing his desire for Charles.

A day or two after I talked to you, I laid down and had a little nap. I was awakened with a dream you and I were playing around, and I was half hard. I took this opportunity to continue playing with myself and had a light sexual experience. It was good, but not as good as I used to have. At least it is a start. I noticed since then that occasionally my breasts get erect, and I have sensation that I had lost.

Smartly and decisively, Charles never writes back.

PART FOUR

Spring 2023

CHAPTER SIXTY

Before I leave for the airport, I tell Claudia over a cup of morning coffee—actually I promise her—that this is my last trip and I won't be going down the Stutzman rabbit hole any deeper. I'd like to think that my wife understands my obsession with the case, and my need to keep a promise to Daniel Gingerich. I have a lot more information now and I hold no doubt Ida was murdered. It is a strong case, though because of the passage of time, it is mostly circumstantial. There are no forensics to speak of, and while Ida's body could be exhumed and examined, I'm not sure that step is really needed.

"Okay," Claudia says, "what happened and who's to blame? And beyond that, what's the outcome you're seeking? Everyone is dead."

"Frost and Stutzman and Levi Levi. Right, all dead. That doesn't mean some form of justice couldn't prevail. It should."

"Fine," she says. "Lay out what happened."

I show her the printed list of bullet points.

"It was completely premeditated," I begin. "Eli might have married Ida to find his way back into the safety of the Amish after the botched and faked attack in Marshallville, but it was never going to work out. The strong pull of his sexuality couldn't be contained."

"Do you think he loved Ida? At any point?"

"I can't say, but I know she really loved him. She wanted to save him, make sure he got to heaven."

"About that night."

"Right. I think his story of the lightning strike was a lucky part of the plan. He went to great lengths to show others it had happened. He's a complicated liar. He seeks ways to bolster his story. The notes he wrote to himself. The lightning. The longing Ida had when passing by the graveyard."

"The lawyer and the will?"

"Planned ahead of time," I say. "I guarantee you that there would have been a fire that night with or without the lightning."

I revisit the evidence I have gathered—Ida's pinned dress, the burning lamps, the fact that the hired boy wasn't wakened—that indicates to me that she was killed between nine, when they went to bed, and about midnight, when the fire was burning.

"She had barely any CO2 in her lungs," I add.

Claudia nods. "Dead before the fire."

"Right. And hit on the head by something and killed. She was posed in the milk house. Vats were lying around the scene. He set it up. All of it to look like Ida had been overcome by smoke in the midst of saving things that weren't worth saving."

"Does your list say what the motive was?"

"Motives aren't necessary to prove a case. They help a jury understand things that are often impossible to truly comprehend. Motive here? Ida was going to tell the bishop something about her husband. He had a car? A camera? She caught him having sex with a man? Maybe Eli tried something with one of her brothers sooner than I thought? She found something in the mail? We don't have to know the real reason. Any of those could be true."

I study the bullet list. It really isn't about the why or how she was killed that matters to me most.

"You know," I say, "I can't really know what happened that night. Not for sure."

"That doesn't make for a satisfying story."

I disagree with her. "It is about the cover-up. That's what this story is about. Not the murder. It's about a sheriff who conspired with a coroner to cover up a crime. That's clear as day to me."

Claudia says something about how she hopes Ida gets justice, but she doesn't feel it's truly in the cards.

"Getting the government to admit it messed up on something is more than a tall order."

I let her have the last word.

Inside, I'm gullible and hopeful enough that isn't so.

It's spring now. My last shot. I've been through each of Ohio's four seasons. Spring feels right. It's about renewal and hope, and I'm telling myself that this trip will provide me with the final pieces of a puzzle and a genuine solution that will bring justice. It's a tall order, but as I sit on the plane and look over the list of bullet points, I have hope they will sway the authorities in Wayne County to take another look at Ida's death and do what I feel they must do. Robbin is telling the fellow in 17A that she tore her meniscus after falling off an adult pogo stick.

It's apparently a thing.

I tell her it sounds like a sex toy, and I'd drop the "adult" part when describing the accident and the reason for her limping gait.

I'm studying my index cards. My old-school index cards. By the time we land in Columbus, I'm ready. The hit list fanned out on my tray table includes another visit to the now-grown hired boy, a couple of Eli's relatives, a meetup with Henry Miller at his work, a stop at billboard responder Jamie Smoot's place and, finally, a meeting with Wayne County sheriff Travis Hutchinson to present those aforementioned bullet points. He told a reporter from the Wooster *Daily Record* back in February that he was "absolutely" interested in taking a look at what I'd uncovered. There are others who I'd like to see out of friendship or added clarity, but this is a fast trip. The book is already in production and I'm testing the limits of my editor and publisher's patience. By a lot.

"Just one more week," I say.

"We're running out of any wiggle room," my editor says.

"You won't be disappointed."

I say that, but I don't know it for sure. I can only write what I find.

Everyone thinks that the hired boy saw something that scared him to such a degree that he never spoke of it again. I don't know if that's true, but I do know that this is my last chance to find out at a time when I might make a difference. Emery Stutzman agrees to take me and Robbin to see Eli Stutzman at his farm in Sinking Spring. Just as was the case when I was there the previous fall, Eli is not home. A boy at the sawmill next to the house directs us to a farm nearby where he's leading a group of Amish raising a barn.

Eli is a thoughtful man, and prodding him to recall something that isn't there won't help. I listen as he unfolds the idea that maybe he had seen something but didn't know what it was. Maybe something lingers in his memory that would break the case open. That's my hope. He tells me that long after the fire and up until Eli's suicide, he allowed himself to wonder if he actually had seen something that he shouldn't, something that wasn't obvious.

And that Eli knew it.

"I think he would have killed me," he says. "If I had witnessed something. I had a fear in me. Someone told me that I should be very glad that I didn't see anything . . . and very glad, I think, that Eli didn't think I did."

"You're remembering something now," I say.

"Not about Ida," he says. He's pulling up a memory from when he was twenty-one and getting his horse shod. The subject, as it had often in his life, came up.

"If I just woke up and saw what happened," Eli recalls saying.

The farrier stopped what he was doing and dropped the horse's foot.

"You're lucky you didn't see anything."

Eli says he understood right away.

"Yeah, and I thought then, *Well, if I think too much or say too much, Eli might come back for me.*"

He doesn't need to hide what he feels is true.

"He killed her that night."

Over the years, the early morning hours of July 12, 1977, haunted him.

"I used to think about Eli maybe coming for me. I would see a car driving down the road after dark. Sometimes at home I would get the feeling that someone was watching me from the outside."

"You were traumatized."

"Yeah," he says softly.

When relatives asked him to go see Eli in prison, he refused.

"I found every excuse I could not to go. I didn't want to face him."

I am at a loss here. I feel the clock ticking and I know that we've plowed this terrain before. I ask him a bunch more questions, hoping for a different outcome, but I get nothing but more of the same. His story is solid, I know that. He says that he didn't really see any discord in the Stutzman marriage, nor did he see anything that would indicate other men were coming to see Eli for a tryst in the barn as others have insisted. He didn't know anything about Eli being gay or involved with the sheriff.

I'm well aware that I'm picking a scab and releasing pinpoints of blood and hurt. Things that will last when I'm gone.

And then, it happens.

"I did see something one time that I shouldn't see."

351

"What was that?"

He tightens his brow. It's a memory he'd rather not discuss, but he's offering it up.

"I found a magazine, a *Playboy*, open in the field where he told me to mow."

"A *Playboy*?"

"Yes, one of those magazines with the naked pictures. It was spread open."

"Naked women?"

The former hired boy shakes his head. "No."

"Men?" I ask.

He nods.

It wasn't a *Playboy* after all. For an Amishman, all skin mags were referred to as *Playboy*s; most probably had no idea there were hundreds, if not more, of porn magazines in the late seventies.

Some for men. Some for women. For gay. For straight. For those fixated on this. Or that.

"I think he put it there so I would find it," he says.

The next question I ask will be the most important of the day. Maybe of the trip. So many of the Amish have told me that Ida was going to the bishop about her husband and something she either saw or found. Maybe it was the camera? Maybe it was that he was gone all the time. Maybe it was that she'd caught him having sex with another man. None of those possibilities could be traced easily—and directly—to a witness.

None of those prove that Eli had married Ida and still carried on his interest in other men. That his coming back to the Amish had been a lie. That Ida's death had been a premeditated act.

"Was it before or after she died?" I ask.

"Before."

Bingo. It is so simple. Yet so important. It isn't on the long list of possible scenarios I presented to Claudia to suggest premeditation based on the concept of Ida telling the bishop something very dark, very wrong.

Something her husband should not do.

Something that led to her murder.

It is probably ugly to think, but I have never been happier than I am right now.

P. Graham Dunn is the Costco of inspirational and religious merchandise, and, God willing, the site of a last-minute interview with Henry Miller, the former Swartzentruber Amish kid who gave Eli the tip to buy the marijuana from the other, non-related Miller brothers. Robbin and I pull into the parking lot of the red-roofed, 250,000-square-foot manufacturing facility and mammoth retail store that sprawls over farmland not far from the Stutzman place on Moser Road. Henry pops out of a side door like a cuckoo clock, right on the dot.

He's wearing a baseball cap, jeans, and a white-and-red plaid shirt. His glasses are speckled with a few drops of misty rain, just ending as we talk. He is not a big man, which makes me think at six four I must seem like Gulliver among the Amish. The Swartzentrubers, in particular, are on the short side when it comes to stature. Five eight could serve as center on an Amish basketball team.

If there is such a thing.

Henry starts out telling me right away that he and his wife attended Ida's viewing. "And here is the weirdest thing. It was just like God told me. We walked out to the car and I told my wife, I said, 'There's something really weird going on here. This is not a normal thing. There is something wrong.' I said, 'I wouldn't be surprised if Eli killed his wife.'"

I ask Henry if he recalls what it was that made him think that.

"Eli wasn't there. They said he had a nervous breakdown. It felt weird."

I ask about his role in the marijuana sting.

He says he was working at Stoll Farms at the time when members of the Wayne County Sheriff's Office came to recruit someone to buy marijuana from the Millers. It's been a lot of years, of course, and Henry isn't sure if it was a deputy or the sheriff who came.

"He wore dark glasses."

"I see."

"Yeah," he says. "Anyhow, I don't know who it was, but it could have been Frost."

The law enforcement officer met with Eli.

"So, I went down to the Miller boys a couple of nights later. Eli calls and wondered if he could buy some marijuana. And I said, 'I don't know. I don't have any.' But I said, 'I know somebody that does.'"

That, it seems, was Henry's undoing. His story differs from the report and the Miller brothers' account in that he says it was a bigger operation than just a little box of pot. That's neither here nor there. Henry remembers Frost being at the center of things and, of course, what happened later at Stoll Farms.

"Me and Levi, which was one of the Miller boys, went to see Eli afterwards. Eli had his TV on. He opened his eyes, and he would not really look at us, you know, really weird. We didn't threaten him or anything. But I think by him knowing that, you know, we knew that he came in and bought something and then we went to jail."

"And after that?"

"Yeah, he did this drama thing. He wrote the letter himself. How somebody was trying to get him. And kill him."

And then the faked stabbing and the very real bloodletting.

Henry can't confirm that Jim Taylor was Eli's lover, but he knows that Eli was good friends with one of the deputies.

"But later, after his wife died," he says, "me and my wife went to visit him just to be nice. It was just him and his little boy. You know, nobody was there. And that day he acted really weird, how he just would look at you and his expression just looked like he was in a different world than we were. Wow. It was, like, weird."

Over the years, Henry has tried to figure out how it was that Eli turned out the way he did. He wonders if his father had something to do with it.

"There was something not quite right, quite good about his father. He was so screwy that you'd have to screw him to the ground just to keep him there."

"I don't follow."

Henry looks over at the side door. He's about ready to go back to work.

"Screwy. People felt that he was dishonest. He was into witchcraft, you know."

"No, I don't," I say.

"Eli's father proclaimed to be a healer."

"Like a prophetic healer?" Robbin asks.

"You can call it that. I call it witchcraft."

Henry lets us take some pictures and we're back on our way.

"Witchcraft?" Robbin asks when we're back in the car.

Like an adult pogo stick, witchcraft in the Amish is apparently a thing.

"Yeah," I say. "I know. There's even a TV show that features Swartzentruber witches here in Amish Country."

"Seriously?" she asks, her eyes impossibly wide.

"Seriously stupid," I say.

CHAPTER
SIXTY-ONE

Before going to the sheriff's office, Robbin and I do a drop-in at Jamie Smoot's house in Kidron. The place has two front doors and what sounds like a pack of dogs. Big ones too. The wind is no joke. The "Fuck Biden" flag planted prominently in the front yard is about to break loose. A gust of cold air pummels my face when I get to door number one, which is a bust. Door number two is rattled by the dogs I'm certain are doing their best to break out and eat me. A second later, Jamie, the woman who reached out to the website with information and then suddenly and inexplicably ghosted me, cracks open the door. A small woman with a take-no-shit attitude, Jamie shoves the dogs back inside and immediately apologizes for not getting back to me.

"My family got so mad at me for talking to you," she says right away.

"That happens sometimes," I tell her. "I'm really sorry."

Jamie, now outside and wisely wrapped in an oversize navy hoodie, gives me a little shrug.

"It's okay. Like they tried to make me feel like I misheard them or something about the house with the gay deputies. I didn't. I even asked my son, who was there when they first told me, and he remembered it exactly the same way."

Source remorse is like buyer's remorse. The act of telling the truth is exciting and even healing for many. A few hours later, especially if you've shared that you've met with an author of such a book as this, you might second-guess your decision.

Sometimes people ghost me after spilling their guts. Others phone or write back with retractions. A few ask later to leave out their names when, in the moment of first telling, they were convinced they were doing the best, most courageous thing they could ever do.

And right now, I'm looking for a little courage. Not from me, but from the officials of Wayne County. The coroner's office ghosted me, after an investigator in the office promised he'd meet me to discuss Ida's case. I came in person to their offices twice. Said I'd wait. I did. For nothing. The candy murder case was also met with disappointing silence. Although the West Salem matter was pronounced closed by Frost, not a single record or file associated with it could be located by the unfailingly diligent women in the records department.

Wonder where all that information went.

My hope for justice for Ida will be in the hands of the sheriff, a man who had zero to do with what happened in 1977 but has the power to do what's right.

Right now.

"Ready, boss?" Robbin asks as she puts the car into gear as we head from Kidron to Wooster.

We wait a minute for a buggy to pass by. The driver and his wife have a black tarp covering their laps and a dour look on their faces. *Swartzentrubers*, I think.

"Boss, they're freezing," she says.

"Yeah. Their lives are the opposite of charming and quaint on days like today."

Robbin talks about wanting to bring her husband and girls to Amish country and how amazing it is as I look over the compendium of distractions, discrepancies, lies, and, yes, the conspiracy to conceal a murder.

That night I play the true crime author's version of bingo and go through every note card, prioritizing, tossing out the unverified "Eli's brother gave the blood for the premarital test" and "Eli's constant erection was caused by venereal disease" and "Ida's tongue was bitten off" and more. Those things could be true, but they wouldn't help in moving the needle from conspiracy to justice.

My bed is covered with the confetti of interviews and details, organized as best I can by the when and how it relates to what I've learned over the past nine months. It's late when I begin typing on my laptop.

Travis Hutchinson
Wayne County Sheriff
Wooster, Ohio
Re: Ida Stutzman

Dear Sheriff Hutchinson,

I appreciate the opportunity to share this with you to right a wrong committed by members of your office in 1977. In the interest of justice, my hope (with the support of Ida Stutzman's family and the Amish community) is that you will work with the prosecutor's and coroner's offices to change the manner of Ida's death from natural causes due to a bad heart to homicide or at the very least, reclassify it as a suspicious death.

Wayne County Sheriff James Frost is at the center of a conspiracy that not only allowed Eli Stutzman to escape prosecution for the murder of his wife, Ida, but allowed a psychopath to go free to kill again. Frost's motivation was his need to keep his relationship with Stutzman and other men secret.

Here's the background and the evidence (more contained in The Amish Wife, *publishing at the end of this year):*

- *Eli's mental instability is well documented and known by Frost.*
- *Sent to Cuyahoga Falls mental hospital by father.*
- *Had a mental breakdown prior to going on a date with Ida.*
- *Placed cryptic notes when living with Moses and Ada Keim.*
- *After a Frost-ordered sting, Eli got cold feet and gave false account of assailants watching him, then wrote fake notes about how he was going to pay for working undercover for the sheriff, and finally, Eli stabbed himself, sprayed blood around the barn and said he was attacked.*
- *Frost was forced into making a statement to the press about the self-stabbing incident.*
- *Jim Taylor, another deputy, was one of two of Eli's best friends and lover at the time.*
- *Eli faked state-required blood test results prior to marrying long-time Amish girlfriend, Ida.*
- *Dr. Morton Bissell was responsible for "fixing" Eli's blood.*
- *Dr. Bissell stayed in touch with Eli up to his suicide; after Eli's death the doctor wrote a letter imagining having sex with Eli's last lover.*

After marriage to Ida

- *February 28, 1977—Stutzmans agree to buy Amish-owned farm on Moser Rd.*
- *May 1977—Eli applies for farm loan.*
- *July 7, 1977—$55k loan is approved to pay off original Amish owner (though payoff came years later).*
- *Eli was not around during the final months of Ida's pregnancy.*
- *Ida wants Eli to stop associating with Levi Levi Hershberger.*
- *Eli tells Ida's father she has a bad heart and asks him to build her steps.*
- *Eli has a camera.*
- *Eli still has a car.*

Ida's death

Leading up to the fire on July 11, 1977

- *Hired boy, age 12, finds a male nude magazine where Eli told him to do some mowing.*
- *Ida tells her mother that she thought Eli didn't love her.*
- *Ida's brother sees his sister crying a few days before the fire.*
- *Eli refuses to go with Ida to a funeral just before the fire.*
- *Eli installs a bed in the milk house.*
- *Eli was sleeping with a sheriff's deputy in the milk house.*
- *The loan of $55k was approved 4 days prior to the fire.*
- *Eli asks lawyer Tim Blosser to come to the house and create a will for him and Ida.*
- *Family visits Ida, and as the family member leaves, Ida chases after him and is sad and wants to tell him something but doesn't.*

Day of fire

- Eli says he sees lightning strike the barn when returning home in the evening. Went to great lengths to make people believe his story—even pointing out "charred" wood in the barn.
- Levi Levi Hershberger was there the day of the fire.
- Lawyer (Blosser) comes to the house to write a will for Ida and Eli.

Fire around midnight

- Hired boy wakes up on his own to an empty house.
- Hired boy notices all lamps in the house are lit.
- Hired boy is told by Eli to get the fire department.
- Hired boy sees Ida's body, confronts Eli, and is told to get "the rescue squad" too.

Neighbor responds

- Howard Snavely rushes to help.
- Eli reports that Ida was stuck in the milk house.
- Howard and Eli carry her body from milk house (suggesting Ida was put back into the milk house).
- Ida's body is moved again, this time to a place across the road.

Authorities arrive

- Ida is already dead.
- Eli claims he gave his wife CPR.
- Eli says his wife had a bad heart.
- Eli says she was saving milk vats.
- Frost tells Deputy Jim Gasser to leave the scene because there is nothing to investigate.

- *Frost never brings up Eli's self-inflicted stabbing incident to Deputies Gasser and Carr.*
- *Frost tells Coroner J. T. Questel Eli's theory on how Ida died and foreshadows that Ida might have Valium in her system.*

Differing witness accounts of that night

Hired boy

- *Young Eli, outside at midnight, saw the elder Eli run toward the front porch ("as if he was waiting for me"). Eli tells the boy go to Harley Gerber's to call the fire department. The boy finds Ida dead and turns around and informs Eli. Eli becomes frustrated and yells at the boy that he should call the rescue squad too. The boy returns from Gerber's and sees Ida has been moved again and that there is a neighbor there now.*

Howard Snavely

- *Neighbor Howard Snavely runs to the Stutzman place to help. The hired boy had already left for Harley Gerber's place. When Howard approaches the burning barn, Eli runs out from behind it and states that his wife is trapped in the milk house. Howard accompanies Eli to the milk house and sees a milk vat placed in front of the door. Eli moves the vat, opens the milk house door, and he and Howard find Ida dead on her back. They carry Ida to the grass across the road. Howard never sees Eli perform CPR.*

Eli

- *Eli says Ida woke first to say the barn was on fire. They both ran outside and started to grab things from the barn. Ida asked to save items from the milk house. Eli agreed she could if it wasn't dangerous. Eli told Ida that once she saved the items, she needed to go and call for help. Moments passed by without Eli seeing his wife and he went to check on her. He found her on her back in the milk house and dragged her out onto the grass. He tried to do CPR, but in doing so, was interrupted by the heat from the flames and saw that Ida was being burned and pulled her away farther from the fire. Eli told the authorities that Ida had a bad heart and that there was Valium in the house.*

Investigation/post Ida's death

- *Sheriff Frost refuses to investigate Ida's death, though he had full knowledge of Eli's history as a liar and evidence fabricator.*
- *Dr. Questel, known to be a father figure to Frost, doesn't conduct a thorough autopsy.*
- *Ida's doctor, Elton Lehman, who is also assistant coroner, returns from vacation and informs Questel that Ida was healthy and did not have a history of heart trouble.*

Coroner's report

- *Ida was fully dressed in daytime clothes.*
- *Very little CO2 in her lungs.*
- *No Valium in her blood.*
- *She was pregnant and healthy.*
- *Ida had cuts on her face.*
- *Her body was not fully examined for additional injuries.*

Post fire

- *The Amish were concerned with how Ida had died but trusted that the English authorities would find the truth.*

- *Eli's behavior did not reflect the characteristics of a grieving father and husband.*
- *Eli had a new barn built for horses, not dairy cows.*
- *Levi Levi Hershberger knew exactly where Eli's medication was kept in the house.*
- *Eli's family members came to visit Eli and saw that he was still in bed with Danny in the room even in the late afternoon.*
- *Eli says before her death, Ida had a longing to be in an Amish graveyard.*
- *Eli says the writing of the will showed God's hand in caring for him and Danny.*
- *Eli acted out and was taken to the clinic but checked out early.*
- *Eli wrote to a widower and said that he was "told" by the authorities that lightning caused the barn fire.*
- *Over the next few months and years, Eli told people that Ida was either rescuing puppies or kittens from the fire, or that she died in a car wreck.*
- *Frost confided to former lover Stanley Smythe that Eli had hit Ida over the head with a rock and placed her in the milk house to make it look like she died from the fire.*
- *Deputy Tim Brown lived with Eli even though his boss, Sheriff Frost, knew Eli was guilty of killing Ida.*
- *Frost attended barn parties at Eli's after Ida's death and after he told Smythe he knew Eli killed Ida.*

After Ohio

- *Eli sells the farm and leaves the Amish with Danny for Colorado.*
- *Several sources suspect that Eli sexually abused Danny.*
- *Eli spins a story about roommate Glen Pritchett's absence from Texas.*

- *Eli sends letters to family pretending to be Danny after he was left in the ditch in Nebraska.*
- *Eli gets someone to pretend to be Danny while talking to family members on the phone.*
- *Eli is convicted of Glen Pritchett's murder.*
- *Eli is convicted of leaving his son's body and not reporting his death in Nebraska.*
- *Questel admits on TV he might have made a mistake in finding natural causes as the reason for Ida's death.*
- *Levi Levi Hershberger confesses that Eli planned to kill Ida but he was unable to stop it.*

Frost's downfall

- *Wayne County Sergeant Ken Kerr, Frost's lover, dies in motorcycle accident.*
- *Frost loses second re-election for sheriff.*
- *Frost moves to Florida and is assaulted with a knife in a men's restroom.*
- *Frost receives multiple DUIs.*
- *Frost sells his condo to a pedophile priest.*
- *Frost loses his job, receives more DUIs, and commits suicide in Houston.*
- *Police recover a shoebox of boys' underwear along with gay magazines from the scene.*

Despite the hour, I send a copy to Robbin, who pings back right away.

"Nailed it," she says.

Her enthusiasm lifts me a little, but only for a minute.

"Let's wait and see."

CHAPTER
SIXTY-TWO

A punch of wind nearly knocks the paper from my hand as Robbin and I cross the street to the Wayne County Sheriff's Office. I hadn't been inside the building since I talked with a less-than-forthcoming Deputy Tim Brown back in the day. A kind of irony isn't lost on me just now. Forward-thinking and then up-and-coming Jim Frost built that structure. I'm here to share the details gleaned from an investigation that suggests Frost's office had blood on its hands when he left the county.

Maybe not Ida's. It is possible, even likely, that Frost didn't know Ida Stutzman was going to be murdered that night in July 1977. However, there is no way around the fact that he, for whatever reason, didn't investigate what anyone could see was highly suspicious—in fact, he clearly did all he could to have Ida's death written off as an accident or natural causes. So let's say he didn't know in advance.

The blood on his hands comes from the other victims—Glen Pritchett, Danny Stutzman, and possibly the pair from Durango, Dennis Sleater and David Tyler.

Our experiences with current sheriff Travis Hutchinson confirmed his idolization of Jim Frost. He told Robbin that Frost gave him his first big break and noted how it was such an honor for him to use the very same desk his law enforcement mentor and idol had when he served all those years ago.

A woman with kind eyes blinks from behind a thick bulletproof window just inside the door to the Justice Center. We speak through a hole cut in the glass.

"I don't have an appointment," I say, "but I am here to see Sheriff Hutchinson. Is he in?"

She says she doesn't think so. "Haven't seen him yet today."

When she asks why I want to talk to him, I tell her that I'm a writer trying to solve an old Amish murder case.

"Does he have an assistant or somebody that helps him?"

She says he has a secretary—actually three.

That's a lot, I think.

"I'll try one now," she says, dialing.

After a false start with someone named Norma, she gets Kristin on the phone after some eye contact that reminds me of the look of the Nurse Ratched wannabe at the psych hospital outside of Millersburg.

I have a sinking feeling.

The woman behind the glass hands me the phone. I tell Kristin who I am and what I'm doing. She already knows, of course. If I think the wind outside is cold, it is nothing compared to Kristin's demeanor over the phone.

She very flatly, and very definitively, says Sheriff Hutchinson will not meet with me.

Stunned. Flummoxed. I'm at a loss for words, which I must say is a rare occurrence.

"Can you tell me—"

She cuts me off. "He already spoke to you on the phone. And that's all he wanted to do. He doesn't want to meet with you. He already said what he had to say."

In the preliminary interview Robbin conducted, there was nothing about the investigation into Ida's death. All the sheriff talked about was how Frost walked on water.

Taught him everything he knows.

Gave him a big break.

Got him to where he is now.

All that kind of bullshit people say when someone is dead, or maybe after a few drinks at a retirement party.

I blurt out to Kristin that I have new material.

"He said in the paper that he would be interested in looking at what new information I have."

I'm referencing a February article in the Wooster *Daily Record.*

"Wayne County Sheriff Travis Hutchinson, who became a deputy after Ida's death and was elected sheriff in 2012, said Olsen hadn't shared his findings but said investigators would look at any new information about Ida Stutzman's death."

"Absolutely, we would," Hutchinson told the paper.

The line goes quiet.

I'm pretty sure that Kristin considers me an annoyance. Or that her boss does. I wish I could see her face, ask her if the county sheriff decided this case is of little importance because it was an Amish person involved or because it happened over forty years ago or if it is because they all know the culpability of the sheriff's office in the cover-up of the crime.

It's a crying shame either way.

"Okay, if you can send me an email regarding that, I will pass it on to him."

Wow. I'm dismissed.

"Okay," I say without thinking. "But for now, it's a no?"

"Correct."

I thread the phone back through the circular hole in the glass and turn to face Robbin.

"She wanted me to email the information."

"Email it?"

"Yeah."

"Fuck that," Robbin says, her big hazel eyes suddenly fierce.

"Fuck that, indeed."

After trying to make some sense of the sheriff's deaf ear, indifference, or whatever, Robbin and I drive west to Eli's home farm on Welty Road in Apple Creek.

We don't say much on the way.

When you've said "fuck that," what else is there?

As we turn up the long driveway, I tell Robbin how my heart hammered when I first visited the Stutzman farm. I was terrified of One-Hand Eli, having heard stories about what a monster he'd been to his son. How cold. How mean he'd been to the boy who would grow up to be a killer. I no longer have that concern, of course. Eli H. Stutzman is long gone. Now I think my fear of that particular door knock was also rooted in my awareness of what I was doing there.

To a family.

"I was writing about their son and the trail of destruction he'd left across four states. It was worse than that. I was digging into something so forbidden, so against who they were as a family, but also as members of a community in which following the Bible and abiding by the Ordnung was the sole pathway to heaven."

"Still, Eli was a monster and they knew it," she says.

"Maybe so, but he was their monster," I answer, getting out of the car.

I tell her to wait while I pick my way across the muddy buggy-wheel ruts to the door.

"But don't smoke," I say.

She gives me a look.

A row of dark blue and black clothing sways on a line along the front of a battered old white house. Hard to say how old the house actually is, but county records put its construction around 1850. I freeze as a greeting committee of German shepherds want to mark the front of my jeans with their muddy paws, but I manage to keep them at bay.

When I knock, a little girl of five or so opens the door. She's a miniature of her mother, who stands behind her. It's a world in which Mommy and Me outfits are not attention-seeking familial branding, but a daily habit. Married to Eli's cousin, Rebecca is thirty-one with six children, including a set of twin boys. Two girls are standing on chairs, washing flatware and plates in tubs on the dining table. A canned chicken—feet and all—sits on the stove, waiting for their mother, Rebecca, to turn it into a simple, but I'm sure delicious, meal.

I'd met Rebecca on a previous visit when her husband was away.

She gives me a warm smile.

I tell her I'm leaving that afternoon. "Going home to Seattle. I hate to impose. I wanted to see Eli's room, if that's all right?"

She motions me inside and leads me through the kitchen. All of her little ones stay silent, frozen in what they had been doing before this English stranger appeared at their door. Playing on the floor. Washing the dishes. Peering from the window at Robbin and the rental car.

The staircase to the second floor is very steep, truly ladder-like. Treads are worn shiny, concave, and smooth by generations of bare feet. There are four bedrooms upstairs, all good sized. Rebecca says two kids per bed and two beds per room accommodate a large family.

Walls, unadorned with wallpaper or artwork, are painted a light blue, a hue that makes me think of the crime scene photo of Danny in his blanket sleeper taken on Christmas Eve in that bitter cold Nebraska cornfield. The ceiling in one room has a jagged tear in it. Rebecca tells me that it leaks and that she and her husband plan to build a new house in the future.

"It gets cold up here," she goes on. "Ice freezes on the inside of the windows."

In the room Rebecca says was Eli's as a teenager, a hired boy gets out from under a quilt and nods a hello in my direction.

"I hated sharing a room with my brother," I say.

"When there is a family," she says, "we have to share."

I look around. "I guess there's no message on the wall that Eli wrote," I say.

Rebecca gives me a smile. "They've probably painted it since he was here."

A beat later, we file down the steep stairs, the youngest crawling backward, step by step.

"You have a beautiful family," I say as I go out the door.

Back in the car, ever-ready Robin asks, "Well?"

"Nothing. Not sure what I expected. Just so much of what happened started here. His father hated that his son was gay. Eli learned to lie about everything."

"To survive how he felt."

"Who he was," I say. "Eli was in an impossible position. Couldn't find his footing anywhere. Not with the Amish, for sure. Neither could he fit in with the English during that time. Everything he felt had to be covered up."

She gives me a look. "So you feel sorry for him?"

I shake my head. "'Sorry' isn't the right word."

But I kind of do.

"Then what?"

"Sadness really. For everyone. Ida and Danny and Glen, of course. And some for Frost and Eli. At least to some degree. All were caught up in something that would turn very ugly. And it all started here."

Right here in this beautiful place, this farm that is now crisscrossed by little blond children with bright-blue eyes and wary, shy smiles.

Robbin catches a flight to Portland, and I wait at the gate for a Seattle flight.

I picture strings of red yarn forming a growing web to and from photos of Eli Stutzman to chiropractor Morton Bissell to Deputy Jim Taylor to the Wyoming foster father Cary Cox to Sheriff Jim Frost to

Levi Levi Hershberger and finally to Dr. J. T. Questel. As the web grows in size and complexity, others unwittingly are ensnared.

So many, in fact, that the image becomes a mass of red, a spatter of blood.

Some caught in the sticky threads, and probably others unknown, decided that their secrets were more important than the life of an Amish wife.

And her little boy.

And the men who met the spider at the center of it all, Eli Stutzman.

As my flight home boards, a variation of what Ida's brother Dan Gingerich said during our first meeting on his frozen Minnesota farm comes to mind. A secret might be worth even less than the shit you hold in your hands.

The flight attendant brings me a gin and tonic, and I watch the quilted fields fade below.

And I hope for justice.

EPILOGUE

"No more material," my editor says. *"The deadline is firm."*

"Understood," I answer back.

Yet I can't help myself. I have a feeling my publisher will hate me. I could try to throw my weight around, tell her that I've sold millions of books, made them money. Draw a line in the sand. Pitch a fit.

Even beg.

As I write this last bit and wonder if readers will see this material in the final draft of *The Amish Wife*, I admit I am unable to avoid including portions of an email prompted by the Justice for Ida billboards. Sent by a Dalton woman named Cherie, it arrived in my email inbox the third week of August 2023. It is a detailed message about her family's relationship with Eli. It seems her brothers were friends with Eli before he married Ida; indeed one of her brothers was one of Eli's lovers. She writes that they all were shocked when Eli married Ida and even more so by the tragic barn fire.

But there's more than that here. In her missive Cherie peels off another layer of the veneer of falsehoods and misdirection in a case that I've been obsessed with for more than half my life. She says that her aunt Mary worked for Dr. Questel as his secretary. One of her aunt's duties was to transcribe the coroner's autopsy reports.

"We all heard that Ida died of a heart attack, smoke inhalation, and severe burns. We all felt sorry that she died saving the farm animals. Mary told my dad that was not what Dr. Questel originally had in his autopsy report. That Ida had a fractured skull and was beaten on the back of her head and around her shoulder area. And she was not burned. Mary would say that Dr. Questel thought Eli Stutzman killed his wife and put her body just inside the barn doors so the Dalton and Mt. Eaton Fire Departments would find her. So she wouldn't be burned up in the fire!"

When I met Dr. Questel, he was evasive, but I was too green to confront him. Honestly, it didn't occur to me that he'd lie or omit the truth. God, I was young and stupid. I wonder if he'd have told the truth if I pushed or pleaded. He knew he'd made a terrible mistake.

And he did it at Frost's request, though not for the reason Cherie writes:

"Later Dr. Questel was made to change the cause of death to a heart condition because Sheriff Frost hated the Amish and didn't want to be bothered or burdened investigating a murder! 'The Amish take care of their own!' he was known to say!"

I find Aunt Mary's obituary from 2017. Mary Baer not only worked as a legal secretary for the National Insurance Company in Wooster but also was a stenographer for the US Federal Courts in Cleveland, Ohio.

Good so far.

I can't take her email at face value. She could be a nutjob or troublemaker.

Robbin, who's arrived at my office for the day to get a jump start on another story we've been working, pulls up scores of phone numbers that could belong to Cherie, and I start dialing. After a half dozen attempts ("Welcome to my life, boss"), I finally get Cherie on the phone.

After a few minutes, I decide she's a hero.

Cherie says her aunt told her what she knew when Cherie showed her a copy of *Reader's Digest* back in 1987.

"Not after *Abandoned Prayers* came out?"

"No. Before."

This is important. In my first book I mention the rumor of Ida being hit over the head with a rock.

Cherie, who talks a mile a minute, sets the record straight.

"She had the *Reader's Digest* with the story about Little Boy Blue. I said, 'Do you know who that is? That was Eli Stutzman's boy.' And she just kind of gave me this look. And then she told me how Sheriff Frost told Dr. Questel to change the cause of death. And she was the one who did it. It was Mary. They told her to change the wording. She changed it, so she made it sound like Ida had a heart attack, and she didn't. She had her head beaten. And Mary told me that she had a fractured skull. She had bruises to her face. And they said bruises to the back of her neck. And she had bruises to the side of her face."

My heart is pounding a little. "Was it the sheriff telling her to change the report, or was it Questel?"

"I think it was Questel," she says.

"That makes sense" is all I can say.

We talk a bit more and the call is over.

Robbin, who's heard the entire conversation, has her jaw on the tabletop. "Holy shit," she says. "This is big."

She's right, I think.

"Let's go back to the original reports," I say. I need another look at Dr. Questel's four pages of notes from Ida's autopsy and the single-page typed report.

Robbin prints out everything and delivers it with the flourish of a top-tier maître d'. She points out how things look as though they've been cobbled together. "Look," she tells me. "The pages don't match. The writer's spacing is more elongated on the second page. The thickness of the pen strokes is different too . . . like maybe a different pen was used."

"Or the photocopier was out of toner."

Robbin won't be deterred. She sandwiches the pages against the window, using the surface as a light box. "That might be, but the writing looks different, boss."

She's a terrier with a bone. I like that about her.

I examine each page without the benefit of her pseudo light box. The first is a neatly rendered description of what transpired at the fire.

According to Eli, that is.

It ends with a description of Ida's body, first with the burns on her hand.

Page 2 two covers burns to her breasts, face, and legs before the coroner describes how her clothing had melted, including her headscarf.

No mention of her head, skull, or neck.

Page 3 is only a half page of content. One paragraph identifies cardiac arrest as the cause of Ida's demise. Another paragraph is information provided by Dr. Lehman, who noted Ida had rheumatic fever as a girl but was a healthy adult who'd given birth without any complications when she had Danny.

I review the last page. Also only a partial, with a paragraph saying it is "probable" that rheumatic heart disease and the fear and gases caused her to die.

"Wait a second," I say.

Robbin pops up from her laptop.

I point to the final two pages. "Here and here," I say. "At the end of page 4, he says the body has been released to the funeral home. And right here on page 3 the same thing . . . right in the middle of the two paragraphs."

"Twice."

"Yeah, because—"

She cuts me off. "Because the third page is a redo. He took out any mention of a head injury. All of his other autopsies mention the condition of the deceased's head."

"As they should."

Next, we review the typed coroner's report. It's either truncated to save space—which no one would ever do—or Dr. Questel had someone eliminate whatever he'd written.

That's where Mary Baer came in. I can't know if she retyped or changed the report for a claim made at the offices at National Insurance in Wooster or if she was doing it as a job for the county through the coroner's office.

Either is plausible.

The first would be interesting even without doctored paperwork. Did the insurance money that rancher/lover Howard Runck alluded to come from National?

There's one thing more. And it's a biggie.

The date on the typed report signed by Dr. Questel is July 12, 1977. How was it that he filed the report on that date when Ida's blood samples weren't received by Analytica Labs in Cleveland for another seven days?

The results were sent back on July 21.

Robbin pipes up. She's emotional. "The only way that could be in the report on the twelfth is if it was added later," she tells me. "We got 'em."

I'm feeling it too. Elated. Sad. Everything. For half my life, I have wondered about Ida Stutzman and the night of the barn fire and the unintended consequences of a conspiracy of silence.

Now I know.

So this is my last word.

Promise.

For now.

ABOUT THE AUTHOR

Photo © Claudia Olsen

The #1 *New York Times* and Amazon Charts bestselling author Gregg Olsen has written more than thirty books, including *If You Tell*, *Lying Next to Me*, *The Last Thing She Ever Did*, and two novels in the Nicole Foster series, *The Sound of Rain* and *The Weight of Silence*. Known for his ability to create vivid and fascinating narratives, he has appeared on multiple television and radio shows and news networks, such as *Good Morning America*, *Dateline*, *Entertainment Tonight*, CNN, and MSNBC. In addition, Olsen has been featured in *Redbook*, *People*, and *Salon* magazine, as well as in the *Seattle Times*, *Los Angeles Times*, and *New York Post*. Both his fiction and nonfiction works have received critical acclaim and numerous awards, including prominence on the *USA Today* and *Wall Street Journal* bestseller lists. Washington State officially selected his young adult novel *Envy* for the National Book Festival, and *The Deep Dark* was named Idaho Book of the Year.

A Seattle native who lives with his wife in rural Washington State, Olsen's already at work on his next thriller. Visit him at www.greggolsen.com.

Made in the USA
Middletown, DE
05 June 2024

55379142R00234